D0270435

Pelican Books
The British Economic Crisis

Keith Smith was born in Australia in 1946 and fled to England twenty years later. After working in the theatre for several years he studied at Cambridge, where he took a first in Social and Political Sciences in 1972. Subsequently he did postgraduate research at the Institute of Development Studies, University of Sussex. Since 1978 he has been Lecturer in Economics at the University of Keele.

THE BRITISH
ECONOMIC CRISIS

Its Past and Future

KEITH SMITH

Penguin Books

*In England the outward aspect of life
does not yet teach us to feel or realize
in the least that an age is over.*

J. M. Keynes, *The Economic
Consequences of the Peace*

PENGUIN BOOKS

Published by the Penguin Group
Penguin Books Ltd, 27 Wrights Lane, London w8 5tz, England
Viking Penguin, a division of Penguin Books USA Inc.
375 Hudson Street, New York, New York 10014, USA
Penguin Books Australia Ltd, Ringwood, Victoria, Australia
Penguin Books Canada Ltd, 2801 John Street, Markham, Ontario, Canada l3r 1b4
Penguin Books (NZ) Ltd, 182–190 Wairau Road, Auckland 10, New Zealand

Penguin Books Ltd, Registered Offices: Harmondsworth, Middlesex, England

First published 1984
Reprinted with Revisions 1986
Reprinted with Revised Introduction and Chapters 1 and 13 1989
10 9 8 7 6 5 4 3 2

Copyright © Keith Smith, 1984, 1986, 1989
All rights reserved

Printed in England by Clays Ltd, St Ives plc
Set in 10/12 Monophoto Ehrhardt

Contents

Acknowledgements

I would particularly like to thank Edward Bennett, who encouraged me to write this book, and Phoebe de Gaye, who asked questions which I have struggled to answer in the following pages. For critical comments and help I am grateful to Stephen Hannah, of HM Treasury, and to colleagues in the Economics Department at the University of Keele: Sylvia Beech, Jayne Braddick, Pamela Davenport, Shirley Dex, Leslie Fishman, Athar Hussain, Peter Lawrence, Leslie Rosenthal and John Proops. I am grateful also to my students at Keele for heated discussions on some of the ideas presented here. A substantial part of this book was written in Norway, and I would like to thank Bjørn Christiansen, Gro Fossen, Knut-Vidar Paulsen, and Peter and Anne-Karin Cleaverley for help while I was there. Finally, I would especially like to thank Kristine Bruland, my wife, without whom this book could not have been written.

Introduction

There is a significant difference between economic *problems* and an economic *crisis*. All economies face more or less severe problems, all of the time. Some may result from the basic structure of the system itself, such as the cycles of unemployment and recession which plague capitalist economies: they are due in large part to the absence of any central coordination in and between such economies. Socialist economies, built on central coordination and planning, are stable by comparison, and rarely face problems of unemployment. Yet their very centralization generates other problems: enterprises are often inefficient compared with those of the capitalist world, because they lack the spur of competition, and they find difficulties in generating and sustaining real technological progress. Such problems underlie *perestroika* in the Soviet Union, as well as China's comprehensive economic reforms. Added to these problems of economic structure, countries often have problems due to accidents of nature or geography – shortages of natural resources, for example, or problems of climate. Then there may be difficulties deriving from the framework of institutions within which an economy functions: the absence of a centralized pay-bargaining system, for example, makes the operation of the British economy very different from that of Sweden, say, where pay is often settled at a national level for whole groups of industries simultaneously. Then there may be problems from essentially unpredictable shocks to the system, such as the OPEC price rises of 1973–4 and 1978–9, or the chaos caused in the international financial system by the way the United States financed first its war effort in Vietnam, and then its huge military build-up in the 1980s. Finally there are problems arising simply from mistakes in decision-making. The Concorde project, or the Russian TU144, are examples; if the projects are big enough, and if such mistakes occur often enough, the economic consequences can be very serious.

The mere existence of problems like these – even in severe forms – does not indicate a crisis. It would, in fact, be wildly unrealistic to think of an economy functioning without at least some of the difficulties sketched above. A crisis, in the sense the term is used in this book, is something more, for it is not a matter of problems within a system, but a question of the viability of the system itself. A crisis occurs when the types of activity on which an economy is based, and the levels of income which it generates, are no longer sustainable. To put it a different way, one could say that economic problems – of the kinds outlined above – can be lived with, they can be adapted to; but a crisis entails inevitable change. Significant transformations become unavoidable, and this can happen either through a positive attempt to overcome the critical difficulties (which may not necessarily involve any earth-shattering upheavals), or a process of decline and maybe collapse. There are plenty of historical examples of these paths.

But can it be argued that the British economy faces a crisis of this type? The view of the Thatcher administration and its supporters is that in the late 1970s Britain was indeed in crisis, but that by the mid-1980s the crisis was over; it had been overcome through the revitalizing effects of Thatcherite economic policy in the 1980s. This was the view taken in 1982 by the then Chancellor, Sir Geoffrey Howe, at the bottom of a recession in which unemployment had increased by 2 million and manufactured output had fallen by 15 per cent. As he stated in his speech at the Mansion House late that year:

> There is plenty of economic pessimism about, at home and abroad. In this country and throughout the world, there are those who question whether there can ever be a return to prosperity . . . But I am certain that the problems we see are those of change, not of decay. To be sure, transition is painful and the pace of recovery slow. But . . . long-overdue change, evolution, innovation are at last being willingly embraced: we are on the right path.

As the British economy has recovered from the 1979–81 recession, the theme of economic success has become more pronounced in government statements. Mr Nigel Lawson has declared, with characteristic modesty, that British growth in the 1980s has proved his critics 'wholly wrong'. For the Trade and Industry Secretary, Lord Young, Britain is no longer the 'sick man of Europe': 'Great Britain is great again'. And Mrs Thatcher herself has repeatedly argued that six years of economic growth – with low inflation, tax reductions, and no government borrowing – mean that Britain is now the most successful economy in Europe.

On the other hand there are those who disagree with these triumphalist views, yet who retain faith in the viability of the present economic system in Britain. They might be described as being, to use a cant term, in the 'centre' of British politics (meaning they can be found in large numbers in all of the political parties). For them, continuing large-scale unemployment, increased poverty, and chaos in publicly funded services such as health and education signify an economic success which is at best partial. They believe that what is needed is a change of government, and a modification or reversal of Thatcherite policies; it is therefore the policies which are being carried out within the present economic framework which are the problem, not the framework itself.

This book shares neither of these views. It argues that the recession of 1979–81, which inaugurated the Thatcher years, marked a fundamental turning-point for Britain, for it was superimposed on a long-term economic decay which has now reached a point of no return. The economic growth which began in 1982 and accelerated in the mid-1980s is unsustainable, for it has been based not on investment and the construction of new production capacity, but on a consumption boom fed by an enormous increase in manufactured imports. This growth has been financed domestically by a fall in personal-sector saving and a massive increase in personal debt, and financed internationally by oil exports. Neither of these sources will sustain continued growth of this type. The key point about the 1980s in Britain is that the 1979–81 recession devastated British manufacturing, and the subsequent recovery failed to restore it. But manufacturing will be central to Britain's future. As Britain enters the 1990s, therefore, it does so on the back of unsustainable growth which cannot in the long term resolve Britain's industrial and economic malaise: the economic structure with which Britain emerged from the Second World War, and which carried the country with some success and much failure through the 1950s and 1960s, is no longer workable. The Thatcher alternative (itself a much less radical change than it appears on the surface) is based essentially on short-term palliatives for a minority of the population. It has relied heavily on about £60 billion in windfall oil-tax revenue and has done little to address the fundamental issues. The British economy is indeed in crisis; without far-reaching changes further sharp decline is inevitable within the near future, and if it occurs may well prove irreversible.

The following chapters explain why this is so. They begin with a description of Britain's relatively poor economic performance over a long period, and establish why this poor performance now has the dimensions of a genuine crisis. Britain's economy, and the jobs and living standards of everyone in Britain, have for many years been dependent upon a complex system of foreign trade and international economic relationships; within this system, the manufacturing sector of the British economy has played a crucial role. The importance of the 'de-industrialization' of Britain since the mid 1960s lies in the fact that the relationship between Britain's foreign trade and its manufacturing capability has broken down. Britain no longer pays its way in the world by exporting manufactures; in the 1980s it became, for the first time for many centuries in peacetime, and on an ever-increasing scale, a net importer of manufactures. Only the fortuitous emergence of North Sea oil has enabled Britain to continue as though nothing has happened. But, by 1988, oil exports were already in decline, and serious trade imbalances – indeed the worst in British history – have appeared. If, as is likely, oil exports continue to decline, Britain will face desperate economic problems: the fundamental issue will be whether, and how, we can reconstruct manufacturing industry so that we can pay our way in the world at reasonable levels of income and employment.

Understanding why this impasse has been reached requires not just a description of events, but also the development of some theoretical ideas in order to explain those events. These are mainly to do with the nature of economic growth, with the relationship between economic growth and technological change, and with the interaction between growth, technological change and the external performance of the economy. Economics is not, unfortunately, a field in which theoretical ideas can be altogether avoided. But the issues are not, even for non-specialists, necessarily difficult to understand, and those which are outlined in the first chapters will form the basis for interpreting the long-term decline which will be described in subsequent chapters. Part One of the book is concerned, therefore, with an account of recession and 'recovery' in the 1980s, set against the background of the long-term decline which has been accelerated rather than resolved by the events of the 1980s. Part Two deals with the theoretical foundations of economic policy, concentrating on the so-called Monetarist–Keynesian debate of recent years; in particular, the intellectual basis of 'free-market' policy ideas is outlined and critically discussed. Finally, problems of industrial recovery are addressed, with an argument for an active policy of government intervention for industrial recovery, perhaps along the lines of that carried out so successfully in Japan.

PART ONE

THE CRISIS

Recession, Recovery and Crisis

During the early 1980s the British economy underwent dramatic economic changes, which in key respects were historically unprecedented. Although the changes owed much to the emergence of the new oil and gas industry in the North Sea, to an even greater extent they were a reflection of deliberate policy: 1979 saw the inauguration of the Thatcher government's attempt to alter the priorities, methods and objectives of economic policy in Britain, and this attempt shaped the economic development of Britain in the ensuing decade. But how well has the attempt worked, in terms of addressing and resolving the problems of the British economy in the long run?

There can be little doubt that some of these long-term problems were the economic basis of Mrs Thatcher's rise to power. The 1970s were years of exceptional difficulty and turbulence for the British economy: the world's exchange rate system had broken down in 1971: the OPEC oil price rises of 1973 had led to sustained inflation and global recession; government attempts to control inflation produced rising unemployment and industrial unrest; and Britain needed a major International Monetary Fund (IMF) loan in 1976. The economic situation which Mrs Thatcher inherited in 1979 was unquestionably a grim one. Unemployment had been on an upward track for over a decade, inflation (though well down from its mid-70s peak) was again rising, and manufacturing industry was shedding jobs and performing poorly in export markets. Many of the nationalized industries, and quasi-nationalized firms such as British Airways and British Leyland (later Austin Rover), were in deep trouble and soaking up large government subsidies. The National Health Service, and public services generally, were starved of funds and investment. Industrial relations were chaotic, and the trade union movement was conspicuously failing to face the realities of the situation. But these complex difficulties were themselves the reflection of a long-term decline, of slow income growth, low investment and inflexibility, which had left the British economy poorly equipped to handle the harsh economic environment of the 1970s.

In order to assess the impact which the Thatcher government has had on these problems we need to examine the economic record of the 1980s in Britain. This involves two distinct phases: a period of recession, worse even than that of the 1970s, during the years 1979–81, followed by a period of recovery to the late 1980s. But, as we shall see below, recession and recovery were more than a matter of falling and rising national income: these phases involved profound changes in the structure of the British economy, and in its patterns of investment, work and income. The central question raised by this record is whether these changes have placed Britain on a new path of sustainable growth, with the prospect of rising levels of productivity and income in the long run. The argument here will be that the growth of the 1980s is in fact unsustainable, for reasons which will be developed below, and the structural changes which have occurred are not those needed for long-term prosperity in Britain. Later chapters will explore the dimensions of the real long-term problems and the changes which are needed to solve them.

THE 1979–81 RECESSION

The Thatcher years began, primarily as a result of economic policy choices, with a recession so devastating that it bears comparison with the 'Great Depression' of the 1930s. In the two years from 1979 to 1981, manufacturing output fell by 15 per cent, unemployment rose by 250 per cent, while overall national income fell by just over 3 per cent. In manufacturing the falls were bigger, and happened faster, than those of the Great Depression. And it should be remembered that these figures, dramatic though they are, are merely *averages*, which means that while some industries and areas were better off than the figures indicate, others had been hit much harder. Regions such as Scotland, Wales, the West Midlands and the North-West, and cities such as Liverpool, had far higher than average un-employment. Industries such as metal manufacturing (output down 25 per cent between 1979 and 1981), textiles (down 26 per cent), clothing and shoes (down 21 per cent), timber and furniture (down 21 per cent) and general metal goods (down 26 per cent) were especially badly affected. Even such normally strong performers as mechanical engineering (down 16 per cent) and chemicals (down 9 per cent) were hard hit. In 1980 also, over 27,000 companies went into liquidation, as opposed to 6,000 in 1977 and about 5,000 in 1978. There were signs of an economy in serious trouble. Why did it happen?

THE 'THATCHER RECESSION'

We can start, perhaps, with a paradoxical feature of the post-1979 recession. This is that the large falls in manufactured output and in Gross Domestic Product (GDP) – or total output produced in Britain – were not accompanied by falls in total personal incomes or consumer spending. As the recession took hold in 1980, GDP began a steady decline, manufacturing output fell sharply, and employment fell spectacularly: yet personal disposable income (that is, the total of all individual incomes after tax) actually rose, as did total expenditure by consumers. Even when disposable income finally fell slightly – by about 2 per cent in 1981 – consumer expenditure continued to in-crease. So the recession did not take the form of falling incomes and demand by consumers.

Yet since a recession is nothing other than a decline in output – either absolutely, or in terms of its rate of growth – it must mean that somewhere along the line the consumption of output is slowing down or falling. For one reason or another, one of the end users of output is demanding and consuming less, and falling production and em-ployment are a response to that falling demand. So where did this happen in Britain? Apart from consumer demand, the other major categories of final demand are capital formation (expenditure on such things as new building, machines, equipment, etc.), government expenditure and exports. However, all of these remained more or less stable. To find the main cause of the recession we need to look to another source of demand, one which is in fact *within* the very companies which are producing output. This is a demand for *inventory*, or stocks of goods: that is, the stocks of raw materials, semi-completed products and completed output which firms hold for various reasons. To see why this 'stockpile' demand collapsed, we need to look first at the broad objectives of Thatcherite policy, then at the measures used to achieve those objectives, and finally at the effects of those measures on companies in Britain.

The Thatcher government came to office committed to the defeat of inflation as its primary goal; this was part of a wider programme for restoring market forces and market values as the basis of 'sustainable growth'. The first step, reduced inflation, was to be achieved through controlling the quantity of money in the system. How to control the money stock is, among economists at least, a vexed question: indeed there is hardly agreement on what the money stock actually *is*. Unassailed by doubts, however, the government decided on a double-barrelled strategy. On the one hand this was aimed at controlling the *supply* of money (controlling, in particular, the activities which caused governments to want to expand the money supply), and on the other hand controlling the *demand* for money (meaning, in practice, restricting the demand for credit from banks). The guilty party in expanding the money supply, it was argued, was government borrowing. The problem was a gap between government spending and its income from taxation; this gap is the budget deficit, the basis of the 'Public Sector Borrowing Requirement' (PSBR). So the policy decision was to attempt to restrict spending and thus cut borrowing. This would both inhibit monetary growth, and also lower interest rates (because when the government borrows it naturally pays interest rates, and excessive borrowing – it was argued – raises interest rates).

The attempt to restrict the impact of the PSBR on interest rates was important, for a related measure in the government's monetary control policy was a *rise* in interest rates. One of the ideas behind this is that the banking system is, in effect, capable of creating money through the overdraft system. The way to restrict the demand for overdraft credit is to raise its cost. Thus a lower quantity of money implies an increase in interest rates. This rise occurred: the 'base rate' for bank overdrafts was 12 per cent when the government took office;

it subsequently rose by 2 per cent, then another 3 per cent, and stayed in the range of 16–17 per cent through most of 1980.

This policy had a devastating effect on industrial and commercial companies in Britain. Since most companies were unable to raise prices in line with the interest rate increases, it amounted to a sharp increase in their costs. This affected in particular the source of demand referred to above, namely for inventory or stocks within the company sector of the economy.

Industrial companies normally maintain three kinds of inventory. They are, first, raw materials – these are held in order to even out possible fluctuations in availability, so that a regular supply of inputs is available. Secondly, there is work in progress, semi-completed output. Finally, there are finished goods – firms may want to meet fluctuations in demand which cannot be met out of current output, and will maintain stocks of their product for that purpose. These stocks can be large: in recent years they have been equivalent to about 30 per cent of total annual output.

But the problem with stocks is that they must be paid for. Both raw materials and the labour which turn them into components or finished products are normally paid for before the product is finally sold. Frequently, therefore, companies borrow in order to finance both current production and stockbuilding. In recent years they have done so increasingly through bank overdrafts, often on a very large scale.

For companies running large overdrafts, the government's monetary policy, and the interest rate rises it entailed, was a disaster. Borrowing costs increased dramatically as interest rates reached 20 per cent. At the time, companies faced increased wage and salary costs. Even though inflation was running at quite high levels, few companies were able to raise prices in line with it: in 1979 the big price rise was oil, and in 1980 it was nationalized industries and V A T increases which accounted for much of the increases in industrial prices. The evidence indicates that manufacturing companies, particularly in export industries, were raising prices at rates below the inflation rate. With costs rising fast, and prices not matching them, something had to give, and it was company profits. The average post-tax real rate of return almost halved in 1980, to the very low level of

2.9 per cent for non-North Sea companies. Many firms began making losses.

Under these circumstances, firms reacted in an obvious way: they attempted to lower their current costs by reducing their current output. Firms began to supply finished goods not by producing them but by running down their stocks of such goods. Simultaneously, they reduced their stocks of raw materials, which lowered the current demand for such materials. This lowering of current output led rapidly to reductions in the workforce. The object of the exercise was to cut day-to-day running costs and to reduce debts to the banks, but the effect was to create a recession. For the amounts involved were very substantial: in 1980 the turnaround in inventories was approximately £3.5 billion, or 3.2 per cent of GDP. This alone more than accounted for the overall fall in output. The government had, in effect, created this response by attacking the financial positions of companies.

So the monetary policy, operating through interest rates, produced an immediate recession. This was compounded by a further effect of high interest rates, namely a rise in the value of the pound. One feature of the world economy is the existence of large quantities of 'free-floating' capital which moves wherever interest rates are highest. When the interest rate rises, the foreign exchange markets either reflect a movement of such capital into Britain, or anticipate it. This happened: the exchange rate rose sharply. Since this meant that the pound was exchanging for more dollars, Deutschmarks, etc., then it also meant that the foreign currency prices of British exports were rising simultaneously. This resulted in problems for export industries, not so much in the short term (because most export goods are ordered well in advance) as in the winning of new orders. Prices of British goods abroad are determined by three factors: firstly their cost of production – especially their labour costs – inside Britain; secondly exporters' profit margins; and thirdly the exchange rate which links Britain to the rest of the world economy. In 1980 both costs and the exchange rate were rising, and British goods became much less competitive in price terms. Between the beginning of 1979 and the end of 1980, the so-called 'effective exchange rate' rose 21.6 per cent. This amounted to a decline in the competitiveness of British goods, according to the I M F measure, of about 50 per cent, a change almost unprecedented over such a short period. In the face of these developments, exports held up fairly well, mainly due to exporters making great efforts to keep their prices down – export prices rose by well under half the rise in costs of production. But imports soared, since the strong pound made them relatively cheaper; the recession intensified as British producers began to lose out in their own home market.

A WORLD RECESSION?

The analysis of the Thatcher recession presented above has emphasized the effects on Britain of its own government's policy. This approach stands in sharp contrast to the government's account of the recession, which leant heavily on the existence of a 'world recession'. This worked simultaneously as a defence of Mrs Thatcher (everyone else faced the same difficulties as us, therefore it wasn't her fault) and as an explanation of our problems, a description of their cause (we suffered unemployment because the world recession hurt our economy). To what extent is this government account plausible?

There is no doubt that the international environment, at the time the Thatcher government began to implement its policies, had taken a turn for the worse. The price of oil had risen by 45 per cent between 1978 and 1979, and by a further 68 per cent in the following year. There was a slowdown in the growth of world trade. Interest rates were fluctuating sharply but also moving upwards in Europe and the USA. And all of this was occurring against the background of general instability and slow growth in the world economy in the 1970s.

Can such developments account for the British recession? Here it is worth asking the obvious question, namely, in what ways can international trends affect the British economy? Two possibilities stand out. The first is that the international economy was for some reason contracting, and this was leading to either a slowdown in the growth of demand for UK exports, or an actual decline in the demand for British goods. This would almost certainly have pushed Britain into a recession. The other possibility is that world interest rates might have risen, forcing Britain to keep pace, and which would have depressed the UK economy, possibly through the kind of mechanisms outlined in the section above on the 'Thatcher recession'.

Only the second of these possibilities seems to have any plausibility. The UK government was, as we have seen, committed to a rise in interest rates because they believed this would help in controlling monetary growth. A rise in world rates might then mean that British rates would have to rise by more than previously would have been necessary to achieve the same effect. On theoretical grounds this could easily be disputed, but it should also be said that, since the government had the option of not adopting this policy, it could have avoided excessive interest rate rises, and therefore it can't blame its problems on the world economy. The first possibility – a decline in the demand for British goods – can also be discounted. This is because, although world trade slowed down in 1979, it was in fact still growing. The crux of the Thatcher recession was an absolute decline in manufacturing, yet world trade in manufactures grew by 5.7 per cent in 1979 and by 4.6 per cent in 1980; this could not, therefore, be the cause of Britain's manufacturing troubles. And in general the so-called world recession took this form: slowdown in growth rather than the absolute falls suffered by Britain. Table 1, which compares Britain with the countries of OECD (i.e. Britain's major industrial neighbours: the USA, Japan, W. Germany, France, Italy and Canada), shows this clearly for national income and employment.

At a time when employment was falling by 7 per cent in Britain, it

Table 1. *Changes in income and employment* (%)

	1980	1981	1982
National income			
Britain	−2.1	−2.2	+1.25
OECD average	+1.0	+1.2	+0.5
Employment			
Britain	−2.3	−4.7	−2.5
OECD average	+0.5	+0.1	−0.5

Source: *OECD Economic Outlook*, July 1982, Table 5, p. 20.

was actually increasing among the UK's OECD partners. Subsequently the picture worsened in those countries. Yet two simple points should be made about the development of the world recession. The first concerns timing. Britain entered its own recession *before* the world recession really got going; on chronological grounds alone it seems difficult to make the world recession the source of Britain's troubles. Secondly, we should remember that all countries have faced much the same sort of international problems. Yet the other OECD countries, facing the same international environment, have not suffered recession on anything like the British scale; Britain's unemployment and output losses have been quite disproportionately greater than those of any other advanced country. Once again, the conclusion is that Britain's problems cannot be laid at the door of a world slump. Mrs Thatcher needs some other line of defence.

THE RECOVERY

In 1982 the recession finally reached its lowest point. Despite proclaiming that it was steadfastly maintaining its course, the government in effect began to abandon its monetary policy; interest rates began to fall, consumer demand began to pick up, and growth began once more. In succeeding years growth accelerated at rates which had not been seen since the late 1950s and early 1960s, and was moreover accompanied by low inflation rates and sharply growing productivity.

What were the sources of this growth? In the first place, as interest rates began to fall the industrial situation stabilized, and the massive 'destocking' of 1979–81 stopped. More important, however, was growth in demand for goods by consumers. From 1980–81, consumers' demand for a wide range of products, especially 'durables' (such as household appliances, television and video equipment and so on) began to grow rapidly; more rapidly than consumers' incomes as a whole, in fact. Between 1981 and 1987, demand for consumer durables grew at an annual average rate of 14 per cent (which means in effect that such demand more than doubled over the period), while disposable income grew at an annual average of 2.3 per cent. Other items of consumer demand grew more slowly and some (such as beer and tobacco) actually fell; but as a whole consumers' expenditure rose

17 per cent over the period, while incomes grew 12 per cent. How was this possible? It was feasible only because the British people began to save less and to borrow more: the 'savings rate' (which is the proportion of income which the personal sector saves) fell every year from 1980, from 14.2 per cent of income to 3.6 per cent in 1988. Over the same period, annual borrowing from banks rose by over 100 per cent, and borrowing from building societies by 230 per cent. In other words, the economy began to recover from the recession not because of improved efficiency, or better export performance, or because of any activity of the government, but because the British people wanted to consume more, and to do it were prepared to save less and to go significantly into debt.

Did this strong growth in demand generate strong growth in the output of British industry? On the whole, the answer is no. Industries such as distribution and retailing, as might be expected, grew steadily, reflecting the growth in demand for goods. Banking and financial services grew, in response to growing demand for credit and the development of an international capital market. And, of course, the oil industry, which had come onstream in the late 1970s, grew by over 50 per cent between 1980 and 1986. But British manufacturing output in the early 80s actually fell in most major categories: for example, between 1981 and 1985, consumers' expenditure on cars and vehicles rose in real terms by 23 per cent, while British output fell by 25 per cent. As consumer demand was maintained through the mid 1980s, it finally fed through to British manufacturing, but not in such strength as to cause major growth. It was not until late 1988 that UK manufacturing finally regained the 1979 level; this experience contrasts markedly with comparable advanced economies, where manufacturing has in general grown significantly during the 1980s. So, as a result, the 1980s has seen an important change in the structure of the British economy: growth in the significance of service industries such as retailing and banking, and in the oil industry, but a decline in the role of manufacturing.

In fact, in manufacturing in the 1980s we have seen an extremely unusual phenomenon: rapid growth in demand for manufactures accompanied first by falling output, then by growth at rates slower than demand growth. In general, the downward trends of the 1970s continued. In measuring the growth of manufacturing output, we need to bear in mind the fact that there are cyclical fluctuations over time, so economists normally measure output growth from the peak of one cycle to the peak of the next. Typically, in advanced economies, peak-to-peak growth is positive, reflecting the long-term growth of the economy. In the 1970s, however, Britain showed the almost unprecedented phenomenon of peak-to-peak *decline*, the dimensions of which are laid out in Table 2.

But just as significant as the unprecedented fall of the 1970s is the absence of growth in the 1980s. Of the eleven industry groups described below, only two – chemical and electrical and instrument engineering – grew significantly, though in neither case could the growth rates be described as spectacular. For electrical engineering, the best performer, the average growth rate between the 1979 and

Table 2. *Peak-to-peak industrial output* (*1980 = 100*)

	1973	1979	% Growth 73–79	'Trough' (81/2)	1987	% Growth 79–87
Chemicals	99.8	110.5	10.7	100.0	131.5	19.0
Man-made fibres	175.6	137.0	−22.0	67.9	62.9	−54.1
Metal goods	141.1	121.2	−14.1	92.2	102.4	−15.5
Mechanical engineering	116.6	108.9	−6.6	86.9	88.5	−18.7
Electrical and instrument engineering	96.3	102.2	6.1	93.9	138.5	35.5
Motor vehicles	137.8	115.7	−16.0	80.1	91.4	−21.0
Other transport equipment	101.5	92.4	−9.0	91.5	100.1	8.4
Textiles	149.2	121.0	−18.9	89.6	102.9	−18.8
Clothing and footwear	111.3	115.2	3.4	92.7	107.9	−6.3
Paper, printing, etc.	110.1	108.4	1.5	91.7	112.0	3.3
Other manufacturing	114.9	112.0	−2.5	89.8	118.0	5.3
Total manufacturing	113.7	109.5	−3.7	94.0	109.9	0.37

Source: CSO Macroeconomic Time Series Data Bank, *Index of Industrial Production*; *Monthly Digest of Statistics*, No. 506, Feb. 1988.

1987 peaks was 3.9 per cent, and for chemicals it was 2.2 per cent.
But six of the eleven industries had negative growth rates; note that
for five of these industries the decline in the 1980s was bigger than
for the 1970s. Growth in the remaining three industries was derisory.
Even if we calculate from the bottom of the recession in 1981–2 to
the 1987 peak, there are few British industries whose growth reflects
the rate of growth of demand. These output figures are reflected in
the figures for investment, that is, for expenditure on increasing the
stock of machinery, equipment and so on in manufacturing. For most
of the 1980s, net manufacturing has actually been negative: scrapping
and depreciation have been outstripping new investment, and the
capital stock has been falling, as Table 3 indicates:

*Table 3. Net domestic fixed capital formation in manufacturing (£ million, 1980
prices)*

1979	1399
1980	237
1981	− 1447
1982	− 1629
1983	− 1562
1984	− 607
1985	37
1986	− 92
1987	454

Source: *UK National Accounts, 1987 and 1988*, Table 13.5.

But if the British people are consuming ever-increasing quantities
of manufactures while British industry is not producing them, it can
only mean that they are being imported. And this indeed is the case.
Over the period 1980–87 Britain's exports of goods other than oil
increased by 15.2 per cent; but imports increased by over 40 per cent
in volume. In 1976 Britain had a surplus in manufacturing trade of
£5.5bn. By 1986 it has become a deficit of £5.5bn. In 1988 the trade
deficit in manufactures was running at approximately £15bn per
year, pushing the balance of payments as a whole into a substantial
deficit, of about £11.5bn.

Accompanying this decline in manufacturing output and trade has been a major change in the pattern of employment in Britain. Between 1966 and 1979 employment in UK manufacturing fell steadily, by nearly 2 million; between 1979 and 1987 it fell by another 2 million. Over this period only one industry, financial services, has employed significantly more people (an increase of about 600,000), and the overall result has been a sustained increase in unemployment (especially long-term unemployment), and increased employment of women (especially in part-time or temporary work in service industries).

Viewing all the above changes as a whole, we can infer a transformation in the structure of the British economy. Since the eighteenth century Britain has been a major producer of manufactured goods, and has paid its way in the world through the export of manufactures. Throughout the 1970s and 1980s the position has changed. Overall, we have seen the following major shifts:

– absolute declines in manufacturing output and employment;
– rapid growth of oil output and exports;
– Britain has become a net importer of manufactured goods, on a scale which outweighs oil export earnings;
– the 'personal sector' is no longer a significant saver, and personal indebtedness has risen substantially: indeed in 1987 the 'personal sector' in the UK was in overall financial deficit, another unprecedented development;
– Britain has become, and remained, an economy with persistently high levels of unemployment.

THE RECORD OF THE 1980s

The above account suggests that Britain's economic record in the 1980s is, at very best, mixed. The record on inflation has been good (though not when compared to similar economies) and productivity growth has also been good: by no means the best in British economic history (the early 1960s were also years of sharp productivity growth) but impressive none the less. On the other hand, there are real grounds for concern over recent UK performance. Growth has been based on a consumer boom fuelled by falling savings and rising debt, neither of which are a secure source of demand growth in the long run. And the most spectacularly growing part of British economic activity concerns the financing, purchase and distribution of manufactured imports. This too cannot continue, for reasons which will be described in detail in the next chapter.

Before we address the question of whether or not the developments of the 1980s have solved Britain's fundamental problems, however, we need first to look at some of the dimensions of the long-term weaknesses of the British economy in the context of comparable economies.

THE LONG-TERM CRISIS: 1945 AND AFTER

Tracing the post-war decline on which the 'Thatcher experiment' has been superimposed involves looking at the economy in a comparative context, setting its performance against those of its competitors. Because of the competitive trading environment in which Britain exists, the 'health' of the British economy depends not only, for example, on how fast productivity is growing within it, but also on how fast productivity is growing relative to Britain's competitors. Britain is only geographically an island; economically it is tightly bound up with an international economy. International comparisons are not simply, therefore, of academic interest, they are part and parcel of understanding what is happening in the UK economy.

The 'performance' of an economy is not necessarily easily captured in figures. How well an economy is working, for those who live within it, depends on a number of things including:
- how fast it is growing;
- how efficient it is, in getting the best from the resources available;
- the level and growth of productivity, or output per person (which helps to determine competitiveness and levels of income);
- the distribution of income.

This section will concentrate on Britain's record in growth and productivity, first looking at the post-war period to 1979, and then at the experience of the 1980s.

The post-war development of the world economy has consisted of two main phases of development. The first runs from approximately 1950, when the problems of post-war industrial reconstruction were at last beginning to be solved, to 1973, when the OPEC price rises installed a period of slower growth which has lasted to the present. In both of these major phases Britain's rate of economic growth was slower than those of comparable advanced economies, as Table 4 indicates.

Table 4. Growth of output 1950–79 (GDP, constant prices)

	1950–73	1973–79
Australia	4.7	2.5
Austria	5.4	3.1
Belgium	4.1	2.3
Canada	5.2	3.2
Denmark	4.0	2.1
Finland	4.9	2.3
France	5.1	3.0
Germany	6.0	2.4
Italy	5.5	2.6
Japan	9.7	4.1
Netherlands	4.8	2.4
Norway	4.8	4.4
Sweden	3.8	1.8
Switzerland	4.5	−0.4
UK	3.0	1.3
USA	3.7	2.7
Average	4.9	2.5

Source: Angus Maddison, *Phases of Capitalist Development*, Oxford, 1982, Table 3.1, p. 45.

Clearly, in each of these periods, Britain's performance was well below average: in fact its growth rate, during the post-war boom, was the lowest of any industrialized country (though it was also, it should be added, the highest that Britain had ever achieved). In the post-1973 recession Britain's performance was second-worst: only Switzerland, which suffered a sharp though short-lived deterioration in its economy, did worse. The ratio between Britain's growth rate and the average growth rate declined during the post-1973 period (in 1950–73 the UK growth rate was approximately 40 per cent below the average growth rate; in 1973–9 it was 50 per cent below). One interpretation of this would be that Britain's performance in the 1970s was not simply due to a slowdown in the world economy; but it was also due to the fact that it handled the slowdown worse than other countries.

Britain's performance in terms of productivity – or output per person – was also weak over these two periods. The level of productivity and the rate of growth of productivity matter for two central reasons. The first is that output per person has a large bearing on income per person, and hence on standards of living; it is not the only determinant of real income, but it is an important one. The extraordinary growth in the amounts of goods and services available to the populations of the advanced countries over the past hundred and fifty years is essentially due to a dramatic growth of productivity. Looked at from another angle, productivity is a measure of efficiency, for it plays a significant part in fixing the costs at which output can be produced. In a competitive world – and a large proportion of Britain's output must compete, either in export markets or against imports within Britain – levels of productivity matter a great deal in determining the costs and hence competitiveness of products.

Rates of growth of productivity are vitally important too. If two countries begin with approximately the same level of productivity, and one then has a higher growth rate of productivity, the high-growth country will tend to generate higher incomes, lower prices and a competitive advantage. This process can become cumulative, with increasing disparities emerging between countries. This is indeed what has happened to Britain. Table 5, which looks again at the two broad stages in the post-war period, indicates something of the productivity gap.

Once again there was a sharp slowdown in the second period, and once again Britain performed worse than average, and much worse than its main industrial rivals (Japan, W. Germany, Italy, France and Canada), though rather better than the USA. This last phenomenon

Table 5. Rates of productivity growth (%), *1950–79* (*Annual average compound growth rates of GDP per man-hour*)

	1950–73	1973–79
Australia	2.6	2.6
Austria	5.9	3.8
Belgium	4.4	4.2
Canada	3.0	1.0
Denmark	4.3	1.6
Finland	5.2	1.7
France	5.1	3.5
Germany	6.0	4.2
Italy	5.8	2.5
Japan	8.0	3.9
Netherlands	4.4	3.3
Norway	4.0	4.4
Sweden	4.2	1.9
Switzerland	3.4	1.3
UK	3.1	2.1
USA	2.6	1.4
Average	4.5	2.7

Source: Angus Maddison, *Phases of Capitalist Development*, Oxford, 1982, drawn from Table 5.1, p. 96.

has a ready explanation, however. For most of the post-war period the USA has been the world technological leader, and one effect of this is that other countries could follow the US path, using US technologies without the pains and problems and costs of developing them. 'Follower' economies can thus often attain higher productivity growth rates than 'leader' economies, though they may not be able actually to overtake them. But Britain's productivity growth has rarely reached the rates achieved by other 'followers', and has in general been markedly lower than comparable economies'. These figures of course refer to the whole economy; but it should be noted that the differentials in productivity have been confirmed by a number of studies at plant level, in which output per worker, even in similarly equipped plants producing similar products, has been shown to be markedly lower (by up to 50 per cent) in Britain.

The most obvious effect of this record of slow growth and slow productivity growth has been a stark relative decline in British incomes, compared with the same group of countries. There are serious problems in making cross-country income comparisons, but the figures in Table 6 give at least a broad indication of the differences involved.

Table 6. National income, per person (1979, US dollars)

Switzerland	13,920
Sweden	11,930
Denmark	11,900
W. Germany	11,730
Belgium	10,920
Norway	10,700
USA	10,630
Netherlands	10,230
France	9,950
Canada	9,640
Australia	9,120
Japan	8,810
Austria	8,630
Finland	8,160
UK	6,530
Italy	5,250

Source: World Bank, *World Development Report 1981*, Table 1, p. 135.

How has this comparative picture altered during the 1980s? Overall, Britain's relative performance has improved slightly, although the improvement cannot be said to be substantial. Table 7 demonstrates this in terms of average growth rates of output and productivity.

It can be seen that Britain's output growth rate remains below the average of its OECD partners, though it is no longer the lowest. Productivity growth has improved, but remains below Japan, France and Germany and is nowhere near sufficient to overhaul the long-

Table 7. Output and productivity in the 1980s: average growth rates (%)

	Output (1980–87)	Productivity (1979–86)
USA	2.3	0.6
Japan	3.9	2.8
Germany	1.5	2.0
France	1.6	2.3
UK	1.9	1.9
Italy	2.3	1.3
Canada	2.9	1.1
OECD Average	2.4	1.4

Source: *OECD Economic Outlook*, 43, Tables 23 and R.1.

term productivity gap between the UK and its major trading partners. If we examine other indicators of performance, we see a similar picture. For example, Britain's inflation record is unimpressive: it continues to have a higher inflation rate than all of the above countries other than Italy. Likewise with trading performance: Britain's exports are growing slower than its export markets (and so our share of world trade continues to fall), and imports are growing at a record rate. Finally there is the question of unemployment. Here measurement is difficult because the UK unemployment statistics have been shamelessly massaged: the method of computing the statistics has been altered seventeen times since 1980, each time with the effect of lowering the unemployment figure. But none of this can conceal the fact that the UK remains a society of mass unemployment, with the highest unemployment rate among the advanced economies.

CONCLUSION

Has Thatcherism overcome the economic crisis which it inherited? The answer is no: we have seen that British growth in the 1980s has consisted essentially of a debt-fuelled consumer boom which has resulted in a massive trade deficit. On the one hand this growth is unsustainable, and on the other hand it has produced structural changes which involve serious reductions in Britain's manufacturing capability. In many industries decline in the 1980s has been worse than that of the 1970s. Britain's relative performance, in terms of inflation, productivity and the growth of output, has not in fact markedly improved. The Thatcher experiment, for these reasons, in no way resolves the fundamental problems of industrial decline and international competitiveness which are at the heart of Britain's long-running economic difficulties. We turn now to an examination of the real dimensions of these difficulties, and their underlying causes.

Growth and Trade –
Components of the Crisis

Improvements in the incomes, living standards and welfare of any country's people are in large part an effect of success in generating economic growth. Of course, growth is by no means the only contributor to these things, nor does it guarantee anything: much depends, for instance, on how its benefits are distributed among the population. And certainly growth brings many new problems in its wake. Even so, it remains the basic process by which problems of poverty, unemployment and low incomes – Britain's problems – can be overcome.

The previous chapter showed that Britain's growth record has been very poor: in the 1950s and 60s Britain's growth rates were the highest it had ever achieved. Yet they were dismal when set against those of comparable economies; and in the 1970s even that slow growth evaporated and an absolute decline began. This chapter sets out an analytical framework for understanding these developments, within which some of the basic elements of Britain's decline can be identified. It is concerned essentially with two types of problem:

1. The nature of economic growth. What does economic growth actually consist of, and what are its mechanisms? In particular, what is the relationship between technological change and economic growth?

2. The role of international trade for an economy like that of the UK. Why does the trading position of the economy matter, and what is the relationship between it and the economy's growth record and growth prospects?

ECONOMIC GROWTH

Economic growth is an increase in the total output of an economy over time. It can result from two quite separate processes. On the one hand there may be a growth in output resulting simply from an increase in the number of workers and an increase – sufficient to employ them – in the economy's stock of machines and equipment. This is, in other words, an expansion of existing activities; it means doing the same sorts of things on a wider scale (in fact, economists sometimes call this 'capital-widening' growth). Such growth involves an increase in total output, but no increase in output per person, or in income per person. We can call this 'extensive' growth.

On the other hand there is a further dimension of economic growth in which, in the words of Professor Simon Kuznets – one of the most influential of modern growth theorists – 'we identify the economic growth of nations as a substantial increase in per capita or per worker product.'[1] Here, economic growth occurs not because of more workers but because of increased output by existing workers: in other words, productivity growth. We might call this 'intensive growth'. Now this 'intensive' productivity growth is a complex process involving many activities ranging from basic scientific research through to the development and application of quite small-scale skills in production. But in general it involves changes in the capital stock; that is, changes in the array of plant, equipment, machines and so on with which workers produce. These changes take the form either of increases in the amount of equipment available for each worker to work with, or improvements in technology which increase either the quantity or quality of output which can be produced with available quantities of capital and labour.

Clearly these two types of growth – extensive and intensive – have gone hand in hand in the course of the development of the advanced economies. But it is the second type, based on productivity growth, which is more important and on which the attention of economists has focused. The reason is obvious: rises in output per head are one of the few paths to rising incomes and standards of living and shorter working periods. Since these are among the central objectives of economic activity as such, the importance of intensive growth stands out. Another reason is that there is considerable research evidence to suggest that productivity increases, resulting from broad technological improvements, have made the most important contribution to the rapid economic growth of the advanced economies since 1850. The massive rises in income, and the dramatically shortened working week, which have characterized Western economic development, are the result of intensive forms of growth.

So what is entailed by this intensive, productivity-increasing mode of growth? What kinds of activity promote it or retard it?

The most general point is that intensive growth involves a process of almost continuous *change* within the economy. This change occurs along three main axes, to do with the kinds of activities on which the economy is based (that is, its structure); with the kinds of products which are produced (its output mix); and with how products are produced (its technology). We can consider each of these types of change in turn:

1. Structural change

Structural change means simply a shift of emphasis within the activities which make up the economy; by itself it can raise productivity and generate growth. For example, in many economies agriculture is less advanced technically and less productive than manufacturing. If workers move, therefore, from agricultural work into a manufacturing job, their productivity will automatically rise and output will grow. These kinds of shifts have historically been important in raising productivity, but are obviously limited; only so many people can be moved out of agriculture, and the productivity improvements gained thereby are a once-for-all affair. But structural shifts of this type remain important. Recently, for example, manufacturing employment has dropped in the UK – as we have seen – while service employment has risen; since services are, on the whole, less productive, the result is a fall in average productivity and in overall output.

2. Changing the product mix

The general mix of products being turned out by an economy clearly changes over time. In the first place, some products simply drop out of production: whale-bone corsets and horse-drawn wagons are no longer made. Others remain but fade from significance, like lace, or horseshoes. And completely new products emerge, such as – in the twentieth century – electrical goods and, more recently, electronic and microprocessor-based products. Finally, within this broad process of change, some things remain in production, yet change their character so much as to be, in effect, new products: transistor as opposed to valve radios, digital as opposed to mechanical watches. We could sum up by saying that there is continuous product change in terms of design characteristics, technical attributes, materials and functions. The question is, what is the *economic* significance of such change?

There is in fact an important relationship between product change and economic growth. We can start by noting that, in order for output to grow, the demand for that output must also be growing. For any particular country within the world economy, product demand can grow for two reasons: either the total market is growing, or that country's share of the market is growing. Now when the world economy grows, when world incomes grow, the demand for all individual products also grows. But these demands for individual products do not grow at the same pace; some, in fact, grow faster than others. Over the past ten years, for example, world income and demand have grown; but the market for stereo equipment, for instance, has grown much faster than the market for nuclear power stations. As a general rule, as incomes grow, the demand for manufactured products grows faster than the demand for agricultural goods.

This suggests that a first condition for growth is that a country must be producing goods for which demand is growing: often, this will mean *new* products, since the expansionary possibilities here will usually be greater than for older products whose demand pattern is more stable. After the Second World War, for example, consumer durables such as refrigerators and washing machines – which in Europe were essentially new products – were in strong demand and became an important motor of post-war growth. At the present time, demand for consumer electronics, notably video equipment, is growing, and this promotes growth in Japan, the only significant producing country.

But it is not, by itself, enough to be producing in new and expanding product groups. Products also have to *compete* to maintain their share of the market, and for both new and old products this also means change: the development of new designs, of new standards of performance, and so on. The motorcar of the 1980s is very different from that of the 50s; in this field, as in many others, world competition relates not just to prices but to the technical standards of the product. If producers are to stay in business they must keep up, therefore, with the frontiers of technical change in the design of the product.

These considerations suggest that product change is central to economic growth simply because without it, demand is unlikely to grow. Thus growth is not just a matter of efficiency, but of efficiency in producing the right sorts of things: there is no percentage in being the world's most efficient producer of whale-bone corsets. Moreover, from this perspective, 'de-industrialization' can be seen not as a bad thing, necessarily, but as a vital concomitant of growth. 'De-industrialization', in the sense of running down industries in declining product areas, and building them up for products with high and rising demand, should be normal practice for a successful economy.

3. New processes: changing methods of production

The other crucial aspect of change is not in products but in the processes of production through which they are made. New products generally entail new production techniques. But even where products remain broadly the same – as in steel, or chemicals – methods of production change. Such changes can take a wide variety of forms. Some may be very dramatic, shifting the whole nature of production: in chemicals, for example, an important shift was from 'batch' techniques to a continuous 'flow' process; the analogous shift in cars was from individual assembly – one car at a time – to the production line. Such 'big' changes can also take the form of changes in power sources (oil and electrical power for coal and steam), or materials (plastics for metals), or methods of work organization (the factory for the artisan's workshop). At present, the rapid introduction of robots into manufacturing assembly – made possible by microprocessors – may well be such a 'big' shift.

At a less spectacular level there are frequent small changes in production processes which raise overall productivity. In a competitive world the economy must be flexible along the whole spectrum of such changes; it must keep in touch with 'best-practice' techniques of production, or lose out to its competitors. In processes as with products, the economy must be in the business of continuous change.

Such 'process' transformations necessarily involve changes in the nature of work, in the numbers of people employed, and in the kinds of jobs they do. Here again there must be flexibility, an openness to the possibilities of de-industrialization. A growing and efficient economy must somehow solve the problem of shifting people from declining to growing industries, from low-productivity to high-productivity jobs; it must be able to absorb the consequences of technical change. As a very minimum this involves recognizing and overcoming complex problems of education, retraining, and relocation; but it entails many further problems of industrial policy.

GROWTH AND TECHNOLOGY

To sum these ideas up, we can say that economic growth implies a continuous, multi-faceted process of change: a process which Joseph Schumpeter called 'creative destruction', as old methods and products make way for new. This is nothing other than the process of technological and technical innovation. So the theoretical point in all of this is that growth and technological change go hand in hand; they are indissolubly linked, for it is technological change that makes growth possible, as Professor Kuznets rightly argues,

a sustained high rate of growth depends on a continuous emergence of new inventions, providing the bases for new industries whose high rates of growth compensate for the inevitable slowing down of the older industries. A high rate of overall growth in an economy is thus necessarily accompanied by considerable shifting in relative importance among industries, as the old decline and the new increase in the nation's output.[2] [My italics.]

This emergence of new inventions and innovations does not, of course, happen by accident. It involves the commitment of resources directed specifically at generating technological progress: in a word, it involves *investment*. Now investment in technology-based growth means that resources must be committed to two types of activity.

First, there are research and development (R & D) activities, which are aimed specifically at producing new technologies. These R & D activities can range all the way from basic scientific research, via forms of applied technological study, through to the design and construction of new machines and products. It is extremely important to note that this R & D activity need not be confined to the direct development of technologies: it can also consist of a search for useful technology imports. At the technological level, the world economy is characterized – as the previous chapter noted with respect to the US growth record – by a distinction between 'leader' and 'follower' economies. Follower economies can and should devote a large part of their R & D activity to obtaining the technologies of more advanced economies. This has been a notable feature of rapid economic development in Western Europe in the mid nineteenth century (using British technology), in the Soviet Union in the 1930s (using US and European technologies), in Western Europe after the Second World War (using American technologies). The most striking example, however, is Japan, which has combined a high level of domestic R & D with a very high level of technology import from Europe and the USA; Japan's remarkable economic growth has been heavily dependent on foreign technologies, but the point is that this has required a substantial commitment of R & D resources aimed at seeking out the most useful, adaptable and profitable techniques for import.

The second aspect of investment is industrial construction itself: the commitment of resources to building up the industries which will either use or produce the outcome of R & D activity.

For an economy to grow successfully, these two kinds of investment must be 'adequate' in two different senses. On the one hand, investment must be 'adequate' in volume or amount: a country must devote enough of its income to such investment, so that it has both the ability and the economic capacity to produce a level of output that will maintain its incomes and employment. On the other hand, investment must be adequate in what we might call *direction*: it must be directed towards viable activities, meaning areas of R & D and production where there actually will be a pay-off and profits.

These kinds of theoretical points about the relationship between technology and growth suggest various propositions about the poor British growth record outlined in Chapter 1. Specifically, they suggest that Britain's growth problems have been tied up with a technological weakness. *Britain has not devoted enough of its resources to R & D and production investment; and the resources it has committed have gone to the wrong areas.* The consequence has been low rates of growth. Conversely, it could be argued that the success of countries like Japan and West Germany is an effect of success in managing the processes of technological innovation and investment.

These propositions form the first part of a framework for understanding the British predicament. The next two chapters will look at some of the relevant evidence, which suggests that technological weaknesses are indeed at the root of Britain's slow growth problem. However, we also need to ask why this slow growth should involve a crisis, a threat to the viability of the UK economy. Here it is necessary to look at the 'external' position of the economy: at its import–export structure, and its balance of payments, and at the economic role they play in an economy like Britain's. Against this 'external' background we can discern the really worrying implications of the slowdown and end of British economic growth in the 1970s.

THE EXTERNAL PROBLEM

Britain's place as part of an international economy is central to its economic functioning. To some extent this is for geophysical reasons: Britain is a small, overpopulated island which needs to import about half its food, and a large proportion of the raw materials used in industry. Obviously it must export to finance such imports. But there is more to the problem of exports than this. This is because the 'balance of payments' – in which Britain's economic relationships with the world are summed up – is not simply a set of accounts. It involves the operation of powerful economic forces which place real constraints on the rate at which Britain can grow, and on the level of income and employment which it can sustain. It sets limits on the kinds of policies which can be adopted. As we shall see, for an economy like Britain's, manufactured exports and imports play an important role within the balance of payments, which is why the growth failures and technological weaknesses − referred to above − have very disturbing implications for the future. But in order to depict the problem accurately, we need to look first at the meaning of the balance of payments and then at its mechanisms; then at the structure of British trade and the prospects for the future.

In essence, the balance of payments records the purchases and sales of sterling and foreign currencies related to two kinds of transaction. The first are called 'current account' transactions; these refer to all imports and exports of goods (such as cars or machinery or food) and services (such as insurance sales or tourist activities). Goods and services are sometimes referred to as 'visibles' and 'invisibles' respectively. The second type of transactions are called 'capital account' transactions; they refer to the shift of money into and out of Britain for the purchase of assets − shares, bonds, bank deposits, land, plant and equipment, etc.

The ratio at which pounds exchange for other currencies within these transactions is, of course, the 'exchange rate'; it plays an important part in keeping all of these transactions in balance, and every country must have some policy on how its exchange rate is fixed. There are in fact a range of possible exchange rate systems, each with different implications for the economy. One is a system of fixed, unalterable rates, such as the 'Bretton Woods' system which governed the advanced market economies between the end of the Second World War and 1971. With this system governments fix a definite set of rates, which are changed only at long intervals; for most of the post-war period, for example, pounds exchanged with dollars at the fixed rate of $2.80 = £1, until 1967 when the pound was devalued to $2.40 = £1. In order to keep the rate stable, governments would hold large reserves of gold and foreign currencies, which in Britain were and are held in a special account in the Bank of England called the 'Exchange Equalization Account'. When, for example, Britain imported more than it exported it would need more foreign currency than it was currently earning to pay for the imports; the Bank of England would supply this by running down its reserves. Conversely, when Britain had a surplus of exports over imports, foreign buyers would need extra sterling to pay UK exporting firms; then the Bank would supply sterling in exchange for foreign currencies, which would go into the Exchange Equalization Account, thus increasing UK reserves. In this way the Bank ensured that the supply and demand of sterling and foreign currencies were always in balance at the going exchange rate, and the rate was thus fixed.

At a polar extreme from the fixed-rate system is the 'floating-rate' regime. Here the government supplies neither sterling nor foreign currencies into the foreign exchange markets. In consequence, the supply of sterling into the market (from importers wanting to buy foreign currencies), and the demand for sterling (from foreign buyers of our exports, who need to change their money into pounds to pay UK companies for the goods), can be out of balance. This causes the exchange rate, which is the 'price' of sterling in terms of other currencies, to move. A surplus of exports over imports means a demand for sterling greater than the supply, and vice versa. Thus, in this system, the day-to-day exchange rate can fluctuate quite sharply.

Apart from holding and using foreign currency reserves, there is one further way the government can affect the movement of currency (and hence, in the floating system, the exchange rate). This is by affecting capital movements through interest rates. A rise in interest rates will induce foreign investors to shift their capital to Britain, since they can now get a better return than elsewhere. This has the effect of increasing the reserves (with fixed rates), or pushing up the exchange rate (with floating rates). In principle, therefore, the government can keep the overall supply of, and demand for, sterling in balance by varying the basic interest rate: if there is a surplus on current account (exports are greater than imports) then it can lower the interest rate to produce a deficit on capital account (more capital goes out than comes in). If the capital account deficit exactly offsets the current account surplus, then there will be no change in either reserves or the exchange rate.

At present, Britain operates a system which is somewhere between the fixed and floating-rate models – it is called a 'managed float'. The exchange rate is allowed to float, but the Bank of England intervenes with its reserves to iron out temporary fluctuations. In addition, interest rates also shift to stabilize the rate.

So in any one year the balance of payments consists broadly of three items:

- the current account balance;
- the capital account balance;
- the 'balance for official financing': i.e., the change in the reserves as a result of Bank of England intervention.

The 'balance for official financing' is equal to the difference between the current and capital account balances; this means that by definition the whole thing sums to zero − the balance of payments really is a balance. In 1980, for example, the current account was in surplus to the tune of approximately £3 billion; the capital account was in deficit by £1.8 billion; and official financing − in this case involving additions to reserves − was approximately £1.2 billion. Net balance: zero.

This particular accounting identity *always* holds true: the balance of payments is always in short-term balance, or 'equilibrium'.

However, the problem of balance of payments equilibrium goes much further than this. Clearly, if Britain had a serious overall deficit, it could not finance this by running down the reserves over an indefinite period, simply because the Bank of England's foreign currency reserves are finite. Sooner or later they would run out. Then, if not before, the exchange rate would begin to depreciate or even collapse. In theory, this could in itself solve the problem of disequilibrium, since a falling exchange rate means that our exports are becoming cheaper and imports dearer; hence exports would rise and imports fall, and we would move back into basic balance. But this mechanism is by no means as certain as the textbooks tell us, and there would be formidable problems of adjustment (including falling real incomes) along the way.

The upshot of all this is that the basic balance of payments − the current and capital accounts − must be kept broadly in equilibrium. Consequently, the British economy cannot develop in ways, nor can economic policies be adopted, which are incompatible with an underlying balance on our external accounts. We cannot, for example, allow the economy to grow if that growth produces large imbalances in our foreign trade. For a concrete example of the problems here, we can look back to the so-called 'stop–go' cycles of the 1950s and 1960s. This is not just a historical exercise: the basic difficulty it points up is still with us.

THE STOP–GO CYCLE

For much of the 1950s and 1960s Britain was characterized by short bursts of expansion in economic activity, followed by bouts of contraction or recession: the 'stop–go' cycle, in which the 'stop' signal was a balance of payments problem. Typically, the cycle would run like this: for one reason or another – possibly to reduce unemployment – the government would attempt to expand the economy. Growth would be induced by raising demand through tax cuts, increases in public spending and so on. This would cause output to rise and unemployment to fall in Britain; consequently incomes would rise, consumer expenditure would rise, and so would spending by firms on raw materials and equipment.

But as this happened, the 'external constraint' would begin to make itself felt. The problem was this: with given prices, Britain's exports are essentially determined – in the short term – by *world* demand, that is, by the level of world income. Imports, however, are determined by the level of income in Britain. So as the government expanded the economy, imports would grow faster than exports, because the world economy would not be matching Britain's short-term acceleration in growth. The result of imports outpacing exports was thus a balance of trade deficit, and a balance of payments crisis. The foreign currency reserves in the Bank of England would fall as Britain used more foreign currency to pay for imports than it earned from exports. The government effectively had only one response to this: to throw the gears into reverse, and slow down the rise in British income. It would, in a word, deflate the economy – reduce spending and incomes by increases in taxes, raise interest rates (which would have the effect of attracting foreign capital), and cut government expenditure, and so on.

The 'stop–go' cycle was essentially a short-term process, and in the context of the 1950s and 1960s was not too serious, since both the world economy and the British economy were growing at record rates anyway. (It should be mentioned, perhaps, that the stop–go cycle cannot be held responsible for Britain's poor relative performance in those years, since other countries – such as West Germany – experienced the same problems, if anything in a more severe form).

But the point of all this – and it is a very important one – is that there was (and is) an *external constraint* on British growth. It was simply not possible for Britain to grow at a faster rate than that which was compatible with balance of payments equilibrium. And this constraint could be extended to unemployment: Britain could not employ more workers than was consistent with external balance.

Moreover, this external constraint is not confined to the short term: it also affects the long-run attainable rate of growth in the UK.

THE LONG-RUN CONSTRAINT

In the long run, Britain faces a constraint which is analogous to that of the stop–go cycle. As the economy grows, demand for imports grows: some are demanded directly, as raw material inputs for production; others indirectly as people spend part of their growing incomes on imported goods. As this happens, exports must expand in order to maintain a basic balance of payments equilibrium. If this does not occur, then there will have to be a slowdown in growth, and a slowdown – or even contraction – in incomes and employment until external equilibrium is restored. This is the problem which policies of tariff protection – widely advanced by such people as Wynne Godley and the Cambridge Economic Policy Group – are meant to overcome.

This problem of an external constraint, of course, confronts all of the successful industrial economies. How have they solved it?

TECHNOLOGICAL INNOVATION
AND EXPORT PERFORMANCE

Here we must return to the process of economic growth, and outline the connection between it and a successful external performance. As we saw earlier, success in economic growth involves success in research and development, in the innovation of new products and processes, and involves directing these activities towards growing, high-demand markets. These markets need not be, indeed cannot be, exclusively home markets. On the contrary, export markets are necessary in order to recoup the large development costs typically associated with modern innovation. But innovation of itself plays a large part in opening up these markets, since a great deal of international competition is not just price competition (though successful innovation does tend to lower prices) but is in the areas of quality and design. This is especially true in high-income countries. Thus it is resources devoted to innovation which open up the possibility of economic growth; but it is precisely the same thing which delivers success in export markets. The Japanese example is, by now, a rather trite one to deploy; but it is simply the most extreme case of a general phenomenon. Cars, cameras, motorbikes, consumer electronics are all areas where the rewards for innovation and product quality are high; these rewards include the expansion of export markets, and by that fact the overcoming of the external constraint on growth. So the successful economies removed the external constraint by exporting the same innovation-based high technology manufactures which made their growth possible in the first place. Moreover the effects were cumulative.

CUMULATIVE GROWTH AND CUMULATIVE DECLINE

Economies which succeed in generating innovation-based growth, and in consequence a high-technology export pattern, can readily find themselves in a kind of spiral of success. Strong export performance and high growth generate the resources for investment in further innovative effort; this in turn produces further export and growth success, and the cycle can repeat itself. Again, this is particularly noticeable of Japan, but the pattern of innovation → export success → growth → further innovation is one which can be found in the export specialisms of a number of countries. We might call it a 'virtuous circle', as opposed to the converse 'vicious circle' of decline, which is equally possible: low growth and low incomes, feeding into low investment and innovation levels, further low growth and so on.

Important consequences, for Britain, flow from such considerations. If this picture of the mechanisms of economic growth is correct, then Britain's low growth rates of output and productivity – which were traced in the previous chapter – cannot simply be shrugged off. This is because they imply that the technological frontier being set by the most advanced industrial economies is moving continuously *away* from the technological levels attained by the UK economy. If both high and low growth are cumulative, then Britain will be falling further and further behind; and because competitiveness at the level of the world economy means *technological* competitiveness, then the possibility emerges of Britain finding great difficulty in competing *at all*. The consequences of that, for a country like Britain, would be desperately serious.

It may seem, of course, that this picture of cumulative decline and potential collapse is overdrawn. Yet it would account, for example, for the fact that Britain's performance, relative to other countries, has worsened over the 1970s. The fact that Britain has entered a period of *absolute* decline would accord with these ideas of a cumulative slide. Finally there are the recent trends in Britain's foreign trade position. Here the situation is very worrying: it seems to indicate that Britain is becoming systematically less able to survive in the world economy. The place of manufacturing and manufactured exports — precisely the products for which technological innovation is so crucial — are central here; and it is here, in the underlying trade position, that the real British crisis is to be found.

BRITAIN'S TRADE STRUCTURE: THE EMERGING CRISIS

Now let us try to combine these ideas about growth and foreign trade to assemble a picture of the problems confronting Britain. First, we need to look at Britain's exports and imports of goods (visible trade) and services (invisibles), that is, at the items which make up the current account of the balance of payments. Three types of traded item are important:
- raw materials, food and fuel;
- manufactures;
- 'invisibles': banking, insurance and so on.

Since the first half of the nineteenth century, Britain has had a quite specific structure of trade in these categories. Firstly, it has run a large *deficit* in the first item: about half of food consumption, and a considerable volume of raw materials, are imported, while historically, exports in these areas have been small, hence a deficit. This deficit on raw materials has been offset by large surpluses in the other items, namely manufactures and invisibles. Overall, the current account was never actually an exact balance – it didn't need to be – but over a run of years this structure generated a rough balance. The general picture can be seen, for example, in the figures for 1972, a year selected more or less at random (see table 8).

Table 8. Current account balance, 1972 (£ million)

Visible balance		
Food, beverages, tobacco	−1,498	(deficit)
Basic materials	−811	(deficit)
Mineral fuels and lubricants	−707	(deficit)
Semi-manufactured goods	+457	(surplus)
Finished manufactured goods	+1,688	(surplus)
Other	+123	(surplus)
Visible balance:	−748	(overall deficit)
Invisible balance	+995	(surplus)
Current balance:	+247	(overall surplus)

Source: *UK Balance of Payments 1983*, Tables 1.1 and 2.3.

The offsetting deficits and surpluses can easily be seen; they have been an almost permanent fixture, in much this form, in Britain's peace-time external accounts for many years.

Recently, however, things have changed. The first development has been a shift in emphasis for the direction of trade: the EEC has taken considerably more of our exports, and developing countries less. Much more important than this, however, has been the emergence of North Sea oil, which has turned Britain into a major exporter of oil, running large surpluses on the current account. As recently as 1976 the deficit on trade in oil was nearly £4bn; but by 1980 there was a surplus of £273 million. The move from deficit to surplus on oil is one reason why the UK is now running a strong current account surplus. It was an unforeseen development, and moreover a very fortunate one indeed.

It is fortunate for a very simple reason: it has come just in time to offset a precipitous worsening of the picture in one of the central categories of Britain's external accounts – in manufacturing. The surplus here which – with the surplus on 'invisibles' – has underpinned the UK's international position, has been eroding fast. Manufactured imports have been growing at a considerably faster rate than exports, and the result, inevitably, is a sharp decline in the trade balance in manufactures. In 1971 the value of Britain's manufactured exports was 97 per cent higher than that of manufactured imports; in 1975 it was 48 per cent higher; in 1980 it was 23 per cent higher. In 1983 Britain's manufacturing trade went into deficit. The trend is steadily downward, and the implication is clear: not only are British manufactured goods competing poorly in international markets, they are competing poorly against imports within Britain itself. The collapse in our manufacturing output – down 13 per cent since 1971 – is reflected in a collapse in our trade in manufactures.

This would not matter if oil was a permanent fixture. But of course it is not: North Sea oil will reach its peak of production in the mid 1980s, and in the 1990s output will begin to decline. This particular item will be removed from Britain's balance of payments, and Britain will return to its historic position, of depending on manufactures.

But the manufacturing output on which Britain will have to rely has disappeared. The consequence of Britain's failure to match the investment levels, the technological standards and the design skills of its competitors is the erosion of its industrial manufacturing base. The capacity to re-enter the world of technology-based manufacturing on the required scale is, as things stand, non-existent.

CONCLUSION

This, then, is the crisis which faces Britain. De-industrialization has undercut the foundations of the precarious structure of economic activities which is the British economy. This process has been masked by the discovery of oil, which has prevented the deterioration in manufactured trade from leading to a collapse of the exchange rate. But sooner rather than later the flow of oil which now sustains the balance of payments – and thus the living standards of Britain's people – will slow and then end. When that happens, the British economy as it now exists will become non-viable, since there seems little likelihood of Britain smoothly replacing exports of oil with exports of manufactures. The actual development of the situation, and its outcome, are virtually impossible to predict. But Britain will then face stark choices: it must either reconstruct its industrial base – a process which will involve heavy investment expenditures, and thus considerable sacrifices in consumption and the living standards of Britain's people – or accept dramatically lower levels of real incomes as the exchange rate deteriorates.

The following chapters trace the development of this impasse, before we move to some of the strategic questions of policy which must be faced if this crisis is to be overcome.

3

The Long Decline

     The path of the British economy since the late nineteenth century has been one of persistent decline relative to its main industrial competitors. While the pace of the decline has altered from time to time, it has never in peace-time been arrested, let alone reversed. It is the background against which our current predicament should be viewed, for some – though not all – of our current problems are nothing more than the cumulative effects of that decline. And some – though not all – of the forces causing the decline are still at work in the modern UK economy. Understanding it, therefore, is a part of understanding our present malaise.

The decline has had two main aspects. The first can be expressed in terms of the figures for national income (or the total value of goods and services produced annually in Britain), and the economic indicators associated with these figures. Since around 1880, Britain's rate of growth of national income has been significantly lower – often less than half – than those of its main competitors. At the same time, the growth rate of productivity (or output per worker) has been slower: again, often less than half those of competitor countries. The productivity measure is particularly important because it affects the overall growth rate, the competitiveness of British exports, and the incomes of the British population. Finally, Britain's share of world trade in manufactures has declined, from about 40 per cent in 1880, to less than 7 per cent a century later.

These disparities in growth rates meant that first Germany and the USA, then France, Japan, Scandinavia and a number of other economies began to grow at a faster pace than Britain, then to overtake and surpass British levels of income per person. In 1981 this group of countries included, for the first time, a socialist one, East Germany.

In 1880, of course, Britain dominated the world economy, in production, in trade, and in finance. As other economies industrialized and grew, a decline from Britain's position of pre-eminence was entirely predictable. But it is important to be precise about what form that decline might be expected to take, for while some aspects of decline were inevitable, others were not. In the first place, as the world economy grew, and as world trade grew, Britain's share in world output and trade would clearly fall. Moreover, during the period of industrializing growth, as other economies reached towards Britain's income level, their growth rates would be higher than Britain's. If they were to attain British levels of productivity, then their growth rates of productivity would also be higher. This much could be expected. But a smaller share of world output and trade remains compatible with high levels of productivity and income. There is no reason why, in the process of world growth, Britain's levels of productivity and income should ultimately have fallen below those of other countries. In recent years, for example, Sweden's share of world output and trade has fallen, while its income and productivity levels remain among the highest in the world. Although it might be too much to expect a levelling out of growth rates and incomes in the advanced countries, large and increasing disparities would be unexpected, particularly in the case of Britain, an economy which had been at the frontier of industrial advance. Yet a gap in incomes and productivity not only emerged, it widened unceasingly over a long period; this was entirely unexpected and certainly was not inevitable. The end result has been that of the European 'industrial market economies' Britain has one of the lowest levels of productivity, and lowest levels of income per person.

Accompanying this relative income decline, and in fact underlying it, is the second aspect of overall decline. It consists in a decline in the technological level of the economy, an inflexibility in responding to the direction and opportunities of technological advance. What is involved here is the problem raised in the previous chapter: the capacity of an economy to transform its industrial structure. Economic growth does not consist of simply performing the same economic activities on a larger scale. It involves not expansion, but *change*: the construction of new industries in response to changing patterns of demand and technological possibility, and the demise of old industries where the demand for their products is falling. Even where a product remains unchanged, it may be necessary to change the process of production in order to remain competitive and to survive. The capacity for such change is an essential component of overall economic growth, and of growth in incomes: British industry turned out to lack that capacity, at least in the degree required. In the late nineteenth and early twentieth centuries the structure of the advanced economies changed. New industries – such as chemicals, and electrical products – emerged, and old ones either disappeared or were transformed from within by new methods of production. To 'decline' in this context meant to stick with the old industries and old methods of production, and to develop the new only inadequately. This is precisely what happened in Britain.

Before describing this process, however, something should be said about the effects of relative decline. Many have consoled themselves, over the past century or so, with the thought that relative decline means only that we are growing slower than others; it does not mean that we are not growing at all. If the total world economy is growing, then relative decline is quite compatible with an absolute improvement in output, exports, living standards and so on. In the period with which this chapter is concerned, from 1880 to the eve of the Second World War, *per capita* income in Britain increased by over 100 per cent, even though in other countries it was increasing faster. From 1880 to the First World War, Britain's share of world trade declined, but the actual volume of exports in fact doubled. Unfortunately these comforting thoughts can involve illusions, in a number of ways. The first problem is that relative decline, although compatible with growth, may indicate that the economy is not performing as well as it could. It may indicate inefficiency, wasted resources, possibilities for better results which are not being explored. In a country plagued, like Britain, with continuing problems of poverty, this possibility cannot lightly be ignored. Secondly, if the overall system begins to stagnate, as it has done in recent years, then relative decline can become absolute decline.

Finally, and most importantly, consistent relative decline can impair the technological basis of the economy, and thus its entire future. If economic growth and technological change go hand in hand, then a poor growth performance indicates a low rate of technological change. Clearly, these aspects overlap each other and are cumulative: low growth = low level of technological transformation = further low growth, and so on. The point is that low relative growth can mean an emerging gap between the actual technological level of the economy, and the technological frontier set by the leading economies. If this gap becomes wide enough, then ultimately an inability to compete internationally may result; there may come a 'critical point' in this process, beyond which absolute decline and industrial collapse set in.

The account which follows describes some industrial aspects of Britain's relative decline. The overall process was very complex, being tied up, for example, with Britain's position as a foreign investor country, with the role of London as a financial centre and the role of sterling as a 'world currency', with government economic policies (which were often suicidally ill-chosen), and with the effects of trade wars and shooting wars. But for the time being these complexities will be put to one side, and the emphasis will be on *what* happened in Britain's industrial economy rather than *why*. This process of development and decline will be contrasted with the experience of other industrialized economies, particularly Germany.

THE STRUCTURE OF BRITISH INDUSTRIALIZATION

British economic growth really began in the late eighteenth century, and was ultimately spread across a wide range of industries and products. The so-called 'industrial revolution' actually had precious little that was industrial about it in a technological sense: it consisted to a great extent of changes in the organization and management of work, in new methods of marketing, finance and the control of enterprises. Inside this broad wave of economic change and expansion, however, occurred a truly spectacular growth in a relatively few industries. These industries came to have a quite disproportionate weight in the economy as a whole, and particularly in exports. Most British capital investment was concentrated in them, and their massive export success made possible a new economic structure based on the import of large quantities of raw materials and a major part of the nation's food supply.

Since they were the bedrock of Britain's economic system, they have become known as the 'staple' industries. They were – in approximate order of appearance – coal, textiles (especially cotton), iron and steel, and engineering (especially shipbuilding, but also railway components and machine manufacture).

Of these, probably the most important was the textile sector. From 1760, when the industry first began to expand, to the beginning of the nineteenth century, the value of output grew from around half a million pounds annually, to approximately £15 million. Throughout the nineteenth century this growth continued, at compound rates of between 3 and 6 per cent per year; the value of annual output topped £100 million in the late 1860s. By a judicious combination of economic efficiency and military/political force the few serious competitors were destroyed, and major international markets were opened up. From the start the industry was export oriented. In 1830 no less than 50 per cent of *all* British exports were cotton textiles. This declined gradually to just under 25 per cent by the eve of the First World War (which even so remains a remarkable percentage for only one commodity group). Within the industry, the proportion of output sold abroad was even more striking: in the early 1820s about half of industry output was exported, but by the beginning of the twentieth century this had risen to 80 per cent. The significance of all this is perhaps obvious. Levels of employment in the cotton industry were heavily dependent on continued success in export markets, so was the balance of trade as a whole, and so were those 'ancillary' industries whose fortunes were in some way linked with cotton (either because they sold inputs to the industry, or because they sold things to cotton workers).

The expansion of coal output during this period was almost as striking. Between 1800 and 1830 output doubled (from 11 to 22 million tons). In the next fifteen years it doubled again, and this dramatic growth was maintained: by 1913 production was almost 300 million tons per year, and nearly a million men were employed in the pits. Once again, exports were an important component of sales, rising from 2 per cent of output in 1800 to over 30 per cent by 1913.

This first wave of growth in the staple industries was succeeded, in the mid nineteenth century, by a second phase of industrialization. This time it involved not just Britain, but other European economies and the United States. The new phase was not simply a prolonged economic boom – lasting from about 1850 to the mid 1870s – it was also an important structural shift. The pivot of the shift was metal: in particular, the development of major steel capacity, and of industries using steel (such as shipbuilding, railways and machines). Even when growth rates began to slow down towards the end of the century, expansion in these industries continued: European steel output increased by no less than eighty-three times between 1870 and 1913. In Britain, production of pig iron grew from 2.75 million tons in the early 1850s, to nearly 10 million tons by 1907; and by the end of the period 50 per cent of output was being exported. Steel output grew even faster, from just over 300,000 tonnes in 1871 to nearly 8 million in 1913. And similar dramatic increases can be traced in the iron and steel using industries, shipbuilding in particular.

This story of growth in the staple industries is, of course, a familiar one, for it forms the centrepiece of most accounts of the industrial revolution. As I pointed out earlier, the emphasis on the 'industrial' aspects of Britain's economic transformation is in some ways overdone, for many industries retained handicraft methods of production, with very few indeed using steam power or mechanized techniques. Economic growth in this period extended into most sectors of the economy, including such non-industrial activities as agriculture. Yet there remains an important justification for focusing mainly on the staple industries. This is that these industries absorbed an enormous amount of investment, provided the bulk of Britain's export earnings, the majority of manufacturing employment, and were in many ways the driving force of Britain's economic growth. As the British economy entered the twentieth century, these four industries provided a quarter of all employment, 40 per cent of all output, and three-quarters of all exports. The structure of British industry was therefore highly unbalanced, concentrated on only four industrial sectors. The fact that the advanced sector of the economy had such a very narrow basis meant that, although the staples were vital to the overall performance of the UK economy, they made Britain intensely vulnerable to shifts in the pattern of world trade. Such shifts might occur because of the declining importance of Britain's 'basic' industries, or because of the rise of competitive pressures within them. Failure or decline in even one of the staple industries might have serious effects not only on employment and incomes within it, but also on export earnings; and through this there might be serious impacts on a wide range of incomes and jobs in Britain. Should any of these industries face significant difficulties, it would have been essential for the British people to develop new industries to take their place. In fact this problem was not an abstract one, but a real development: by the late nineteenth century difficulties in the staple industries were not just appearing, they were accumulating.

THE COMPETITIVE CHALLENGE

In terms of world trade in the staple products, two kinds of problem had to be faced in the late nineteenth century; more precisely, two forms of competition. The first of these was within the domestic markets of the other developing industrial economies. Their economic growth obviously meant the expansion of their own industries, often on the basis of imported British machines and even British workers. In many cases they developed textile industries first, but soon followed up with iron and steel, machines and so on. American and German textile, steel and engineering firms emerged. France and Italy began less vigorous but still significant industrialization, while in the east the nascent Japanese textile sector embarked on a rapid expansion. The initial impact of these industries was felt, naturally enough, in their own home markets. But for Britain, these were export markets: the development of an Italian textile industry, for example, selling to its own domestic market, would inevitably mean a contraction of British exports unless other markets could be found. This was the first type of competitive problem.

However, it was the second type of competition which held greater dangers, for it concerned the finding of 'other markets'. In their own markets the emergent foreign industries had certain intrinsic advantages which meant that they could sell their products even if they did not match British levels of efficiency: the protection of tariffs, for example, and lower transport costs. However, if they could match British costs of production, then their goods would be cheap enough to compete with British goods elsewhere, in 'third country' markets. This might be achieved through the use of a more advanced technology, or through better management, or cheaper labour, or a combination of these factors. Moreover such a challenge might be thrown out by a number of economies simultaneously, and thus could be world-wide in scope. It could erode Britain's share not only of the domestic markets of other industrializers, but also of the expanding markets of the European periphery, of Australasia, of Latin America. These were vital to continued British export success, and ultimately to the pattern and rate of economic growth in Britain. This second form of competitive challenge to the British economy was potential in 1870. By 1900 it was real.

Let us take, as an example, the iron and steel industry. In 1870 Britain was the leading producer by far, turning out five times more pig iron and over twice as much steel as Germany, its nearest European rival. But the German industry began to expand, taking over its home market, and towards the late nineteenth century its growth accelerated. Between 1895 and 1913 its production of pig iron grew at nearly 7 per cent per year, compared to less than 1 per cent growth in Britain. At the same time German steel output grew at 8.5 per cent per year, as opposed to 3.6 per cent in Britain. More significant than these growth disparities, however, was the fact that German growth was based on larger plants and the most modern processes, while the doubling of British output over the same period involved no major new technical processes. In 1870 British plants had been consistently larger than those of Germany. By the turn of the century, however, the position had been reversed: new German steel plants were typically three to four times the size of new British plants, and the output of the *average* mill in Westphalia was equal to that of the biggest mills in Britain. At the same time the US industry was growing fast, also on the basis of larger plants. These size differences were important, for they led to so-called 'scale economies'. These occur in a number of industries: as the scale of output grows, the plant becomes more efficient, and costs per unit of output therefore fall. This is because

THE LONG DECLINE · 63

of, for example, economies in the use of fuel, or in the handling of bulk raw materials. The possibilities for such economies were aggressively explored in the German industry, and successfully put into practice. To give just one example of the order of the economies involved, it has been pointed out that, in post-smelting processes, British plants used over seven times more coal per ton of output than their German counterparts.

The result of all this, for the German industry, was cheaper steel. Between 1883 and 1910 German steel prices fell by 20 per cent; British prices were up to a third higher. Inevitably the cheaper prices of the German industry led to increased demand which promoted further growth. In 1893 German steel output was for the first time greater than that of Britain; by 1913 it was two and a quarter times as great. By 1910 German exports of iron and steel were larger than Britain's. They were penetrating markets – such as Australia, Southern Africa, Canada – which had hitherto been regarded as a British preserve. German steel was even selling rather well in Britain itself.

This pattern of foreign production, then foreign competition, leading to a falling UK share of world trade, can be traced as a gradual but inexorable development in the other staple industries. In 1880, for example, Japanese firms such as Mitsui and Co. began importing cotton spinning machines from the Lancashire firm of Platt and Co. They produced cotton themselves, and acted as an agent, selling the machines to other firms. Soon Japan no longer imported textile manufactures. By the late 1890s it was successfully exporting to the Asian markets which had until then been dominated by Britain. (As a postscript, it might be added that in the 1980s Mitsui is busy consolidating its position as one of the largest companies in Japan and indeed the world; in 1982 Platt's went bankrupt.)

Developments such as these, in the late nineteenth and early twentieth centuries, produced sharp changes in the shares of world trade of the major industrialized economies. Britain's share began the downward trend from which it has never permanently recovered, as table 9 indicates.

Table 9. Share of World Trade in Manufactures (%)

	1883	1913
Germany	17.2	23.0
USA	3.4	11.0
Britain	37.1	25.4

Source: D. H. Aldcroft and H. W. Richardson, *The British Economy 1870–1939*, London, 1969, p. 154.

At the same time the rate of growth of industrial production and productivity was slowing quite significantly in Britain. From the early nineteenth century, industrial output had grown at rates of between 35 and 40 per cent per decade; this growth slowed to under 25 per cent in the 1870s, then to only 16 per cent the following decade. A slight recovery in the 1890s was followed by a further slowing of growth in the early twentieth century; 9 per cent growth in the first decade was followed by a 5 per cent fall in the second (under the destructive impact of the war). The overall growth rate of net national product from 1899 to 1924 was only 0.5 per cent per year: Britain had entered a period of stagnation.

It seems natural to ask about the relation between the weakening export performance and the slowdown in growth. There are those who attribute the deceleration in growth to falling demand for British exports; on the other hand it is possible to argue that it was the other way around, that emerging weaknesses in British industry were generating export failures. However, to put the problem in terms of one-way causal relationships like this seems misleading, since growth and export performance are clearly interrelated. Poor industrial performance in terms of growth and productivity is likely to affect the prices and quality of output, which in turn will certainly inhibit export sales. At the same time, restricted export markets will reduce overall demand and profitability, which may reduce the desire and ability of firms to invest in new plant and new techniques; this will further limit performance, and at worst the whole process can become cumulative.

It should be said at once that export performance is affected by many things other than the technical efficiency of particular industries and the quality of their products. The rate of growth of the world economy, the level and composition of domestic demand, and the structure of exchange rates can all exert a big impact on export sales. However, the efficiency and technological level of industry remains a central issue, and a weakening export performance is an indication that something may be seriously wrong in this area. It was this which, at the turn of the century, began to give rise to increased concern in Britain, and to widespread discussion in the press, in Parliament, and elsewhere. The principal issue bothering those who thought about it at the time was an apparently increasing technological gap opening up between Britain on the one hand, and Germany and the United States on the other. In part their success was built upon substantial technical advances within the staple industries on which Britain depended so heavily: in those countries such industries were transformed from within, while in Britain they remained static and rigid in their technical structure. However, these technical gaps within the staple industries were only a part of the problem. The competitive problems for Britain within the existing industrial structure were being overshadowed by another development, which was ultimately to be of greater significance. This was a shift in importance between industries, a change in the structure of the industrial economy as a whole. In the face of this new transition, the UK economy once again appeared rigid and inflexible. The problems of decline were multiplying.

THE NEW INDUSTRIAL ECONOMY

The advanced capitalist economies are characterized by relentless technical development and large-scale transitions. The process of industrialization and the growth of the staple industries was itself such a transition, away from an earlier capitalist economy dominated by handicraft manufactures, by woollen textiles, and by agriculture. In the late nineteenth century a new phase of transition began, as new and dynamic industries emerged. These became the leading echelons of twentieth century industrial advance. They are often described as 'science-based' industries, though this can be misleading since the relationships between science and industry are far from direct. Nevertheless, they all bear a distinct relation with research and development skills, and most of them – both products and the processes by which they were made – depended on new R & D techniques and institutions. Many of them also required large-scale and long-term finance, and a degree of industrial coordination between firms.

The most important of the new industries were chemicals, electrical engineering and vehicles. Around them were ranged an array of subordinate but also important industries, such as glass, precision instruments, optical devices, and so on. In the first two of these industries – chemicals and electrical products – and ultimately in the third, vehicles, the German economy proved outstandingly successful, while Britain barely rose to the challenge of the transition. Where it did, the results were often incomplete, or in some way at odds with the main tendencies of twentieth century industrial development.

The first stages in the transformation were felt in the German chemicals industry. They began with the unglamorous and seemingly unexciting product of textile dyestuffs, which had previously been based on such natural products as cochineal, but which were now the outcome of chemical processes. German firms rapidly secured dominance within the product group: by 1880 they held 50 per cent of the market throughout the world. Within twenty years this had risen to 90 per cent, and a number of the major German firms had gone multinational. The significance of this, in the words of the historian David Landes, lay in the fact that dyestuffs 'were only one corner of a new world: the scientific principles that lay behind artificial colourants were capable of the widest application'.[1] These principles were exploited in the development of an enormous range of products, from explosives, to film, to artificial fabrics and ultimately to the first plastics. In all of these products German firms were pioneers in development. The British chemical industry, by contrast, was not only smaller but less innovative, being oriented around the production of much less sophisticated products, such as soap, bleach and the earlier types of dyestuffs. By the beginning of the First World War the German chemical industry was undisputed world leader in an industry which was becoming increasingly central to the operations of the industrial economies.

Similarly impressive were German achievements in electrical engineering. The world-wide growth of this industry was staggering by any standards. In 1880 the German electrical industry consisted of less than two thousand people, working mainly on telegraphic equipment. In Britain at the same time, numbers were roughly comparable, with something under one thousand workers. Neither country possessed a public power station or a grid, and anyway there was no commercially feasible light bulb, let alone domestic electrical equipment. Sixty years later both countries were covered by unified power grids; Germany was generating 60 million kilowatt-hours of electricity per year, and Britain 33. Over 140,000 people were employed in the German industry by 1907.

But although the industries developed rapidly in each country, they did not develop in an equivalent way. It is worth quoting Landes once again, on the growth of, first, the electrical supply industry, and then electrical manufacturing:

> Here, as in chemicals, the most striking achievements occurred in Germany. The parallels are numerous: the belated start, the rapid rise based on technological excellence and on rational organisation, the concentration of production, the strong position on the world market ... Even more impressive was the German electrical manufacturing industry. It was the largest in Europe – more than twice as big as that of Britain – and second only by a small margin to that of the United States. The firms, as in the chemical industry, were large well-financed enterprises, strongly supported by the capital market and the great investment banks ... Their products were ingenious, solidly made, competitively priced; financial support made possible generous credit to customers. As a result, German exports on the eve of the war were the largest in the world, more than two and one-half times the United Kingdom total, almost three times the American.[2]

German exports made up, in fact, half of all world trade in electrical goods. And it is in the changing pattern of trade that the new industrial transition can be seen reflected. In table 10, which shows the composition of exports by Britain and Germany, the breakdown is a fairly crude one, yet it clearly indicates important differences in industrial emphasis.

Table 10. Composition of exports by commodity group, 1913 (%)

	UK	Germany
Coal	13.3	11.0
Metals	16.7	28.9
Machinery	10.0	17.7
Transport equipment	6.1	4.2
Chemicals	5.1	14.4
Textiles	48.8	23.9

Source: A. Levine, *Industrial Retardation in Britain, 1880–1914*, London, 1967, p. 35.

The most notable thing, perhaps, about this table is the way in which British exports remained so overwhelmingly dependent on textiles – nearly half of all exports – and on coal and metals. All of these industries were, as noted above, intensely vulnerable to foreign competition. The German export structure, on the other hand, placed far more emphasis on the new growth sectors, on steel, chemicals and machinery (which in table 10 includes electrical equipment). Within these categories, German performance was far superior. In chemicals, for example, Britain's exports, in the words of one historian, 'consisted largely of older products produced with older technology',[3] while in such 'new industries' as electrical goods, scientific instruments and so on, British exports made up well under 3 per cent of export earnings.

Britain's declining share of world trade, outlined in table 10 above, thus consisted of two quite separate processes. The first was an increasingly poor performance in the old 'staple' industries. The second was a failure to construct adequately the new industries whose importance was growing at the beginning of the twentieth century. This latter problem played a large part both in weakening export performance and slowing growth.

Once again, it should be emphasized that the world economy and world markets were growing at that time. So British products and industries were not wiped out by their competitive failures; on the contrary, output and exports grew, but at a slower pace than Britain's main competitors, and slower than the world average of industrialized countries. Table 11 indicates this, and shows also that the differences were quite marked.

Table 11. Production and exports of manufactures (volume in 1911–13 as percentage of volume in 1881–5)

	Production	Exports
UK	162	175
Germany	363	290
USA	377	537
World average	310	239

Source: I. Svennilson, *Growth and Stagnation in the European Economy*, Geneva, 1951, p. 219.

However, although the British economy *was* growing, it was entering a new economic era with an industrial structure still organized around the main activities and technologies of the previous industrial phase. In the face of an increasingly sophisticated industrial challenge, British industries and enterprises had three broad strategies available. The first was simply to do nothing: to accept exclusion from an increasing number of world markets, to become an essentially marginal supplier of manufactures. The second was to retain the existing structure of industries, but to seek markets in which Britain had a built-in advantage. In practice this could only mean Empire markets. The third strategy was to engage in major programmes of reinvestment, modernization and technical change.

British manufacturers essentially accepted the first of these alternatives, though with growing world trade in manufactures the consequences were not fully apparent until after the First World War. However, one immediate result was that British exporters did not share fully in the major growth of the European and American markets in the pre-war period (and after the war Britain's already declining share collapsed utterly).

To some extent, the second strategy came into play: British exports to the Empire steadily expanded, from about 30 per cent of UK exports in the mid nineteenth century, to nearly 45 per cent in the mid 1930s. Moreover some of the staple industries – particularly textiles and iron and steel – depended on Empire markets even more heavily than these numbers indicate. Yet even here, British perform-ance was surprisingly weak. In one group of fifteen manufactured goods, for example, British exports to the Empire increased by 91 per cent between 1895 and 1907. Yet in the same period German and US exports of the same goods to the same Empire countries increased by no less than 129 and 359 per cent respectively.

More significant for the future was the strategy of re-equipment and structural change which was *not* adopted. Its absence meant that the British economy faced an incipient crisis of exports and growth. Two things masked the underlying problems. The first was improve-ments in the terms of trade, or the relationship between export and import prices. Prices of imports over this period became cheaper, which meant that Britain could afford to pay for more imports with a given quantity of exports. In practical terms, this meant a rise in the standard of living, as the prices of, for example, foodstuffs fell, even though export performance was not good. The second factor was the astonishingly large investment incomes being earned by Britain's wealthy investors abroad. Between the 1850s and 1913, the interest and dividends received in Britain from British investments abroad were substantially greater than the total net outflow of investment funds; this overall inflow of funds enabled Britain to import quan-tities of goods which would have been out of the question if financed by exports alone.

THE FIRST WORLD WAR: CRISIS AND REORGANIZATION

We have seen in the previous section that British economic per-formance in the forty years before the First World War was char-acterized by an increasingly weak performance in the old staple industries, compounded by the non-development of the new, research-based industries which were growing rapidly elsewhere. Inevitably, the economic demands of the First World War forced substantial industrial changes. It was a matter of more than embarassment when it emerged that the dyes for British army uni-forms were imported from Germany. And the German lead in chemicals – and in consequence, explosives – clearly had to be cut back.

The government faced formidable economic problems. Firstly, there was the difficulty of organizing any production at all in the context of a severely restricted labour supply. Over five million men were called up in the course of the war, and it became necessary for the government to intervene heavily in the allocation of labour to industry, and in the training and employment of women workers. Secondly, there was the problem of ensuring that resources went to the right industries: that luxury goods production, for example, did not grab inputs needed for munitions and so on. Thirdly, there was the problem of creating industries which either did not exist, or which were too small for the needs of war. Finally, the population had to be fed.

These problems were all successfully solved through an increasingly complex system of government control and intervention. The government ended up rejecting decisively the frenetic calls to fight the war with 'business as usual', with which the war had opened. First, it took control of imports and exports, and of a large proportion of British shipping. Next, and perhaps most importantly, came the munitions industry. Government direction here involved not just the manufacture of arms and ammunition, but complete control of raw material supply and purchase, of all ancillary industries, and even of the manufacture of the necessary tools. By the end of the war the ministry had organized a major supply process involving three and a half million workers, and over twenty thousand production establishments. This effort was a formidable achievement, and arguably the basis of eventual military victory, if victory is the appropriate word. But it was certainly an economic success, as the official history of the Ministry of Munitions pointed out: 'the practical application (of control) to munitions and non-munitions industries, aided by the control of materials and the operation of the priority principle, resulted in an enormous increase in output, more efficient industries and great economies of production'.

At the same time, the government engaged in a wide range of other economic activities. Some of them, as Professor Sidney Pollard has indicated, were of epoch-making significance:

Scientific research, for example, unduly neglected by British industrialists, was stimulated by the government which set up in July 1915 a department to promote scientific research in industry ... The discovery of applied science by British industry may be said to have dated from those years, though it was still in an embryonic state.[4]

And the government was instrumental in establishing such industries as ball bearings, scientific instruments and modern chemical products, tungsten manufacture and so on. It also played, for obvious reasons, the central role in the expansion and modernization of the tiny aircraft industry, and in the rapid growth of car and truck production. It controlled imports rigorously, and marketed about 80 per cent of all food sold in Britain, which was done through a controlled price system which prevented profiteering and contained inflation; purely in terms of nutrition, the British population survived the war in much better shape than the German. Economic and industrial achievements such as these were surely the only positive result of a period which was otherwise one of unremitting horror. Britain entered the war with an outdated industrial structure. It emerged from it, despite the economic chaos of the post-war world economy, with at least some of the technical basis for modernization.

WASTE, TURMOIL, RECOVERY: THE INTER-WAR YEARS

The economic control system of the war had unequivocally succeeded, and one might think that the problems of reconstruction could have been tackled with the same administrative apparatus (or at least some version of it). Certainly the problems facing the post-war economy justified the term 'emergency'. Yet, in the words of one economic historian, 'contrary to the explicit intentions of the War Cabinet and the Ministry of Reconstruction, the controls were frenetically disbanded by Lloyd George's government elected in 1919'.[5] Britain was returned post-haste to the free-market, *laissez-faire* economics of the pre-war period. This happened, however, in an infinitely more hostile economic environment.

Nevertheless, against heavy odds, new industries began to emerge in the post-war world. The economy finally began the transition into modernity: unfortunately it did so in an incomplete way, producing a curious mixture of success and failure.

For the first time, the 'new industries' came to have a significant weight in the economy. The motor vehicle industry, for example, began a dramatic expansion, doubling its number of workers between 1923 and 1938. In 1913 Britain had produced about 34,000 cars and trucks; this reached nearly 150,000 by the mid 1920s, and no less than 493,000 vehicles in 1937. This was nearly a quarter of the net output of the entire engineering sector. During this period also the chemicals industry expanded and was reorganized, with the formation of ICI in 1926 out of a myriad of smaller, uncoordinated companies, the bits and pieces which had hitherto comprised the industry. It rapidly moved into new products and processes, to become a major success. Entirely new products, such as artificial fibres and fabrics (meaning essentially viscose, or 'artificial silk'), emerged, to become the basis of large-scale companies – such as Courtaulds – and industries. And between the wars the electrical engineering industry more than doubled its size, employing nearly 350,000 people by 1938. All of these 'new industries' grew rapidly in the 1930s, both in terms of output and employment.

Yet against this expansion had to be set stagnation if not outright collapse in the old staple industries. Output in textiles, shipbuilding and mining grew very slowly, and employment fell. The massive unemployment in these industries in the early 1930s was only the worst phase of a prolonged depression. Recovery came only in the late 1930s, and even then was weak (with the exception of steel: but its sharper recovery was entirely due to rearmament demand, and was facilitated by high tariff protection). The collapses were in part caused by a general decline in the level of world trade, and the wider use of tariff barriers around the world. But they were exacerbated by the way in which low productivity in Britain inhibited the ability of these industries to compete. One historian has spoken recently of

differences in productivity between British and foreign industries of such an order to be unattributable to statistical error. For 1936 ... in relation to the corresponding British industries, physical productivity per man in German coalmines and coke ovens was 50 per cent higher, in cotton spinning, rayon and silk between 20 per cent and 25 per cent higher, and in blast furnaces, steel smelting and rolling between 10 and 20 per cent higher. Comparative figures for the USA were even more striking: productivity was substantially higher in all US industries and enormously higher in some, with a maximum difference of 200 per cent for blast furnaces.[6]

To a certain extent, dependence on the staple industries for export receipts declined, from 42 per cent of export earnings in 1929 to 37 per cent in 1937. But the volume of exports in 1937 was only 77 per cent of the 1929 figure, which indicates the seriousness of the collapse of the staple exports. This led, of course, to serious unemployment in those industries; in each of them, unemployment at least doubled between 1929 and 1931, and was slow to recover. In coal, over 40 per cent of the workforce was unemployed; in iron and steel about half; and in shipbuilding about 60 per cent were out of work. Since the average level of unemployment for the whole country, at the bottom of the slump in 1931, was 22 per cent, it can be seen that the old staple industries bore the brunt of the depression. Unemployment in Britain was therefore not just an effect of a major world recession; it was also the price to be paid for the concentration of industrial resources in mines, mills and shipyards – 'unwanted places', in Professor Sayer's words[7] – producing products which were of declining industrial importance and, moreover, doing so inefficiently. Growth in the 'new industry' products ameliorated but did not offset this collapse.

Overall industrial development during the inter-war period was therefore a complex mixture of success and failure: success in actually generating new industries, failure in either improving the performance of the old, or in having the new grow fast enough to absorb the masses of unemployed thrown out by the contraction of the staple industries. Despite the expansion of the chemicals industry, for example, by 1938 it was still employing less than half the number of workers who had been employed in the German industry before the First World War (and this was only partly the result of labour-displacing technical improvements).

Furthermore there were potentially serious problems within the new industries, likely to inhibit their competitiveness, export performance and indeed whole future. These were to do with their technological level and the technical character of their products. The future of these industries lay in mass markets, in high-volume production, in innovation both in the products themselves and in the process of their production. This in turn placed a premium on design, where new standards were required which could link high quality with cheapness and large-scale production. But in many of the British 'new industries' another route was taken. In cars, for example, the market was restricted to the well-off, largely because of a very uneven distribution of income in the society as a whole. In 1938 there were 39 cars per 1,000 inhabitants in the UK; in the USA it was 194. This led car producers to aim not at a mass market, but at high-quality specialization:

In 1939 the six leading British producers, making roughly 350,000 private cars, turned out more than 40 different engine types and an even greater number of chassis and body models, which was considerably more than the number offered by the three leading producers in the US, making perhaps 3,500,000 cars.[8]

At the same time German production, though initially lower than the British, was growing faster and on the basis of mass-market, low-priced cars. Its methods were exemplified by the Volkswagen 'beetle', a type which eventually sold 20 million world-wide. In Britain, because car ownership was so restricted, it came – as so many things do in Britain – to be tied up with social status. This meant that it could be positively dangerous to produce a low-priced car, as Ford found to their cost in the 1930s: 'nobody wanted to keep down with the Joneses', as some recent commentators remarked of one Ford failure.[9]

Similar problems of design and method and market strategy can be found in other 'new industries'. Employment in electrical engineering doubled, it is true; but so did the level of imports into the UK, particularly from the USA. In terms of design, quality and price British radios, vacuum cleaners and so on were little match for the American competition. The flood of imports was only stemmed in 1932 with the introduction of protective tariffs; unfortunately, while these did protect employment in the industry, they also sheltered its limitations in terms of design, quality and production.

CONCLUSION

This chapter has been concerned with what happened in the UK industrial economy between 1870 and the late 1930s, rather than why it happened. Some explanations will be considered in later chapters; for the time being, what matters is the course of British economic development, not the reasons for it. Two broad trends have been identified. The first is a weak growth performance, both in terms of output and productivity. This is true both in relation to Britain's own historical record, and also in comparison with its major trading rivals. Table 12 tells the story to the eve of the First World War.

Table 12. Long-term growth rates, 1870/1–1913 (% per year)

	Industrial production	Industrial productivity	Exports (1880–1913)
UK	2.1	0.6	2.2
USA	4.7	1.5	3.2
Germany	4.1	2.6	4.3
France	3.1	n.a.	2.6

Source: D. H. Aldcroft, ed., *The Development of British Industry and Foreign Competition 1875–1914*, London, 1968, p. 13.

The trends visible in this table were continued after the war, as the USA recovered in the mid 1930s, and as Germany reflated its economy vigorously, behind tariff barriers, after Hitler's accession to power.

The second trend, far less easily captured in figures, was a rigidity in the face of technological change. The British economy did not respond with the flexibility and vision necessary to take advantage of new technological opportunities, and thereby to solve – or help to solve – its competitive and employment problems. 'Britain's industrialisation process was exceptional,' as two historians recently pointed out, 'as one in which there was a period (two or three decades after 1870) when the birth rate of new industries in the British economy was very low indeed.'[10] And when those industries finally emerged, their growth was in many ways restricted, and their development inadequate. It was this rigidity, combined with the non-modernization of the old staple industries, which underlay Britain's relatively poor growth performance.

It should be pointed out that there has been a major debate in recent years, among economic historians, over whether or not the British economy 'failed' in some sense in the late nineteenth century. Was its performance due, for instance, to a failure by entrepreneurs to recognize and exploit new opportunities in products and processes? Was there a failure by the banking system or by investors in the providing of industrial finance? There are some influential economic historians who take the view that, given Britain's particular circumstances (its available resources, its inherited industrial structure, the world economic context) it is unreasonable to expect anything other than what happened. They reject the idea, therefore, that anyone should be blamed for what happened. But even the strongest proponents of this view accept that the consequences of what happened were serious: they accept that, 'with the benefit of hindsight we can see that twentieth century Britain has paid a considerable price for the industrial concentration that led to the export of a few commodities to relatively few markets by the eve of the First World War ... the loss to the economy was enormous.'[11]

The long-term significance of the industrial rigidity of the British economy, and the decline which it generated, lay not just in the unemployment and misery of the 1930s, tragic and pointless though they were. It lay in the fact that the industrial structure developed at that time, with all its inadequacies and failures, was the basis for the next phase of development: that of the Second World War and its aftermath. Though British economic performance was to improve dramatically, it remained handicapped by its industrial heritage, and indeed was to continue to repeat the errors of a previous generation.

The Post-war Boom

The post-war economic era, for the advanced economies of Europe and North America, divides into two distinct phases. The first runs from about 1950 to 1973: a phase of full employment, relatively low inflation and of sustained economic growth at unprecedentedly high rates. Then the 1970s ushered in a period of much more hesitant growth, of high inflation and unemployment: an experience in marked contrast to that of the previous quarter of a century. This chapter deals with the factors underlying the post-war boom; it discusses the main areas of expansion which motivated it, and then moves on to consider Britain's performance during those years. Two central points will emerge. The first is that the boom will not easily be recreated; in fact it may have gone for good. The second is that, in Britain's performance in those years, we can clearly discern major problems in industrial performance and technological development. We are living with the legacy of these problems. Much of the following discussion is inevitably in outline form, for our understanding of both the boom and the stagnation/inflation recession which followed it is at a very preliminary stage. But the main lines of development can certainly be identified.

The boom itself was far from inevitable. Few, at the end of the Second World War, can have foreseen the path of economic development which lay ahead for Western Europe. Where the economies were not in physical ruins, they faced enormous problems of conversion from war production. Where there were not ghastly scenes of hunger and deprivation, there were seemingly intractable difficulties in creating jobs for the demobilized millions of men and women. It would have been a rash economist indeed who predicted a future of prosperity and full employment emerging from this post-war chaos.

And indeed, most economists held out little hope, feeling that the best which could be achieved would be an avoidance of the grim years of instability and depression which had followed the First World War. In Britain, influenced by policy ideas coming from Keynes and his associates, the government had committed itself (in a 1944 White Paper called 'Employment Policy') to policies aimed at maintaining 'a high and stable level of employment'. But what did this objective of 'full employment' actually mean? Most, including Keynes himself, thought it would involve at least 5 per cent of the workforce permanently out of work, and few gave much for the prospects for growth.

The actual outcome was, of course, very different from such gloomy prognoses. There followed a quarter of a century of rapid growth at rates which had never before been achieved by capitalist economies. As we saw in Chapter 1 the European economies expanded at about 5 per cent per year. Over the whole post-war period to 1973 this meant a doubling of annual output every 14 years, or a staggering 400 per cent increase in incomes in about one generation. Japan, especially from the late 1950s, grew even faster. There were many sceptics when Prime Minister Ikeda announced a plan to double income in ten years, with a projected annual growth rate of 7.2 per cent. In fact, from 1959 to the early 1970s, the Japanese economy grew at nearly 11 per cent per year, doubling its output every seven years. Prices rose surprisingly slowly; even in Britain, which had the worst record on inflation, the average inflation rate between 1948 and 1973 was under 4 per cent. And unemployment was in effect no problem; on the contrary, almost all of the advanced economies pulled in immigrant labour to satisfy growing demand for labour.

So for the advanced economies these were years of outstanding success. It was a success in which Britain shared, though in a hesitant and ambiguous way which complicates assessment of Britain's record. The facts are that over the post-war period Britain grew at a rate of just under 3 per cent per year; thus, over the twenty-five years, annual output doubled. Incomes, in terms of real weekly earnings, doubled also. The proportion of national income devoted to new investment in the economy more than doubled in relation to the pre-war era. In even more striking contrast with the pre-war world was the employment picture. In the twenty years before the war unemployment was never less than a million; for thirty years after the war, until 1975, it never, except for a couple of weeks, rose above a million. The average proportion of the workforce unemployed between 1920 and 1938 was 10.6 per cent; between 1951 and 1973 it was 1.9 per cent. All of this implied a spectacular improvement in the standard of living of the population, as incomes rose, as working conditions improved and the working week shortened, as nutritional and housing standards improved, and as ownership of consumer durables such as washing machines expanded. At the same time the construction of the National Health Service meant better access to medical care, while the improved provision of unemployment pay, child allowances and sickness benefits sharply reduced the economic risks to which the pre-war British population had been exposed. Harold Macmillan was right in 1959: Britain had indeed never had it so good.

There is a problem in evaluating this record, however. Should we regard it as one of success or failure? The difficulty is a simple one: if we are to say it was a success, then we should really ask, a success in relation to what? In fact, two quite different pictures seem to emerge depending on what we use as a standard of comparison. If we compare post-war Britain with its own previous history, then the 1950s and 1960s are years of unqualified success. Table 13, outlining the growth of output and of output per worker points this up.

Table 13. Growth of GDP and GDP per man-year in the UK (%)

	GDP	GDP per man-year
1856–73	2.2	1.3
1873–1913	1.8	0.9
1924–37	2.2	1.0
1951–73	2.8	2.4

Source: R.C.O. Matthews *et al.*, *British Economic Growth 1856–1974*, Oxford, 1983, p. 22.

Note that after the Second World War the growth rate accelerates; but even more noticeable is the growth in productivity – in output per worker – which jumps to nearly two-and-a-half times the pre-war rate. What makes the post Second World War growth all the more remarkable is that it occurred in the context of full and expanding employment, something which was really quite new for Britain. Moreover it was relatively steady growth: the earlier periods in table 13 contained sub-periods of slump and stagnation – from 1899 to 1924, for example, income grew at barely 0.5 per cent per year. So in these historical terms the post-war years are years of straightforward success.

The picture changes sharply, however, when we make the comparison in international terms. Table 14 gives us both a historical comparison and an international one; it picks up the way Britain's growth accelerated after the war, but also shows its poor performance relative to others.

Table 14. Long-run GDP trends in Europe (% inc. per year)

	1870–1913	1922–37	1953–73
France	1.6	1.8	5.3
Germany	2.8	3.2	5.5
Italy	1.5	2.3	5.3
Austria	3.2	0.8	5.7
UK	1.9	2.4	3.0

Source: A. Boltho, ed., *The European Economies: Growth and Crisis*, London, 1982, p. 10.

These higher growth rates of the European economies were not simply a matter of catching up from a lower level, or recovering from lower levels of output due to war damage. Many European economies had indeed been hit harder by the war than Britain, and one might expect them to grow faster while they rebuilt. But the important thing is that their growth rates were maintained, and they soon overtook Britain. Having done so, they continued their rapid growth until Britain's income levels were far surpassed.

Thus we have a contrast between Britain's performance seen in a historical light, and its performance seen in an international context. 'Hence,' as the authors of a major recent study remark, 'arises the persistent dilemma in the study of British economic growth in the post-war period: is the task to explain why Britain did so well or why it did so badly?'[1]

Resolving this dilemma seems to depend on what it is we want to know. If, for example, we want to assess the effects of some change within Britain – such as the adoption of new types of government economic policy – then we should use Britain's own historical record; in that case the post-war period is one of success. If, however, we are concerned with Britain's competitive position, then international comparisons are appropriate, and Britain's record looks much less happy. For our purposes it is the international context which matters, since we are concerned with the way Britain's record in technological development affected both its trade performance and its growth path. So in assessing Britain's past and present performance we need to begin with the post-war boom itself, looking at the factors underlying it, the extent to which Britain lagged behind comparable economies, and finally at the reasons for this lag.

THE BOOM

At the end of the Second World War the United States exercised unequivocal political, technological and economic leadership over the non-communist countries of the world. The war had massively expanded the US economy and produced an acceleration of technical advance, where others had barely survived. And the US government grasped the opportunity which this offered: to refashion the world economy, if not in its image, then at least to its liking. American foreign policy thus laid exceptional emphasis on economic objectives in the reconstruction of the post-war world, and developed forceful and on the whole clear ideas about the instruments which would achieve those objectives. The objectives were in fact complex and various, but one had overwhelming priority: to prevent the further expansion of communist regimes in Europe, and to enhance the ability of Western European capitalism to survive any socialist challenge. Clearly this implied flourishing European market economies. The American strategy to achieve this had three main components. They were:

1. *Marshall aid.* In order to raise their levels of both consumption and investment, the European economies needed to import both goods and technology from the US. But how could they pay, when they were unable to export enough to the USA to generate the dollars needed for American imports? The US government was acutely conscious of this problem. It therefore eschewed the rigid demands for reparations and repayments of war loans which had followed the First World War, and instead granted aid under the so-called Marshall Plan. Over a four-year period from 1948 some $12.5 billion in grants and credits were extended tò Europe. This helped to overcome what one writer has called 'the fundamental imbalance between the heavily strained European economies and the technologically-superior productive apparatus of the United States'.[2]

2. *Trade liberalization.* Perhaps the most uniform reaction to the depression of the 1930s had been the adoption of policies of *protection*. In order to prevent or slow the rise in unemployment, governments had tried to cut imports by protective tariffs, quotas and duties. International trade slowed down in consequence, and this in turn hampered growth and recovery. The Americans, partly though not solely in their own self-interest, were desperately concerned to prevent both a return to a 'protectionist' trading environment, and the re-establishment of protected zones like the British Empire. They unhesitatingly used their political influence, in a most determined way, to restore free international trade. The ultimate result was GATT – the General Agreement on Tariffs and Trade – 'the world's first multilateral trade order', a significant move towards free international trade.

3. *A stable international financial system.* If the advanced economies were to grow then international trade must grow; this implied the need for a regular system of finance and payments. The central requirements for a world trading and finance system were that it should be stable and predictable, with a basic 'world' currency which was in adequate supply. At the Bretton Woods conference of 1944 the Allies agreed on a structure based on fixed exchange rates, pegged against the dollar, which was itself pegged against gold at the rate $35 = 1 oz of gold. Two new institutions – the International Monetary Fund (IMF) and the World Bank – were set up to aid countries with balance of payments difficulties, and to finance development projects.

The US dollar thus became the basic currency of world trade, the supply of dollars into the world economy eventually being assured by persistent US balance of payments deficits, which the US covered by, in effect, exporting dollars.

These three building blocks – Marshall aid, trade liberalization and the Bretton Woods system – made up the basic framework: there were, however, expansionary factors at work, which promoted the dramatic burst of growth outlined above.

The first was the technological lead of the USA itself. Since the USA was the clear technological 'leader' others had the opportunity of drawing on its technological knowhow by importing US equipment. And since a large backlog of technological possibilities had built up over the war years, European enterprises had the opportunity to cut their costs sharply and raise profits by deploying US technologies. This led to a wave of investment in Europe: the rate of growth of the stock of capital – factories, machines, etc. – accelerated, from under 2 per cent per year over 1913–50, to nearly 5 per cent per year over 1950–73. The result was sharp increases in the growth of output and also increases in productivity.

The second factor at work was government economic policy. Much though the Keynesian era is now decried, the policies of expansionary demand which were widely adopted produced results, as Angus Maddison rightly points out:

> The main achievement was success in nurturing a buoyancy of demand which had been created during the war and Marshall Plan period and which kept the economies within a zone of high employment. The lowered attention to risks of price increases or payments difficulties, and the absence of crassly perverse deflationary policies were the most important features differentiating post-war demand management from pre-war policy. The payoff was much bigger than could have reasonably been anticipated ... given the favourable supply factors in Europe and Japan, growth performance reached unparalleled proportions.[3]

The pay-off was so big because, in a context of high and stable demand, enterprises were acutely conscious of the risks of *not* investing: they would face an inability to meet demand, a loss of market share, and reduced profits. So they invested, and the 1950s and 1960s were thus years of exceptionally high investment. This was the biggest single contributory factor in the accelerated growth of the post-war boom.

Accompanying these developments was the final factor: a major expansion of world trade. Exports from the industrialized countries grew at 7 per cent per year in the 1950s and 10 per cent per year in the 1960s. Within this expansion of trade, the most dynamic and important part was played by trade in manufactures between the advanced capitalist countries.

We can, then, sum up the post-war boom as follows. Within the context of a stable international financial system, policies facilitating growth and full employment were adopted; Western governments in general promoted buoyant demand within their economies. These measures met a ready response on the production side of the economy. Enterprises took full advantage of available technological opportunities in meeting rising demand. The high levels of investment which ensued led to rising productivity, profits and incomes; and this maintained the impetus behind further investment and growth. Over this period prices were relatively stable for three reasons. Firstly, the growth in productivity kept down costs of production even though incomes were growing; since industrial prices are based on costs, then price increases were constrained. Secondly, raw material prices – especially for oil – were low. Thirdly, the fixed exchange rate system inhibited the inflation rates of individual countries (because, with fixed rates, if a country raises prices then it loses out in export markets, and must then depress demand in order to get the balance of payments back into equilibrium; this tends to return the rise in prices back to the international 'norm').

This account of the post-war boom has concentrated, so far, on quite general pre-conditions for accelerated growth. In previous chapters, however, it was emphasized that economic growth is very much a matter of technological change: of new processes, and new products. This involves the commitment of resources to research and development, to innovative improvements in the performance and design of products which are in growing demand. So we turn now to the products on which post-war growth was based, and then to the growth records of different countries in terms of their innovative performance within these product groups.

FAST-GROWING PRODUCTS
IN POST-WAR GROWTH AND TRADE

Post-war Western European growth was founded on the construction of a consumer society. As income grew, and as income inequalities evened out somewhat, markets for consumer goods expanded. Large numbers of people now had access to products which had previously been the preserve of an affluent minority. Pre-eminent among such products were cars, and consumer durables (record-players, radios, refrigerators, freezers, washing machines and so on). Expansion in these areas naturally promoted expansion in the production of inputs to such goods: in steel, chemicals, machine tools, electrical and electronic components and so on. The growth of all of these products was rapid, but that of cars was particularly spectacular, as table 15 indicates.

Table 15. Output of private cars (*thousands*)

	W. Germany	France	Italy	Britain	Spain
1950	219	257	100	523	0
1960	1,817	1,136	596	1,362	42
1969	3,380	2,168	1,477	1,729	379

Source: drawn from B. R. Mitchell, *European Historical Statistics 1750–1970*, London, 1981, Table E25, p. 469.

The table shows that total car output increased, in these countries, by 730 per cent in less than thirty years; note that Britain's increase was considerably lower (about 230 per cent), and that despite an initial advantage it was rapidly surpassed by France and Germany. Consumer goods matched this kind of expansion: Lars Anell has pointed out that, in effect, 'homes turned into small factories for the production of an ever increasing amount of goods and services ... a person working at home now draws on greater machine investments than a factory worker before the First World War'.[4]

In general, the growth of world trade reflected this pattern of production growth. Particularly fast-growing products in international trade included office machinery, consumer durables, cameras, machine tools, cars and trucks, plastics and general chemicals.

Within this structure of growth and trade, two questions arise in evaluating the performance of any particular economy. The first concerns its output mix. Was it actually producing and exporting within the fast-growing sectors of world production and trade? Secondly, if it was in the right product groups, was it actually producing them well enough? Was it matching its competitors in terms of product performance, quality and price? Concretely, this means, was it devoting enough in the way of research and development resources to the task of innovation; was it keeping pace with technological advances in products and processes?

On the first of these questions – was the output mix right? – there are some formidable statistical problems in making inter-country comparisons. But the evidence indicates that Britain's output composition has not been wildly out of line with that of other major industrial economies. Similarly with exports: a study some years ago suggested that the proportion of UK exports in the fast-growing sectors of world trade was much the same as other advanced countries.

But if there seems no problem in the broad types of goods being produced, there may remain considerable problems in the detailed characteristics of these goods. Britain may, for instance, be producing cars and radios, but what if they do not match the performance standards, quality, reliability and general technological level of competing cars and radios? This is very much a matter of the commitment of research and development (R & D) resources. So in examining Britain's relatively poor post-war performance it remains to look at the question of industrial R & D, and the contribution it has made to Britain's economic performance. It is in this area, in fact, that we find serious problems; it is the weaknesses here which underlie Britain's economic decline.

BRITAIN'S RESEARCH AND DEVELOPMENT (R & D) RECORD

An important first point to make about R & D and technological change is that there are no simple measures of innovative performance. In this section the level of R & D expenditure in any particular area is taken as an indicator of the commitment to technical innovation in that area. But it should be noted that technical change can occur without formal R & D spending. New technologies can be imported rather than self-developed, for example. However, in practice it turns out that output growth and export success are closely linked with direct spending on R & D, so there is a strong case for taking that as the first measure of innovative activity.

Two central aspects of R & D are important. The first is the level of spending on R & D activity, the amount of funds actually devoted to such work. So question one is, is the *scale* of R & D expenditure adequate? This is important because the amounts of money spent on R & D often need to be very large. Recent research on the aircraft and computer industries, for example, has shown that 'research, development and design costs exceeding £100 million are by no means uncommon for a new generation of products and they have been known to reach £1,000 million'.[5] Scale is thus important because there is no point being in some industries at all unless an adequate level of R & D funds are committed. The sums involved in modern R & D are frequently so vast that governments often play a large part either in the provision of such funds, or in the overall coordination of R & D expenditure.

Next on the agenda is the *direction* of R & D, or its allocation: that is, it must be spent on the right sorts of activities. Given that the sums involved are huge, they invariably require a large volume of sales of the subsequent product if the development costs are to be recovered. This means that R & D expenditure must be directed towards products and processes where demand is strong and growing. And if possible it must be used in areas where a country has some kind of competitive advantage.

Against the background of these considerations, how has Britain performed? In terms of the level of R & D expenditure things do not seem serious: Britain devotes about the same proportion of industrial output to R & D as other major countries. But because our output and income are less than other countries, this means that the absolute level of spending is less. Moreover, it has been pointed out that 'Britain was the only OECD (i.e. advanced) country where industry-financed R & D activities decreased absolutely between 1967 and 1975'. [6] More significant than the level of R & D for Britain, however, has been the activities on which it has been spent.

Recall that the central products on which post-war growth and trade have been based are vehicles, machinery (including consumer durables) and chemicals. These are *not*, as it happens, the areas on which Britain has concentrated its research and development effort. Rather, Britain has poured massive R & D resources into three other areas: aircraft, defence products (especially military electronics), and nuclear reactors. These preoccupations absorbed over 50 per cent of British R & D in the late 1960s (total industrial R & D in 1968-9 was approximately £650 million; just over £360 million went on aerospace, electronics and reactors). This pattern of R & D expenditure in the post-war years was very different from that of our competitors, as table 16 shows. It looks at the way R & D expenditure is distributed among activities by five major countries in a typical year of the post-war boom.

Table 16. *Industrial distribution of R & D expenditure in 1962* (%)

	UK	France	W. Germany	Japan	USA
Aircraft	35.4	27.7	—	—	36.3
Vehicles and machinery	10.3	9.0	19.4	12.7	15.6
Electrical machinery and instruments	24.0	25.7	33.8	28.0	25.5
Chemicals	11.6	16.8	32.9	28.3	12.6

Source: C. Freeman and A. Young, *The Research and Development Effort in Western Europe, North America and the Soviet Union*, Paris, OECD, 1965.

Thus, Britain put 35 per cent of its R & D effort into aircraft; Germany and Japan – zero. Rather, Germany and Japan concentrated on electrical products and chemicals. The thing which stands out about this table, therefore, is the way in which German and Japanese R & D has been concentrated in the really dynamic growth areas, the areas where markets were big and growing.

Table 17 below, in a wider and more general way, also shows this. It is based on research into the R & D specialisms of a range of advanced economies, and it highlights the way in which the fast-

Table 17. Some comparative strengths and weaknesses in innovative performances

	Comparative strengths	*Comparative weaknesses*
Belgium	Ferrous and non-ferrous metals; stone, clay, glass; chemicals	Transport equipment; household appliances
France	Railroad equipment; motor vehicles and bicycles; soap and cleaning products	Radio and TV; household appliances; machinery
W. Germany	Machinery; chemicals; motor vehicles	Petroleum; food; ship and boat building; radio and TV
Italy	Household appliances; textiles; chemicals	Radio and TV; ship and boat building; electrical transmission and distribution equipment
Japan	Radio and TV; ferrous metals	Petroleum products; machinery; ordnance and missiles
Netherlands	Electrical and electronics; petroleum; chemicals	Aircraft and missiles; transportation equipment
Sweden	Metals and metal products; household appliances; motor vehicles; machinery; ship and boat building	Chemicals; petroleum; textiles; radio and TV
Switzerland	Drugs; chemicals	Petroleum; transportation equipment
UK	Aircraft and missiles; engines and turbines; non-ferrous metals	Household appliances; radio and TV

Source: K. Pavitt, ed., *Technical Innovation and British Economic Performance*, London, 1980, p. 56.

growing economies of Europe and Japan concentrated their innovation effort on the mundane but vital commodity groups – vehicles, machinery products, chemicals – which provided the real thrust behind post-war growth.

Britain's areas of specialism were thus ill-chosen, to put it mildly. Aeroplanes may be glamorous products, but they were simply not very significant in terms of market size. In 1961, for example, total exports of the products in table 16 above, by the nine biggest market economies looked like this (table 18):

Table 18. Export markets 1960–61 (total exports of nine economies)

	($ million)
Machinery, general	7215.2
Chemicals	6086.6
Vehicles	5062.4
Electrical machinery and instruments	3837.6
Aircraft	1551.2

Source: drawn from 'Fast and Slow Growing Products in World Trade', *National Institute Economic Review*, no. 25, 1963, Table 2, p. 24.

This picture has, alas, altered very little since the early 1960s (except that the level of British R & D has declined). When the same group of nine European countries was surveyed in 1975, Britain was still carrying out 42 per cent of total aerospace research; and Britain still lagged badly in research in chemicals, mechanical engineering, and electrical and electronic engineering.

In terms of government-financed R & D the picture is especially depressing. Government-backed R & D is particularly important in view of the large sums involved. The distribution of this crucial expenditure is especially interesting. In 1975, Belgium, Denmark, Germany, Italy and the Netherlands all put 50 per cent or over of R & D funds into basic scientific and technological research. Britain put in under 20 per cent. Only one country, France, spent over 11 per cent of such funds on defence R & D (France spent 29.6 per cent). Britain however put 46.4 per cent of government R & D into defence.

This pattern of research expenditure by Britain – that is, concentration on aircraft, military electronics and nuclear power – inhibited Britain's economic growth for three reasons. The first is that these were not and are not products on which major economic growth could be based, for the markets were simply too small. As we saw above, the export market for aircraft in 1960–61 (where Britain put 35 per cent of its R & D effort) was about a quarter of the size of the export market in chemicals (where Germany spent 33 per cent of its R & D funds). The nuclear reactor market appears to be neither large nor profitable, and the enormous research and development programme in Britain has resulted in the export sale of precisely *two* reactors (and those sales were twenty-five years ago). Secondly, these are all product groups in which Britain not only has a competitor, but the most formidable competitor it would be possible to have: the USA. Any rational policy for R & D should involve specialization not just in areas of growing demand, but also in areas where competitive pressures are not overwhelming. Even if Britain's aircraft R & D had produced the best aircraft in the world, which it did not, it would anyway have been difficult to sell them in the American market. One cannot but agree with Sir Arthur Knight, former chairman of the National Enterprise Board:

It seems that much of our massive programme of investment in defence-related high technology products was directed towards products which the Americans were bound to be able to manufacture more competitively . . . but these new activities were interesting and exciting and so they attracted a high proportion of our best young technologists; whereas in Germany the best young people were attracted into building up export-oriented, more down-to-earth mechanical engineering activities.[7]

Thirdly, these are not research areas which generate 'spin-offs', that is technological breakthroughs which have other uses and applications. We saw in Chapter 2 that German chemical expertise in dyestuffs generated a range of new products ranging from explosives to plastics (indeed a German book on applied chemical research in the early twentieth century bore the evocative title *One Thing After Another*). These spin-offs have played a large part in the continuing success of the German chemical industry; but they are not a conspicuous feature of British post-war R & D.

One could, therefore, sum up the post-war British technological record in this way. Even when British R & D resources were larger than those of competitors – which they are no longer – they were ludicrously misallocated. Britain concentrated on 'glamour' areas where markets were in fact derisory and the competition overwhelming. Furthermore, these problems, writes one R & D expert, Christopher Freeman,

were exacerbated by some extraordinarily inept public decision-making in relation to 'big' technology throughout the 50s and 60s. Concorde is the extreme example of unproductive but huge investment. Commercial and market factors were frequently ignored ... it took a long time before any government was prepared to stand up to the expert but special pleading of a high technology lobby in full cry. This applies particularly to aircraft and nuclear reactors, where prototype development and testing can be very expensive.[8]

The consequence of this research and development disaster was that British industry was progressively outstripped in technological terms by rival producers. New products and processes do not just happen – they require resources, and the resources simply were not committed to the job. Inadequate R & D meant that the UK lagged as the technological frontier was pushed further out by competitors; Britain increasingly failed to meet the new standards of product design, performance and quality which research was generating elsewhere. First this meant a declining share of markets, and economic growth which was slower than more innovative rivals. Hence the relatively slow growth of the 1950s and 1960s; Britain really prospered mainly because world markets were expanding. Then, as the world economy slowed down, inadequate R & D meant industrial collapse and unemployment as British manufacturing failed even to be in the same game as competitors, let alone to compete.

The eventual outcome [writes G. F. Ray] can best be seen in the penetration of imports of all types of products into the UK market, probably manifesting itself most clearly in consumer goods. To take just two examples: the British audio industry, which had been significant, lost most of its markets because it neglected the growth areas of the tape recorder, the cartridge and the cassette; in the past five years about 10,000 jobs have been lost in the television industry through lack of R & D ... but the best illustration can be found in the pathetic record of the UK motorcycle industry ... its market was first flooded with Italian scooters and mopeds and later by Japanese models which offered better performance at very competitive rates. The outcome is the virtual disappearance of the British industry.[9]

And this pattern of inadequate R & D, leading to loss of market share and then stagnation and collapse, has been amply documented in other industries.

SUMMING UP: BRITAIN IN THE BOOM

The argument, then, is that Britain performed poorly during the years of the post-war boom. Economic growth depends on the emergence of new products and processes which provide the focus for major programmes of investment. Britain failed to devote adequate resources to appropriate forms of research and development; and since R & D is the activity by which opportunities for new investment are searched out, this had serious long-term effects on Britain's growth prospects. The problems were masked during the long boom, because growing world markets offset Britain's increasingly poor performance. The reckoning arrived with the end of the boom, and it took the form of declining manufacturing employment and output: 'de-industrialization'.

THE END OF THE BOOM

The analysis outlined above suggests that Britain's post-war prosperity was largely an effect of a world boom in which Britain performed, on the whole, poorly. A return to economic growth will thus imply overcoming economic problems internal to Britain, but will also involve restoring some semblance of stability to the world economy. The latter, however, will not be easily achieved, and it would be rash to think either that a world recovery will happen, or that it would benefit Britain if it did.

The post-war boom collapsed in the early 1970s under the impact of a series of strains and shocks. The strains began with the Vietnam war. The United States faced the prospect of financing this very unpopular war in the context of considerable social upheavals; these upheavals, particularly among the poor in the decaying central city areas, had led to a vast increase in government spending on health, education, employment and welfare programmes. This warfare–welfare combination was hideously expensive and the obvious need was for tax increases to finance it all. The government, however, was desperately concerned about opposition to the war, and had no desire to fuel it further. So there were no tax increases; and the first consequences were massive deficits in the government budget, as well as increases in the money supply. A further consequence was balance of payments deficits, as the US increased its imports to maintain its consumption levels as its own industry switched towards expanded production for war.

These balance of payments deficits were financed simply by paying out dollars. This was possible because the basic currency of the post-war world economy was the dollar. In effect, people would accept dollars in payment for goods, knowing that the dollar was backed by gold (at the rate $35 = 1$ oz gold). However by the late 1960s, the combination of US budget deficits and balance of payments deficits had pumped a huge volume of dollars – far greater than the US gold reserves – into the world financial system (and particularly into the European financial system). Dollar holders in Europe began to switch out of dollars. In the second week of August, 1971, this movement accelerated dramatically as nearly $4 billion moved through the exchanges. US gold and foreign currency reserves could not stand the strain. In order to solve this problem the US government needed first to control its expenditure (and the war was still continuing, under President Nixon), and then to devalue its currency (and thus accept a reduction in income). There was, however, an alternative. In the words of an eminent banker, 'it appeared preferable to the US government simply to destroy the international monetary system'.[10] The Bretton Woods system of fixed exchange rates based on dollars collapsed, as the United States devalued, imposed import controls and stopped converting dollars into gold. No agreement could be reached among the advanced countries on a system to replace the Bretton Woods arrangements. For want of anything better, a confused system of floating rates emerged, injecting considerable uncertainty into the world economy.

The world of floating rates permitted a sharp increase in inflation. Previously, fixed rates had constrained inflationary pressures – no one could inflate out of line with everyone else without a balance of payments crisis. Now, inflation simply resulted in a depreciation of the exchange rate. Within the uncertain framework of the post Bretton Woods system, governments were almost uniformly anxious about exchange rate and balance of payments problems. Invariably, therefore, they adopted policies based on restriction of economic activity; caution was carried to recessionary lengths, and contributed in a major way to the slowing down of growth.

At the same time, for Western Europe, the technological opportunities which promoted post-war growth began to shrink as Europe caught up with the American technical lead. This was a main aspect of a slowing down in productivity growth which began in the late 1960s, in almost all of the advanced economies, and which in turn slowed down the possibilities for growth.

Finally, of course, came the OPEC price rises in 1973–4, and subsequently in 1978–9, which exacerbated inflationary pressures and generated major problems in the world financial system as the rises pushed many countries into serious balance of payments deficits. Many countries filled these deficits by borrowing from private banks, and the consequence has been a major international debt crisis.

The international context of the market economies is, therefore, now one of uncertainty and fluctuation. Some of its problems – such as the slowdown in productivity growth – are not well understood, and may not be solvable. Some problems – such as those of the international financial system – may be capable of solution; but solutions here will require a degree of political consensus and commitment which appears very unlikely to emerge. The post-war boom is unlikely, therefore, to reappear. 'World in dishevelled condition' reads a memorable entry in the diary of Keynes's Russian-born wife Lydia; she was writing in 1945, but things are the same and are likely to remain so. However, even in the unlikely event of a renewed international boom, Britain's internal problems will remain. Indeed, the material presented in these chapters indicates that the problems

of low and misdirected innovative activities, hence poor investment
and growth record, now threaten the viability of the British economy.
It is these problems on which Britain must concentrate, and it would
be foolhardy indeed to pin hopes on an international recovery.

5

The Crisis in Prospect

Previous chapters have argued that Britain's problems are long term in character, and have become cumulative, self-reinforcing. One central feature of Britain's industrial development is easily found: it is a low rate of growth, compared to similar economies. We have seen that relatively slow growth characterizes Britain's performance for at least the past century, and is particularly noticeable over the whole of the post Second World War years, a period in which Britain has declined from relative prosperity and economic health to relative poverty and economic debility. It has been possible also to outline some of the mechanisms underlying that performance. Economic growth is based on flexibility, on technological renewal, on constant transition, on the systematic development of new products and processes. This requires the commitment of resources to research and development, which is the process by which opportunities for investment and growth are searched out. Britain's slow growth record is based on a lack of dynamism, and on some very poor decision-making, in this area: it has failed in the development of new products and processes, and has failed to match the technological standards being set elsewhere. To an important extent responsibility for this predicament must be laid at the door of government, since the research and development resources needed by a modern industrial economy are so large that governments inevitably play a major role in their provision, coordination and use.

So Britain's modern economic development is based, like that of any advanced economy, on a particular pattern of technological development. Rigidity and a lack of dynamism in technological research have led to lost markets and restricted demand, and to a consequent slowing in output and income growth. Failure to develop new techniques of production means that productivity growth is restrained or non-existent, and opportunities to produce at lower cost are missed. Slow growth and stagnating incomes in one period mean that resources for developing new technologies in subsequent periods are limited. Limited profits, limited investment, further limited growth – this cycle can rapidly become self-perpetuating. These problems have been spelled out in Chapters 3 and 4, which tell a dismal story of persistently inadequate and misallocated research resources, and of increasingly worrying economic performance by the economy as a whole. The cumulative character of this cycle of development opens up the possibility of a critical point being reached in the long run, a point at which Britain will not merely be a poor competitor and slow grower, but will be unable to compete and will begin to decline not relatively but absolutely. But as we saw in Chapter 1, that absolute decline has happened: it has in fact been with us for a decade. The long run has arrived.

This growth record underlies the rather stark claim made in the introduction to this book: that the British economy is in crisis, in the sense that its traditional structure is no longer viable. It was suggested that those who think that the crisis is actually over, that we are leaving the danger zone rather than about to enter it, are mistaken. Mistaken also are those who think that a mere change of government will suffice to improve matters. This is because the first group misunderstand the nature of the transition which Britain is experiencing, while the latter seem to deny that it is taking place. The remainder of this chapter discusses the kind of 'structural' crisis which Britain is undergoing, and then goes on to consider some of the problems and possible futures before us.

A STRUCTURAL CRISIS?

In the first place, what is meant by talking of a 'structural crisis'? The 'structure' of an economy could refer, for example, to its pattern of ownership and wealth, its institutions (firms, unions, government agencies, etc.), to its political and legal character, and so on. And 'crisis' could mean anything from unforeseen difficulties to major cataclysm. In this book the 'structure' of the British economy has referred to three things, and their inter-connections. They are:

1. the division of economic activities which characterizes Britain; that is, the framework of sectors – agriculture, services, manufacturing, primary industry, government – which make up the British economy; the composition of output which they produce; and the pattern of employment which they involve;

2. the pattern of trade, that is of imports and exports, which connects this economic framework to the wider world economy;

3. the levels of income and standards of living which this framework of production and trade makes possible.

The 'structure' of the British economy can be summed up as follows. Britain, like most advanced economies, consists of a small but productive agricultural sector; a large industrial sector with manufacturing as its focus; and a service sector which has been increasing consistently in size. Agriculture employs less than 3 per cent of the workforce. The other sectors are characterized by marked changes: in the 1950s, manufacturing and services each employed about 42.5 per cent of the workforce. Since then manufacturing has declined sharply, to less than 30 per cent of the workforce, while service employment is now somewhere over 50 per cent. This domestic economic structure is connected to the world economy through a particular pattern of trade: Britain has traditionally been a net exporter of manufactures and financial services, and a net importer of food and raw materials. The trade pattern underlies Britain's balance of payments, which forms a major constraint on its rate of growth and level of income. The real incomes and standards of living of the British population are an effect both of its level and type of domestic economic activity, and its ability to trade with the world and thus consume imports.

To say that Britain is in crisis is to say that it is no longer capable of supporting this structure of production, employment and trade. If the pattern of production and trade is not viable, then Britain's levels of income are also unsustainable. It cannot support, in other words, its traditional pattern of consumption.

In fact, as previous chapters have shown, the assertion that the 'traditional' structure might, at some time in the future, no longer function, is not quite correct. It no longer functions *now*. Britain is no longer a significant net exporter of manufactures, their place in our export structure having been taken by North Sea oil. This erosion of Britain's trade surplus in manufactures is not a recent development: the general trend has been adverse for many years. Thus, in 1971, Britain exported manufactures which had a total value approximately twice that of manufactured imports; now the value of imports is greater than that of exports. One way of showing this trend is to plot the ratio of the value of exports to the value of imports in manufactures. When the ratio is greater than one, we have a surplus; when it is equal to one the surplus has disappeared. The following diagram (fig. 1) plots precisely this relationship, and the downward trend is clearly evident.

Figure 1. Ratio of value of manufactured exports to manufactured imports, from 1971

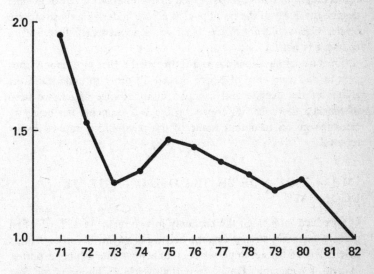

Source: Calculated from Table 2.3, 'Analysis by Commodity', *UK Balance of Payments 1982*, p. 15.

One important point to note about this diagram is that the downward trend began well before North Sea oil came onstream. We cannot, therefore, ascribe this structural shift – as various economists and government spokesmen have done – purely to the effects of North Sea oil. One of the central supports of Britain's international economic position has, in effect, crumbled.

So the crisis can be summed up in terms of Britain's decline as a major producer of manufactures. Manufacturing industry has been at the core of Britain's output, employment and export structure. Yet in the period 1970 to mid 1981, employment in manufacturing declined by 2.9 million workers, or 32 per cent. Output declined by 10.2 per cent and the export surplus in manufactures disappeared. Were it not for North Sea oil, Britain would be confronting desperate economic problems now. Instead, oil has permitted Britain to continue to consume imports as though nothing had changed. Since the ability to consume imports is part and parcel of our real income, i.e. of our real standard of living, it has helped to maintain our levels of income despite the decay of the traditional structure underlying those income levels. This would not matter if oil was a permanent fixture. But of course it is not.

The critical questions for the future of the British economy thus turn on the transience of North Sea oil. In order to understand the effects of the decline and eventual disappearance of oil, we need to consider first what its impact on the UK economy has been; we can then go on to outline some of the possibilities implied by its removal.

IMPACT OF NORTH SEA OIL ON THE UK ECONOMY

Oil produces effects on the economy in two main ways. In the first place it massively strengthens the balance of payments, since it turns Britain from a big net importer of oil to being a smallish net exporter: in 1976, for example, Britain imported nearly £4 billion of oil; four years later in 1980 this had completely turned around and became a net export of approximately £300 million. This strengthens the pound against foreign currencies, and enhances Britain's ability to consume imports (which can be paid for with the dollars earned from oil). It might also be expected to improve Britain's growth prospects by removing to some extent the external constraints on growth which were outlined in Chapter 2. In any case, as the pound strengthens, imports become relatively cheaper and this is one of the main mechanisms by which the benefits of North Sea oil are delivered to the British population generally. In the second place oil affects the government budget, via taxes on the profits being made in oil and gas production. Other things being equal, this would reduce the amounts of tax which individuals would need to pay (a second mechanism by which benefits are delivered), or it would enable the government to expand its activity (in, say, public investments) without increased general taxation or borrowing.

In fact the enhanced prosperity and government opportunities made possible by oil have largely been swamped by the effects of recession. Recessionary economic policies meant that prospects for growth were rejected. The collapse of manufacturing meant that instead of increasing prosperity, North Sea oil simply enabled us to stay where we were. The possibility of tax reductions or increased government activity were lost because of increases in government expenditure on unemployment pay and the other expenses of recession.

POSSIBLE EFFECTS OF DECLINE IN OIL

The fact that the prospective benefits of North Sea oil were missed does not mean that the decline of oil will be of little consequence. Because it has not permitted prosperity but only masked the effects of crisis its advent has had little noticeable impact on Britain; its disappearance is a different matter. The critical problem is this: when oil begins to decline, Britain's non-oil exports will need to expand significantly if current levels of income are to be maintained in the long term. Can Britain adjust to a world in which it must export manufactures or services on a much larger scale than it does at the present? If not, then it must reduce its consumption of imports, and hence its real income and standard of living, in order to maintain a basic balance of payments equilibrium. As oil declines, what are the prospects for reestablishing that structure or something like it?

What, in other words, are the prospects for the development of the crisis? The key things to consider are firstly the likely developments, and secondly their time-scale. Here we face some major difficulties, since we are talking about an uncertain and unknowable future. It would be rash to hazard any particularly definite predictions, especially since this book is not an exercise in forecasting or futurology. Nevertheless the main elements in the situation can be outlined, as well as some of the tangible and intangible factors governing the chronology of developments.

The key factor must clearly be the rate at which oil output will decline in the late 1980s and early 1990s. A long slow decline in oil production would certainly be easier to cope with than a more or less sudden cut-off. Part of the problem here is that medium- and long-term projections for output are very uncertain. On current estimates however, oil output in the North Sea will reach its peak in 1984–5 and will begin to decline thereafter, probably at a rate of about 4 to 5 per cent per year. Britain will remain self-sufficient until the early 1990s, possibly even as long as the turn of the century. From a peak annual production of approximately 100 million tonnes it will still be producing significant amounts (i.e. to be counted in tens of millions of tonnes) well into the twenty-first century. For Britain, 'self-sufficiency' means something in the region of 75 to 80 million tonnes of oil per year. So if these figures and rates of decline are roughly correct then Britain will be self-sufficient in 1990, but will need to import 15–20 million tonnes per year by 1995, and about 30 million tonnes per year at the turn of the century. At current prices, this would take us back – very roughly – to the 1976 position, of importing about £4 billion of oil products per year.

Of course all of these projections are fraught with uncertainty. Recoverable reserves in the North Sea are not known with any great accuracy, and there is always the possibility that new fields will be discovered which will alter the general picture. This is unlikely, but not out of the question. On the other hand any increase in GDP in Britain would increase our oil consumption and thus affect our overall oil balances.

What will be the effects of a slowing of oil production? The most important concern the exchange rate and Britain's external position. As oil output begins to decline in volume (leaving price changes out of account here) the contribution by oil to the balance of payments and to the government's budget will also decline. This will exert downward pressure on the exchange rate. But much hangs on the extent and speed of any exchange rate slide, and this is unpredictable to say the least. If the exchange rate was determined only by current transactions (exports and imports of goods and services) then we might expect a steady gradual slide, if there were no offsetting increases in other exports. However, there are also capital account movements to consider. On the one hand the government may be able to engineer movements of capital into Britain, and this would ameliorate an exchange rate depreciation. On the other hand, holders of capital might take a longer view, and feel that in the face of a steadily deteriorating trade position Britain was not the place for their money. In that case we could expect a large-scale movement of capital out of Britain, and a more or less sudden and catastrophic collapse of the exchange rate. This seems to be the most likely development.

Either way, the ultimate effect will be on the living standards of the British population. Exchange rate depreciation means that the prices of imports rise. This has an inflationary effect, but more importantly it reduces the real incomes – that is to say, the real amount of goods and services that are consumed – of the British people. Ultimately, the result of an unrestrained exchange rate collapse is a sharp contraction in incomes, though it may also have dramatic effects on inflation (as in Weimar Germany and many developing countries today) and on employment. One of the characteristics of underdeveloped countries is precisely this form of exchange rate and balance of payments constraint: such countries are unable to export enough to pay for the imports which would be needed if the economy were to increase its levels of employment and income. It is this kind of prospect which faces Britain as a result of the decay of its traditional export structure and manufacturing capability. A great deal depends, therefore, on whether anything will happen to offset or prevent this kind of exchange rate collapse as oil output declines.

CAN BRITAIN ADJUST TO IMPORTING OIL?

The crucial question is whether Britain can adjust to a world in which we must increasingly import oil and consequently raise net exports to pay the bill. One approach would argue that this is no problem, that the declining exchange rate would cause an automatic readjustment: as the exchange rate slides, exports from Britain become cheaper and imports to Britain become dearer. This would increase the sale of exports and decrease the volume of imports, thus keeping the balance of payments in constant equilibrium and generating a structural change in our economy to cope with our changed economic environment and resources. Elementary economic theorizing tells us that this is how things will pan out: in this view, the spectre I have raised above simply will not and could not materialize. However as the next section of this book argues, there is a great deal in elementary economics – and even in advanced economics – which is not to be trusted. Will exchange rate depreciation increase our exports by cheapening our goods? An important point to bear in mind – one emphasized in earlier chapters – is that manufactured exports are successful not simply because they are cheap, but because they are of high quality, good design and so on. Their technological characteristics are at least as important as their price, which is why in the past devaluations and exchange rate depreciations have not had strikingly successful effects in improving Britain's manufactured exports record.

There is little reason to believe, therefore, that an exchange rate slide will somehow suffice to reinstate manufactured exports in Britain's export structure. And here it is important to recall that we will be facing the decline of oil with a seriously eroded manufacturing base. It is no use, for example, for Britain to be able to manufacture machine tools cheaply if Britain does not in fact possess a machine tools industry. At the moment, that industry has in effect collapsed, and no amount of exchange rate depreciation will bring it back to life. These thoughts are even more worrying if we reflect that there seems little evidence that the present collapse in manufacturing will be reversed over the coming five to ten years. What evidence is there that the sharply downward trend in British manufacturing has been arrested, let alone that the basic industrial framework needed in the future is being restored and reconstructed? Given that no significant change has occurred in the overall technological level of British manufacturing, that there has been no sign whatever of significant increase in the levels of research and development work, and continuing decline in productive investment, it would be surprising indeed if the whole trend of post-war development was suddenly reversed, and 1995 finds Britain with a manufacturing sector capable of dramatic export expansion. The conclusion must be that the decline of oil will *not*, in all probability, result in some smooth adjustment process by which manufactures regain their former place in Britain's trade pattern.

DEVELOPING SERVICE EXPORTS – AN ALTERNATIVE?

But of course there is no law of economic life which says that Britain must export manufactures; there are other possible exports, notably services of various kinds. There are many who argue that Britain can and should develop its service exports as part of the solution to our economic problems.

However the arguments for increased service exports are often less than convincing. The question should be asked, what kinds of services can Britain sell, and what quantity of them? In the past, Britain's main earnings from services have been derived from two areas: travel (i.e. tourism) and financial services (insurance, banking, investment services and so on). What possibilities are open to expand earnings in these activities? In terms of financial services, the City of London is in many ways a very efficient and competitive centre, but that does not mean that it is capable of accelerated growth. For a start, the world market for services is not growing particularly fast (it is growing more slowly than the market for manufactures, for example). More important perhaps is the fact – often forgotten – that Britain faces increasingly severe competition in this area. For a long period Britain had an effective monopoly in financial services, with London as the principal world centre; even after that monopoly disappeared, there were relatively few major world financial markets. But recent years have seen a rapid expansion of regional and offshore centres, and major new markets (as in, for example, Hong Kong). These increasing competitive pressures in the financial arena parallel the competitive pressures which British manufacturing faced in the middle and late nineteenth century. They make it very unlikely that Britain can hope to solve its forthcoming balance of payments problems through increased exports of financial services.

Similar considerations apply to tourism. When people talk glibly of expanding earnings here it is simply necessary to ask, how many more German tourists, for example, do we need to make up the shortfall in export earnings elsewhere? Suppose we were to go back to the position of 1976, with a £4 billion deficit (in 1976 pounds) on our trade in oil, and assume no significant increase in present manufacturing or financial exports. Then, assuming that every tourist who enters Britain converts £2,000 of foreign currency into sterling, we would require a mere two million extra tourists. Given that world tourism is in decline at the moment such a development would be remarkable, as well as ghastly to experience (for both Britons and tourists). In any case, it is simply not on the cards, and we cannot look to it for any important contribution to the balance of payments problems we face.

Much the same can be said for other developing areas in service trade. Computer software, for example, is often held up as an expanding, dynamic activity, with export markets open to it. This is indeed true, and certainly Britain has skills in this field. But other countries have such skills also, and competition is increasingly fierce. Of course Britain should develop this industry, as vigorously as possible, but it is sheer fantasy to think that it is likely in itself to provide any sort of basis for sustained economic recovery. As with other sectors of the service economy, we can find here no panacea for our problems.

THE CRISIS AND RECOVERY

Britain is in the throes of a serious economic crisis, in which its traditional economic structure is no longer viable. As North Sea oil output declines, we must face the prospect of a serious worsening of our foreign trade position, which will ultimately affect the lives of most of the British population. As we have seen, there seems little likelihood of solving Britain's problems by recourse to expansion of other sectors of the economy, such as services. Just as the decline of manufactures is at the heart of Britain's decline, so the reconstruction of manufacturing industry must be the central component of a re-invigorated British economy. Even the so-called 'old' manufactures such as steel and vehicles remain dynamic and growing sectors in world trade and output. The manufacturing sector retains its historic and characteristic role as a central focus of the growth of demand, output and international trade. Recovery from the crisis is in large part a matter of reversing the trends of the past century, of setting a flexible, dynamic and forward-looking manufacturing industry in place of one which has proved so technologically rigid and ultimately moribund.

But how is this reconstruction to be achieved? In the first place, major decisions must be taken with respect to economic policy. These concern the principles which should guide overall policy making, and the kinds of institutions and mechanisms which should exist to carry out policy decisions. To discuss the problems here, even in outline, is an enormous and complex task, well beyond the scope of a single book and perhaps of a single author. Yet the task should not be dodged, and the following sections of this book try to outline some of the problems in two important areas. The first is in the field of general economic policy: specifically, the kinds of ideas about the economy which guide the formation of policy. Economic theory is often misunderstood and misapplied, yet it also often forms a strategic guide for the formation of broad types of economic policy which have far-reaching implications for all of us. In order to begin thinking about policies for recovery we need at some point to tackle the question of what economic theory can and cannot do in assisting with the task at hand. So the next section looks at recent debates and advances in economic theory, at their relevance and irrelevance to the concrete and urgent problems ahead for Britain. The final section of the book considers industrial policy: the problems it must solve, the ways in which it is formed and carried out in some other countries, and the changes which might be needed in this field in Britain.

PART TWO

THE ECONOMISTS

Introduction

Advanced research, in economics as in other sciences, often appears arcane and obscure; often it *is* arcane and obscure. But the basic ideas which guide economic theory can be set out straightforwardly, and it is important to do so for a number of reasons. Foremost among them is that the formation of policies to solve the present crisis must depend in part on theoretical ideas about the workings of the economy. Economic theory is far from being the only basis for policy making but it can be a crucial component of it. And recently, theory and policy seem to have become more and more intertwined: the most important single issue in contemporary theoretical debate concerns the effectiveness of government policy, while policy disputes in Britain have increasingly taken the form of wrangles over theoretical matters. An interesting symptom of the closer relation between theory and policy was the recent double appearance of a major theoretical article, more or less simultaneously, in a specialized academic journal and a House of Commons policy report. If, then, policy discussion is increasingly dependent on economic expertise it is important that we should be able to assess – at least in general terms – the pronouncements of economists. And for this it is necessary to have some grip on the issues which are really at stake in economic debate.

However, the relation between economics and policy has another dimension, to do with the general social and political influence of economic ideas. Keynes once remarked, in a much-quoted passage, that

the ideas of economists and political philosophers, both when they are right and when they are wrong, are more powerful than is commonly understood. Indeed the world is ruled by little else. Practical men, who believe themselves to be quite exempt from intellectual influences, are usually the slaves of some defunct economist. Madmen in authority, who hear voices in the air, are distilling their frenzy from some academic scribbler of a few years back.[1]

There is an important degree of truth in this passage. Certainly in Britain one particular academic economic idea has been of quite exceptional importance: this is the notion that private-enterprise, free-market economies are efficient, necessary and socially desirable. Clearly, such an idea is central to monetarist economics and conservative political thought; yet it is also to be found in Keynesian economics and all parts of the British parliamentary political spectrum. But to what extent is the idea correct? It is often assumed – both by supporters of Thatcherite *laissez-faire*, and supporters of the 'mixed economy' – that there is an adequate theory of the free-market economy which lends support to economic policies focused on a private-enterprise market system. This is not so. Certainly there is a considerable body of sophisticated theory – which the following chapters will describe – but when it is examined closely, one can see few grounds for applying its conclusions to the UK. This does not mean that market systems and market economics can or should be rejected in making policy. But the case for *some* kind of state intervention and state economic activity becomes overwhelming; the crucial questions for the future concern the level of intervention and the forms of intervention. There are many possibilities. And here lies a further reason for examining economic theory: to understand some of its limitations, what it can and cannot show.

However, there are some real difficulties in understanding the structure of modern economics and the sources of dispute within it. These are mainly to do with the way that the divisions have been presented, in recent years, in terms of a distinction between 'monetarists' and 'Keynesians'. What is the basis of this distinction? It often appears as though purely technical questions are at issue, concerning monetary policy, or the nature of inflation; and many economists do in fact assert that the disagreements are essentially practical in character. But this is seriously misleading. The reason is that many of the 'technical' disputes only make sense in the context of different theoretical starting points, different basic concepts. Looked at in this way, the main disagreements concern not straightforward technical matters, but ideas about the elementary structure and properties of market-type economies. This is where the differences begin, and the divergences which emerge can be very sharp indeed. The following chapters are principally concerned with these basic theoretical points of departure, and their broad implications for policy.

6

Free Markets and Monetarism

Monetarism is simultaneously one of the most widely known and most misunderstood of economic doctrines. It owes its fame to three main sources. The first, within the economics profession itself, is a group of monetarist economists who have successfully forced the profession to sit up and take notice of some analytical problems which it had preferred quietly to ignore. The second is the ebullient personality of Milton Friedman who – through books, articles, his television series and any other medium of publicity springing to hand – has insistently claimed public attention for his 'Chicago' version of monetarism. Finally there is the government of Mrs Thatcher. Hers is not the first administration to attempt a systematic application of monetarist policy principles – various Latin American military dictators beat her to it – but the 'Thatcher experiment' is by far the most important of these attempts. Since these 'sources' are really quite diverse it should not be surprising that they do not always see eye to eye on what 'monetarism' actually means. And this is, perhaps, the first point which should be made about it: it is simply not a unified doctrine, particularly at the level of practical policy.

As an example of this one might take the Thatcher administration's policies on government spending. A central policy aim of the Conservative government has been to narrow the gap between what the government spends – on health, education and so forth – and its income in the form of taxes: it has done so by cutting expenditure and increasing the tax burden. This 'gap' between expenditure and tax income is the deficit in the government's budget, and it must be filled by borrowing: it is the basis of the Public Sector Borrowing Requirement (PSBR). Mrs Thatcher's economic ministers believe that a large PSBR generates increases in the money supply, which in turn fuels inflation. Since inflation is a supreme evil, they argue, we must cut the PSBR in order to cut the money supply, which will cut the inflation rate. But other monetarists believe no such thing. For some, monetarism is quite compatible with high levels of government spending and large amounts of government borrowing: they may not like government spending, but that is not because they think that it increases the money supply or is necessarily inflationary. Milton Friedman has taken this view, and recently wrote that he 'could not believe his eyes' when reading the British government's economic strategy document setting out these ideas. To give a further example, at the risk of labouring the point: Sir Geoffrey Howe, the former Chancellor, once appeared on television armed with two graphs, one showing the increase in prices, the other showing the increase in unemployment. Pointing to the fact that they have risen more or less simultaneously, he concluded that rising prices *caused* rising unemployment: 'Higher inflation means higher unemployment,' he announced, concluding that we must beat inflation to cure unemployment. Many monetarist theorists believe nothing of the sort. For them inflation is a purely price phenomenon with no 'real' effects: when the money supply increases, prices rise but output and employment are in theory entirely unaffected or are affected only temporarily.

Such discrepancies in belief could be multiplied without any trouble at all. What they imply is that monetarist theory should not be identified with Thatcherite policy. But it is nevertheless important to set out the broad theoretical foundations of monetarism, since they have to do with a theory of markets, and it is of course the beneficial properties of free-market systems which are at the core of Conservative economic policies. But the proponents of free-market economics often seem to understand little of the theory which is supposed to support their views. At the same time, monetarist theory has often been misinterpreted by its critics. Both as a theory and as a principle of policy making it is frequently denounced as a 'narrow dogma', an attempt to bring a single idea – control of the money supply – to bear on economic problems which are so numerous and complex that they require an approach which is much wider in scope. Yet the portentously named 'neoclassical general equilibrium theory' which is the real core of monetarist thinking is by no means narrow. In fact it is an economic theory of wide horizons, of considerable structural complexity, logical rigour and breadth of scope. Even though it is rarely well understood, even within the economics profession, its ideas and its conclusions have a pervasive influence both among economists and among those, such as journalists and politicians, who are prone to refer to what they think economics proves. The most important disputes within modern economics concern the properties and the applicability of this general equilibrium theory, even though it is usually in the background rather than the foreground of much economic analysis.

MARKETS AND EQUILIBRIUM

General equilibrium analysis is the study of the interactions of large numbers of economic agents (individuals, firms) who are connected by systems of markets. It sees the economy not as a conglomeration of separate markets, but as a set of interrelated markets, where what happens in one market affects what happens in another. It is concerned with the implications of this market interdependence: if markets, and the prices which are established in them, are interdependent, then the decisions of economic agents must also be interdependent to some greater or lesser extent. The relationships of such an economy are likely to be very complex; general equilibrium theory attempts a rigorous analysis of this complexity.

The theory starts from the idea that a fundamental problem for any economy is *coordination*: the desires of consumers for various products must be coordinated with the production system (so that the right amounts of different goods are produced); at the same time, the production system must be coordinated with suppliers of raw materials, machines and labour, so that the right quantities of inputs are available to produce the required goods. In a word, if the economy is to be viable at all, there must be *compatibility*; the economic needs of consumers must be compatible among themselves, and also with the capacity of the system to produce. Any economy will therefore need some mechanism which will allocate its resources of labour and materials among different types of production so as to produce a coordinated, compatible configuration of output.

Since the late nineteenth century, the mainstream of economic theory has seen markets and prices as precisely such a coordinating mechanism. In this approach, prices are normally seen as *signals*, delivering two kinds of information which should be harmonized in any efficient economy. On the one hand, price signals the intensity with which consumers demand any particular product, while on the other it signals the costs incurred, the resources used up, in producing it. This idea is associated in turn with a theory of how prices are formed in individual markets, a theory which accords with what many people often regard as elementary and reasonable. It runs as follows: as consumers, we do not normally have a need or demand for any *specific* quantity of a good to be produced. The amount which we will want to buy is variable, depending primarily on the terms on which it is available. In other words, if a product bears a high price we will want to purchase a relatively low quantity of it; if the price falls we will tend to buy more; and at a low price we will buy a relatively high quantity. In the jargon of economics, there is an inverse relation between the price and the quantity purchased. So for every price at which goods might be offered, a different amount will be purchased by consumers; and since there is therefore a whole range of possible price–quantity combinations, there is no way – at this point in the analysis – of saying what the ruling market price might actually be, or what quantity of goods will be sold.

However, a similar, though converse, line of analysis can also be applied to production. If the costs of producers rise as they increase output then they will require the incentive of a higher price if they are to produce more and still cover their costs. Therefore at low prices they will supply low quantities of goods into a market; as prices rise they will supply more, and at a high price they will supply a relatively high quantity of the good. Producers also have a range of price–quantity combinations, but in the opposite direction to consumers: for them, the higher the price the more they want to trade in the market. Such considerations lead to a theory of what the market price will actually be. The argument is that there will normally be one price – and one price only – at which the quantity demanded by consumers is equal to the quantity which producers will wish to supply. This is called the *equilibrium price*. It is the only price which will clear the market, meaning that all demand will be satisfied and all goods sold. It is the only price which will leave producers and consumers satisfied with – not wanting to change – the quantity of goods being traded (if the price is above the equilibrium price, then the market will not clear: producers will want to sell more than consumers want to buy; their responses to the price signal will no longer be compatible).

Now there are some interesting problems even at this early stage in equilibrium analysis, which are often skated over in economic theory. Firstly, these concern whether equilibrium prices exist, even in theory, for particular markets: it is quite easy to envisage markets exactly like those described above for which there is no equilibrium price. Secondly, there is the question of whether these prices are stable. The stability problem concerns what happens when the price is not at the equilibrium level: when the market is in what the jargon calls *disequilibrium*. Under such circumstances, does the market work to restore the equilibrium price and the equilibrium quantity traded? Again, it is a fairly simple matter to envisage wildly unstable markets, which show no tendency to restore the equilibrium price if they are disturbed.

But suppose these problems are suspended or ignored or regarded as trivial in practice? What then happens if a market is in disequilibrium? If the price is above the equilibrium price then there will be unsold stocks, because producers will supply into the market more goods than consumers want to buy. Producers might then be expected to lower their prices in order to induce consumers to buy these stocks. As they do so, consumers *will* buy more, but at the lower prices now ruling, producers will want to produce less. In effect, there will be a succession of changes in prices and quantities traded until the equilibrium price is reached or restored. If prices are flexible in this way, then it is straightforward to see how this kind of market might act as a mechanism of coordination. Suppose that consumers, considered as a group, decide for whatever reason that they want more of a product. This means that, at the ruling price, they will want to buy a quantity larger than the existing equilibrium quantity.

Another way of putting this is to say that they are prepared to pay more for the presently available quantity; they will bid up the price since they are in competition with each other for the going amount. As the price rises producers will supply more, because it will be profitable to do so, until a new equilibrium price–quantity combination emerges which satisfies the increased demand. The market, with its changing price signals, will have smoothly transformed an increased desire for the product into increased output. Producers can pass on cost information in a similar way. If oil reserves begin to diminish, for example, then costs of producing a barrel of oil will rise; the market price will rise and consumers will buy less. Once again the price system is coordinating, encouraging a level of consumption which will conserve oil, making demand conform to resources.

This kind of theory of individual markets is known as partial equilibrium analysis. The harmonious picture it presents involves some rather obvious flaws as an image of reality, and some subtle theoretical problems. Before looking at them, and before seeing how a 'general equilibrium' of the whole economy might be conceptualized, it is important to say something about one other individual market: the market for labour.

THE LABOUR MARKET

Sellers of goods (producers) will in the main be sellers in one market and buyers in another; they usually need to purchase labour in order to manufacture output. Now the basic equilibrium 'model' of the economy normally describes the labour market in a similar way to the goods markets outlined above. That is, it suggests that buyers of labour (producers, firms) will buy more labour as its price falls, and less labour as its price rises. Sellers (workers) will supply increasing quantities of labour as the price rises, and vice versa. As with any commodity, there will be an equilibrium price at which the quantity of labour demanded equals that supplied. The 'equilibrium price' thus established will be the going wage rate, while the 'equilibrium quantity' will be the number of workers employed.

One very important point should be made about the labour market when it is analysed in this way. This is that the equilibrium quantity associated with the equilibrium price can be described as 'full employment'. The reasoning behind this is as follows: at the equilibrium price, everyone who wants a job can get one. Anyone who is unemployed, and wants a job, can get one by offering to work at a lower price, a lower wage rate. By lowering the price of labour employers will be induced to raise the quantity employed. This means that no one can, in general, be unemployed against their will; and this is a working definition of full employment. This, in turn, explains why monetarists are apt to describe unemployment as 'voluntary', and it underlies the remarks of more than one government spokesman on the need for workers to 'price themselves into jobs'. Thus a central interpretation of unemployment in the general equilibrium approach – though it is not, as we shall see, accepted by all general equilibrium theorists – is that unemployment is a temporary phenomenon associated with a quite restricted range of causes: these are invariably to do with wage rates being too high, perhaps because of trade union activity, or a mistaken reluctance to take a pay cut.

GENERAL EQUILIBRIUM: A FIRST PICTURE

A 'general equilibrium' can be defined as an economic state in which all individual markets are simultaneously in equilibrium. If such an equilibrium is possible, and if the economy tends towards it (both rather big ifs, as it happens), then the general equilibrium state will clearly be of considerable interest and importance. This is because the particular character of such an equilibrium will determine some very important things about the economy. If all markets are in equilibrium then we will know – from the prices and quantities which are established in them – the following: the overall level of income, the number of people employed, the rate of wages, the profit rate, the types of output which are produced and the quantities of each type, and the relative prices of all goods and services. All of these things interlock. The wage rate will determine the quantity of people employed; the quantity of people employed, in conjunction with the available capital stock, will determine the quantity of output; the quantity of output will determine the total level of income, because the value of output will be equal to the value of the incomes (profits, wages) earned in producing it. The way in which people spend their income will determine a structure of demand, which will in turn affect the relative prices of goods. The intensities of demand for the various goods will determine which goods it is profitable to produce, and hence the composition of output. All of these relationships and quantities will moreover be fixed simultaneously.

All of this depends, it should be emphasized, on the operation of the separate and apparently unconnected markets which make up the economy. Since the time of Adam Smith (a particular hero to monetarists like Milton Friedman), but more particularly since the late nineteenth century, it has been a central theme of mainstream Western economics that market economies do work in this kind of way. It is argued that if all markets operate freely, then the structure of the economy and the amount it produces will be fully determined by the choices made by individuals. In choosing which products to buy, and how much of them to buy, in deciding where we will work and for how long, we are in effect engaged in the formation of a collective decision concerning the making and working of the economy. And in attempting to get the best value for money, in attempting to maximize our incomes, in seeking out the most profitable opportunities for business, we are certainly helping ourselves as individuals, but we are also doing something more. We are improving the efficiency of the economy, raising its output, increasing the economic welfare of all. Moreover, this co-operation and coordination can extend world-wide, as long as there are markets freely operating internationally as well as within our own country.

In many respects this vision of the economy is a noble one. It places the responsibilities for economic decision-making squarely on individuals. It gives short shrift to political elites or economic vested interests who might want to usurp crucial economic decisions, either from private greed or from the belief that they know, better than the rest of us, what is good for us. This 'free market' theory is, in one sense, thoroughly libertarian; its impact on the economics profession in the West would be difficult to exaggerate.

THE ECONOMICS OF 'WELFARE'

It seems a natural extension of the approach outlined above to suggest that the outcomes which emerge from freely operating market systems are beneficial; in fact, could not be bettered. Once again, such views can be traced back to Adam Smith. But in modern 'neoclassical' economics such positive assessments of the market system are not regarded as just matters of opinion. There is a major branch of economics, 'welfare economics', which studies the effects of economic processes on the welfare of individuals and groups. It takes a highly formal, abstract and mathematical approach to the topic and for that reason it would be impossible accurately to describe its procedures here. But it is important to set out one of its most famous results, which has had a deep influence on the thinking of many economists. This result is frequently used as an argument in support of the free-market economies analysed by general equilibrium theory. Welfare economics shows (that is to say, *proves* in the sense of a logical or mathematical proof) that a fully free-market economy produces, out of all the economic outcomes which could be produced, the best for the welfare of its people (given the income distribution, the available technology and people's preferences for goods). This best-possible outcome is known in the jargon as a 'Pareto optimum', and although a free-market economy is not the only way to achieve it (in abstract theory Soviet-type centrally planned economies could do just as well) it is the method which, for obvious reasons, has fascinated Western economists. The relation between welfare economics and general equilibrium theory is simple. It turns out that a competitive economy in general equilibrium is also a Pareto optimum. This result is *the* scientific basis for claims, which are frequently heard but rarely justified, that the free-market capitalist economy is the most efficient, welfare maximizing economy possible.

However, it is always prudent to be a little suspicious of those who start talking of the best of all possible worlds. And since it is not for nothing that the monetarist version of general equilibrium theory has been described recently by a distinguished critic as 'the economics of Dr Pangloss', it will be useful to look in more detail at the theoretical difficulties which lurk in the background of Milton Friedman's rather euphoric picture of competitive capitalism. What kinds of limitations are there in the theoretical methods which general equilibrium theory uses to depict the economy? How far do these limitations vitiate it as a theory of the real-world economy? Are the conclusions based on it sound?

GENERAL EQUILIBRIUM: THEORY AND METHODS

We can start by reconsidering the idea of 'general equilibrium' itself. It was defined as a simultaneous equilibrium, simultaneous balancing of supply and demand, in all markets of the economy. What is involved in this?

In the discussion of partial equilibrium (equilibrium in one market) earlier in this chapter it was suggested that the quantities demanded and supplied for any commodity depended on its price. In fact I should have said, depended *mainly* on its price: there are some further factors to consider. For example, the prices of other goods will be an important matter. The quantity of butter demanded might depend partly on the price of margarine (because they are 'substitutes': if the price of margarine falls then people might just buy more margarine and less butter) and partly on the price of bread (they are called complements: if the price of bread rises people might eat less bread and hence less butter). The quantity of butter demanded also depends on people's incomes, which in turn depend on the prices of other commodities. If the price of carpets falls, then the incomes of those who manufacture them are likely also to fall, and they may demand less butter in consequence as they 'economize'. It can easily be seen, through this kind of argument, that the equilibrium quantity of butter demanded will depend on its own price and the prices of a great many other, perhaps *all* other, commodities. This means that the market equilibria of most or all goods are completely interdependent: we cannot describe what is happening in one goods market without taking into account what is happening in all. This is why it is necessary to study equilibria as both *general* and *simultaneous* in the market economy.

There are a number of reasons why the study of 'general equilibrium' is important. Firstly, there is the question of whether a market economy is actually viable. Clearly, market systems are only worth supporting and maintaining if they actually *work*, in particular as mechanisms of coordination. But in theory they only work insofar as general equilibrium is possible: if equilibrium in the butter market is not compatible with equilibrium in the carpet market, then something has to give. One way or another people's demands for goods will not be effectively coordinated with the production system (because disequilibrium in the carpet market means that there will be either overproduction or unsatisfied demand). Of course, if just one market is out of equilibrium, then there is no great problem. But what if equilibrium in half the markets of the economy means disequilibrium in the other half? Or if, because of the interdependence of all markets, no equilibrium is possible in any market? The result will be chaos. Markets will not be solving the basic economic problem of what should be produced, in what quantities, etc. Market economies tend to look rather chaotic and unstructured; if general equilibrium is possible in theory, then there is at least the possibility of an underlying order.

Secondly, there are questions about the properties of a general equilibrium. Does it generate full employment? Does it encourage economic efficiency? Finally there are questions about 'movement' in the economy. Can we explain shifts and changes and modifications in the economy in terms of movement towards general equilibrium? Does it give us some insight into the dynamic forces which are in play in the economy? These kinds of concerns make the existence of general equilibrium an important theoretical problem.

Now for the sixty-four-thousand dollar questions. Seeing that any one market equilibrium depends on most or all other markets, it is likely to be a very complex matter. In view of this complexity, is it at all possible that a general equilibrium of *all* markets might exist? If such a general equilibrium position is attainable for the whole economy, is there only one equilibrium state, or two, or three, or what? Is such an equilibrium stable? If general equilibrium is reached, does the economy stay in it, or return to equilibrium if some unforeseen shock to the system (such as a basic rise in the price of oil) occurs? These questions turn out to be far from easy to answer.

But the investigation of such problems has been a core preoccupation of Western economists in the modern period. The most influential line of attack on them has derived from the pioneering work of the nineteenth-century French-Swiss economist Leon Walras (1834–1910), usually regarded as the first to pose and solve the big conceptual problems of general equilibrium adequately. His work is frequently praised in rather reverential terms; as one major authority, Joseph Schumpeter, has put it:

His system of economic equilibrium, uniting, as it does, the quality of 'revolutionary' creativeness and the quality of classic synthesis, is the only work by an economist that will stand comparison with the achievements of theoretical physics.[1]

The Walrasian method, set out in his *Elements d'économie politique pure* (1874) runs broadly as follows: the specific price–quantity combinations which describe consumer demand in any one market can be represented by mathematical means, with an equation. The quantity demanded will be related to the price of the good, and all other relevant prices. In mathematical terms, the quantity demanded will be an inverse function of the good's price, and functionally related to other prices. Similarly with the quantity supplied: this will also be some multiple of prices, a direct function of the price of the good itself, and functionally related to other prices. Since we know that, in equilibrium, the quantity supplied will equal the quantity demanded, we can bring these two equations together to form a small simultaneous equation system. If the equations can be solved, then it means that an equilibrium exists; the specific values of the variables, when the equations are solved, will give the actual price and quantity.

However, the equations describing any one market are related to the equations describing most or all of the other markets. So in fact the simultaneous equation system must be very large. The whole thing rapidly becomes very complex, because a very wide range of descriptive equations is in fact needed. The system requires equations specifying the relationships between the welfare of consumers and the number and composition of the goods they consume; it needs equations describing the production system, in particular the relation between output and the quantities of labour and capital input; it needs supply and demand equations derived from or related to these types of equation. Appropriate equations are needed in description of every consumer, every product, every process, every market in the economy. And this very large set of equations, with an enormous number of unknown variables, must solve simultaneously if this mathematical picture of general equilibrium is to be viable. It may seem an abstract, perhaps rather far-fetched approach, and in some ways it is. But it is worth emphasizing that it is simply a precise statement of what we must be able to prove, if more general statements (to the effect that market economies are efficient, welfare maximizing and so on) are to hold water. Another way of putting it is to say that if this mathematical picture of the economy does not work, then there is no completely sound theoretical basis for economic policies aimed – as Mrs Thatcher's are – at extending the free-market, private-enterprise economy. So does the equation system solve?

It turns out to be possible. It has been shown that the equation system is solvable, that in theory a state of general equilibrium in all markets can exist, that the equilibrium is unique (there is only one possible equilibrium to which the economy will tend), and that it is stable.

This was a considerable achievement. Admiration for it, however, should be qualified, for there were some marked peculiarities in the way the results were achieved. These are not necessarily particularly important in theoretical terms; but they are absolutely crucial when conclusions from Walras's theory are applied in practice. The problems in Walras's approach relate, firstly, to the simplifications he had to adopt about the nature of the economy, and secondly, to the way in which equilibrium was actually achieved.

First, the simplifications. An economy, however small, is clearly a complex thing. Any mathematical 'model' of it will therefore need to simplify many features of it; these simplifications are known in economics as 'initial assumptions'. They are the restrictions which must be put on the complexity of the economy in order to make the mathematics of the model of it workable. The restrictive assumptions of Walrasian General Equilibrium theory include the following:

1. There is full and free competition (known as 'perfect competition') in the economy. If all prices are established competitively, then no buyer or seller is in a position to fix prices – they are 'price takers',

they must take the prices established in the market. This means that there must be no monopolies (markets with only one seller) or oligopolies (markets dominated by a few large producers), since such firms can set their own prices.

2. There is no historical *time*: the approach is static, the problem being set up as one concerning economic organization at a particular moment in time, not as one of an economy moving through time.

3. Everyone has 'perfect knowledge'; everyone can get, immediately and costlessly, all the information – and specifically price information – which they need about the economy. There is no uncertainty about the future.

4. There are no 'externalities' in the economy. These are costs (such as pollution) or benefits (such as the acquisition of skills) which are not included in private transactions. There are also no 'public goods' (broadly speaking these are goods or services for which no market price can be easily or realistically charged: defence, street-lights, radio or television programmes).

5. Products in any particular market are 'homogeneous', meaning that they are exactly the same in terms of qualities – the only differences between them can be their prices. There is no 'product differentiation'.

6. There are no 'economies of scale'. This means that there are no production processes where efficiency can be improved by increasing the size of the operation (i.e. where doubling the inputs might lead to more than doubled output).

This is not a full list of the necessary assumptions; there are also usually some quite stringent assumptions made about the nature of production processes. Subsequent research has shown that some of them can be removed or qualified without affecting the existence of general equilibrium. But there is one which remains essential if it is to be claimed that the market system maximizes social and individual welfare, and that is the first. There must be perfect competition. In particular this means that prices must be *flexible*: if there is any change in consumers' demand, or conditions of supply, then prices must shift in response.

'Assumptions' like these clearly take us a long way from the real world economy, which in the case of Britain is characterized by imperfect competition (monopolies like telecommunications, oligopolies like cars, oil, chemicals, bread); considerable uncertainty about the future; many externalities; some public goods; strongly differentiated products; industries with marked economies of scale; and some *very* inflexible prices. But these are only the most obvious difficulties in applying the 'general equilibrium' approach to the real economy. Some more subtle, but ultimately more devastating, difficulties emerge when the question is asked, how is equilibrium attained, and how quickly is it reached? This question is clearly of considerable interest if general equilibrium theory is to be used to argue the merits of free markets in general and Mrs Thatcher in particular. Yet it is precisely in this area – how equilibrium is reached – that intractable problems arise.

It is worth considering this matter in some detail; but why is it so important? Suppose, for instance, that the economy is in disequilibrium. This means that markets are not clearing – quantities supplied are not equal to quantities demanded. Consequently there may be unsold stocks combined with shortages, less than capacity output, unemployment and so on. It is obviously vital to know whether there are forces which will cause equilibrium to be attained. The speed of adjustment to equilibrium is also important: if it takes twenty years for full equilibrium to be attained after an oil price rise, then it might not be advisable to rely on free market forces. Walras solved neither of these problems in a realistically acceptable way.

On the first problem – how is equilibrium attained? – he employed a method which might politely be described as 'mythical'. The difficulty is this: establishing general equilibrium means establishing a set of prices which will enable all markets to clear. This implies that prices must actually be set or changed. But it has already been assumed (in the first assumption noted on p. 128) that all economic agents are price *takers*, not price makers: nobody sets prices, they have to take what the market offers. By what agency then, are prices established or changed? In order to get round this impasse, Walras assumed the existence of a mythical 'auctioneer', overseeing the economy in a rather god-like way. The auctioneer would take 'advance bids', as it were, for all the goods in the economy. Where demand exceeded supply he would raise prices, and vice versa; then a new set of bids would be taken. The auctioneer would keep on adjusting potential prices until the bids revealed a set of prices which would equate supply and demand in all markets. These prices would then be declared the ruling prices, and all trades would take place. The process is one of successively getting nearer to the equilibrium prices; Walras called it '*tâtonnement*' (normally translated rather inelegantly as 'groping'). This approach also solves – if that is the word – the problem of how fast equilibrium is attained. Since the whole thing is set up in advance by the auctioneer, equilibrium occurs *instantaneously*. (Time therefore does not enter Walras's theoretical world; how it might be brought into this kind of analysis is a complex matter, susceptible to a range of interpretations.) Finally, general equilibrium occurs simultaneously in response to the final bids; so there can be no shortage of demand in the economy – demand is simply not a problem.

One might sum up the story so far by saying that Walras achieved a great deal, but at a great cost: that of realism, of applicability to the concrete world. But his work should not idly be rejected on that account, however. No one can solve all theoretical problems at once, and very drastic simplifications may be in order to help work out intractable problems. There is nothing new, in scientific work, in this kind of thing, at least as a starting point. On the other hand it must be said that general equilibrium theorists have not made notable progress on some of the problems noted above in the seventy or so years since the death of Walras. No really convincing theory has emerged on how general equilibrium is attained in a fully competitive economy. The theory remains mired in its central contradiction: if the market economy is to be the best of all possible worlds, then we must all be price *takers*; but attaining equilibrium requires price *makers*. You can't have it both ways. This problem is not a trivial one: it means that if some measure of realism is introduced into the analysis, then the conclusion that the free-market economy maximizes efficiency and welfare cannot be sustained.

MONETARISM
AND GENERAL EQUILIBRIUM THEORY

In the light of the story presented above, monetarism can be seen in terms of two distinct ideas. The first and most important has nothing to do with money. It is simply that monetarists treat the general equilibrium model as the appropriate starting point for discussion and analysis of economies like Britain. Certainly the model is a simplification – but it is an accurate and realistic one. Consequently they regard conclusions drawn from the theory as applicable and relevant to real-world economies in general, and Britain in particular (despite the fact that few would claim that the theory gives a full and complete description of the economy). Monetarists tend to be prepared to use ideas drawn from general equilibrium theory to answer questions about the actual operation of real economies. To take an example: monetarists believe that there is a 'natural rate' of unemployment, a rate which cannot permanently be reduced by expansionary government policies. What determines this rate? Milton Friedman's answer is as follows: the natural rate

is the level (of unemployment) which would be ground out by *the Walrasian system of general equilibrium equations*, provided that there is embedded in them the actual structural characteristics of the labour and commodity markets.[2] [My italics.]

Using the general equilibrium system in this way seems to lead more or less directly to a belief in the self-regulating properties of the market economy. The model demonstrates desirable properties if markets are free. Therefore if the economy is left to its own devices it will not only reach full output and full employment, it will also – because of competition – produce goods and use labour in the most efficient way.

Monetarism involves one further central idea, which concerns the money supply. More precisely, it concerns the role of money in general equilibrium type models. The idea is that money is simply a means of accounting, something which expresses the prices of goods relative to each other, and which facilitates transactions. This leads to a 'quantity theory of money' (actually a theory of the price level), in which the general level of prices is determined by the size of the money stock. As an influential economic idea this has a long history, stretching back into the eighteenth century if not beyond. In essence it is very simple: if commodity A costs £10 and commodity B costs £5, then doubling the money supply will cause A to cost £20 and B to cost £10. This is inflation, a change in the general level of prices. It changes only 'nominal' prices, not the real relationships between the commodities (A still costs twice as much as B). Modern monetarism puts this idea to use in opposition to an idea associated with Keynes: when there is unemployment, the government can increase the money supply in such a way as to increase overall demand in the economy. This will lead to an increase in output (as producers satisfy the increased demand) and in employment. The monetarist argument is that this is an illusion: we know from the quantity theory that increasing the money supply can ultimately only lead to an increase in prices. An increase in the money supply can therefore have no 'real' effects: it changes the general level of prices, though not their relation to one another. It cannot alter the amount of goods being produced, or the number of people employed (in which case, of course, it is difficult to see why inflation is such a significant economic problem).

CONCLUSION

What the above discussion has tried to indicate is that monetarism consists of a set of technical propositions – mainly concerning the price level and the money supply – grafted on to a more general theory of the market economy. It is perfectly possible to reject the former while accepting the latter. And many economists, politicians, journalists and so on do precisely that, though they rarely have any serious understanding of the scientific limitations of free-market economics. Arguably the single most influential economic idea in British society is the notion that free markets work: that they generate efficiency, 'consumer sovereignty', and freedom of choice. Yet the rigorous scientific theory of market systems – Walrasian general equilibrium theory and its derivatives – shows if anything that such notions are true only under very restrictive conditions. In fact those conditions are not met and cannot be met in any real economy. Although this does not mean either that market systems do not work, or that they are inferior to available alternatives, it does imply that we should hesitate before accepting the arguments of free-market apologists, especially concerning economic policy. The next chapter will discuss some aspects of general equilibrium approaches to economic policy, both to outline the basis of free-market policies, and to show how general equilibrium theory can generate alternative policies; the suggestion will be that, even in terms of the Walrasian free-market theory, there is no case for free-market economic policy.

Market Economics and Economic Policy

This chapter will discuss some of the implications for economic policy of free-market economics, concentrating in particular on the general equilibrium theory outlined in the previous chapter. On the face of things, that theory has clear limitations as a basis for policy making. For one thing, it is a highly abstract theory, meant to be an aid to the study of *all* market economies; it therefore has nothing to say about the differences, the peculiarities, of particular national economies. Many of these 'peculiarities', however, are precisely what make up the British predicament, and they cannot be removed to make the economy more like the model. Yet 'free-market' theory has been influential in policy discussion in Britain, in two ways. The first is quite direct, in the formation of policy and in the advice given to ministers: the Thatcher administration has employed economic advisers and policy-makers deeply committed to free-market economics, and their policy statements have shown that they are strongly influenced by theoretical considerations.

The second is less direct, but nevertheless of great importance; it will doubtless survive Mrs Thatcher. This is the way in which free-market economics influences public discussion of economic problems, in the press and on television and radio, for example. One of the startling aspects of British financial journalism is its readiness to apply conclusions drawn from monetarist and general free-market theory to the British economy with no mention of the underlying theoretical difficulties. Can it be that serious financial journalists are unaware of these difficulties? Certainly they are influential: the editorials of Mr Rees Mogg and the writings of Peter Jay in *The Times* in the mid 1970s had great effect in spreading the monetarist gospel; and the writings of Samuel Brittan in the *Financial Times* always exert great influence – his collected articles could perhaps stand as a systematic statement of the free-market position. This is not the place for a discussion of the role of financial journalism in forming the climate of opinion in Britain. But it could be suggested that it is a significant role; and not the least significant thing about it is the utterly uncritical character of its acceptance of free-market positions (even where it has swung away, under the impact of events, from support for hard-line monetarism). For that reason it is important to set out the theoretical basis of support for free-market policy positions, since the solution to Britain's problems must involve a challenge to them.

THE 'NEW CLASSICAL MACROECONOMICS'

Within the economics profession, monetarism is normally associated with a wider body of ideas – also based on general equilibrium concepts – usually known as the 'new classical macroeconomics'. It is distinguished by a thorough-going opposition to government policy interventions in the economy, claiming to prove the case for *laissez-faire*, for leaving the economy to its own devices. Hence the reference to 'classical' economics – in the tradition of such writers as Adam Smith and David Ricardo – which is supposed to be essentially *laissez-faire* economics, and also the foundation of *laissez-faire* economic policy in the nineteenth century. What is the basis of this new argument against policy intervention?

At one level, matters are very simple. Suppose that one takes the free-market, general equilibrium model of the economy seriously, either as a description of the real economy or as an appropriate starting point. That model, as many have assumed and as Walras proved (albeit rather oddly), works beautifully in economic terms without a government. It seems to follow directly that government intervention should be avoided or minimized or restricted to enforcing contracts. That kind of argument is hardly convincing when one remembers the very restrictive assumptions necessary to make the theory work, but none the less it is an important component of monetarist and free-market thinking. They *do* believe in the self-regulating properties of market economies. The advantages of a privatized, competitive economy have been frequently cited by Conservative spokesmen as the rationale behind the Thatcher government's attempts to sell off publicly-owned enterprises, to cut government expenditure and so on.

But the 'new classical macroeconomics' goes further than this rather general position; the theory claims also that government policy interventions in the economy are either completely ineffective, or positively harmful. This section examines the two most influential arguments advanced in support of such claims: the 'crowding out' theory, and the 'rational expectations hypothesis'. The first of these has probably been the more important in terms of practical policy making, while the second has obsessed academic economists.

There are, in this kind of analysis, essentially two kinds of government activity in the economy. They are *fiscal policy* and *monetary policy*. Fiscal policy concerns the economics of the government budget, that is, its tax and expenditure decisions. When the government decides to spend a certain amount, say on defence or on hospitals, it is affecting two things initially: the level of its control over the economic resources of society, and the level of total spending in the economy. When it makes tax decisions it is affecting the amount of income left to the population after tax, and thereby it affects the level of people's consumption expenditure; once again, this affects the level of total spending in the economy. The problem is this: suppose the government runs a deficit in its budget; suppose it spends more than it earns. This obviously increases total expenditure. But does it increase total income and output (and, in consequence, total employment)? The other main policy instrument, monetary policy, concerns the size of the money stock and the level of interest rates (if the government increases the money supply then interest rates tend to go down, and vice versa). Suppose the government increases the money supply. The question is, does the resulting increase in demand generate increases in real output and employment, or not?

The arguments mainly concern fiscal policy, though they also have a monetary aspect, since the way in which government expenditure is financed can have effects on the money supply. The 'crowding out' thesis has a number of variations, of which two are particularly important. The first concerns the implications of increasing government control of real economic resources. The second concerns the effects of the ways in which government expenditure is financed.

'CROWDING OUT'

The first of the 'crowding out' arguments runs as follows. Suppose that the government increases its expenditure on health or defence, financing the increased expenditure with increased taxes. This will reduce the share of national income available to the private sector, which is made up of employers and employees. One or both of these groups will therefore have to accept a reduction in their real income. If workers bear the brunt of the reduction then there are no adverse effects for the economy as a whole (in terms of output, employment, exports and so on). But if they do not accept the wage reductions implied by increased taxation, if they insist on higher money wages to compensate for the increased tax burden, then one of two things will happen. *Either*, exports will be reduced, as a result of increased costs. This will lead to a balance of payments crisis of one form or another, and the government will have to contract economic activity in order to reduce imports. The end results are likely to be unemployment, a decline in national income, and inflation. *Or*, on the other hand, increased wages could mean reduced profits (it is argued by 'classicals' and Marxists that this occurred on a significant scale in Britain in the post-war period to 1974). If the profits of firms decrease, then they will be reluctant to invest in new plant and equipment. Lowered rates of investment mean lower output and national income, and fewer jobs. Once again, unemployment and recession are in store. So, either way, increased levels of government intervention are positively harmful.

The second part of the 'crowding out' thesis concentrates on finance. Suppose that the government increases its expenditure but does not increase taxation. It must then finance its expenditure, which it can do in two ways. Firstly, it could increase the money supply, in effect printing money. If one accepts the 'quantity theory of money' this must be purely inflationary with no permanent real effects. Secondly, it can sell bonds to the public: at the moment it sells many billions of pounds worth of various kinds of bonds per year. If this happens, then people – mostly through insurance companies, pension funds, etc. – will spend money on bonds that might otherwise have been spent in the private economy. In other words, if the government spends £10 billion more than it 'earns', financed by bond sales, then £10 billion of private expenditure is 'crowded out' of existence. The overall effect on demand must be zero. However, there is a further aspect of this to be considered: the government must pay interest on the bonds that it sells. If it wishes to sell more bonds in order to spend more, then it must raise the rate of interest. This of course raises the cost of borrowing for firms (and everyone else) and lowers the amount of investment they are prepared to undertake. Once again, the effect is to depress the level of activity in the economy. The conclusion, in consequence, is that government activity is either useless or positively harmful.

The crowding out thesis raises some important problems which have been neglected by those who take the view that government economic activity is automatically beneficial, and that government expenditure can be raised almost without limit. But it is also true that important criticisms can be directed against 'crowding out' ideas. The 'real crowding out' variant assumes, for example, that private economic activity is the only 'productive' activity in the economy, on no very clear grounds; moreover it is not obvious that the poor investment and growth record of the UK economy is due to crowding out and low profits. It could be that profitability and investment are affected more by a whole history of poor investment and technology decisions, than by relatively recent government actions. The issues here remain unresolved; all that can be said is that they are important. As for 'financial crowding out', it can perhaps simply be said that there is little evidence that investment is significantly affected by interest rate changes in the UK (although the American picture appears to be different).

THE 'RATIONAL EXPECTATIONS HYPOTHESIS'

Although 'crowding out' theories are of considerable interest, they have taken second place – as a theoretical approach – in recent years to attacks on government intervention deriving from the so-called 'rational expectations hypothesis' (which will hereafter be called 'REH').

Non-monetarists often seem slightly embarassed in talking about the rational expectations approach. As Frank Blackaby, of the National Institute of Economic and Social Research, recently put it:

> When I try to explain this hypothesis to non-economists they tend to stare at me with wild surmise, and accuse me of joking when I say that serious economists have serious conferences devoted to the examination of this proposition.[1]

The reason for his diffidence is that the REH is built on what at first sight appears to be an absurd idea: this is that all individuals, all economic agents, in the economy act as if they are in possession of a full-scale theoretical model of the economy, which they use in taking decisions and plotting their economic activities. The model is a correct one, and can be used to assess the likely results of government policy actions; agents therefore act in the light of such assessments (which are necessarily correct). The model which they possess just happens to be the monetarist version of the general equilibrium approach.

Stated as baldly as this, it must inevitably seem ridiculous. But this is to neglect the way the argument runs; some important points are made along the way. REH starts with the idea that people's expectations of the future are a central aspect of the choices which they make today. Suppose a firm is considering borrowing money to finance a new plant, and the rate of interest is 18 per cent. Then the expectation of the firm's planners about the rate of inflation, or future interest rates, will be of great importance in its decision. If they expect a general rate of inflation of say 12 per cent over the next year, then they will expect their money earnings to be higher than they are today. They will therefore be more willing to borrow than if they expect a rate of inflation of zero. The REH suggests that economic decision-makers – individuals or firms – will do two things in forming their expectations:

1. They will use all available information which is relevant to their decision, and they will process and evaluate the information in an intelligent and rational manner.

2. They will reflect on their past performance in expectation-

forming, and in particular on their errors. They will not keep on making the same old mistakes. This means that they will not make systematic errors in their expectations of the future. (REH is not particularly clear about how expectations are formed and the correct model developed. But it seems to be that it is the revision of past mistakes, the elimination of errors, which leads to a sort of evolutionary adaptation towards the correct monetarist view of the world.)

So, expectations of future developments are central to current economic decisions. Since people consider all pertinent developments in making those decisions, it follows that they will take the effects of government policy into account. This means that the actual effects of any government policy adopted today will be determined in large part by the expectations which people form concerning those effects. This is a simple point, and it is true that it has been neglected in many forecasting models of the economy. How does REH put this idea to use?

REH asserts that, if the government adopts an expansionary fiscal or monetary policy (that is, if it tries to expand economic activity by spending more or increasing the money supply) then people will expect inflation. They will be correct in this, having learnt the truth of the monetarist position through bitter experience. These 'inflationary expectations' will ensure that inflation does occur, because prices will be adjusted to accord with expected inflation. More importantly, people will not think that the inflationary price rises represent real increases in demand in the economy, and hence an opportunity for growth. This is a very important step in the argument: people will not be deceived; they will not mistake inflation for a higher level of demand.

But how can this lead to the proposition that the government cannot increase the level of output and employment? Here it is necessary to return to the so-called 'natural rate of unemployment'. In discussing the general equilibrium model of the economy, it was suggested that there was an equilibrium price–quantity relationship in the labour market, this being defined by 'classicals' as 'full employment'. The corresponding unemployment defines the 'natural rate of unemployment'. Once the equilibrium price and quantity are reached, then unemployment can be reduced only in two ways. Either, workers can accept a lower wage (encouraging employers to use more labour), or employers can offer a higher wage (encouraging workers to supply more labour). Consider the second of these cases. Under what circumstances will employers offer a higher wage? One way would be if they thought they were facing increased demand, and consequently higher prices, for their products. What happens if the government tries to generate such an increase in demand?

The 'classical' argument is that unemployment could be reduced below its 'natural rate' by inflationary government action, in the following way. People could mistake the general price rise for a real increase in demand. Firms will think they are facing an increase in demand for their particular product; workers will think that any increase in wage rates is an increase in the real wage. But both are mistaken. If the inflation consists of all prices rising simultaneously, then all prices remain the same in relation to each other. However, while the mistake persists, employers will demand more labour in order to meet what they think is an increased demand for output, and workers will supply more labour in response to what they think is an increase in the wage rate. Once people realize their mistake, once they see that it is inflation which is occurring – and not a real increase in demand and wages – then output and employment will fall back to their original level (but at a higher level of 'nominal' prices). One of the explanations of why all this occurs is that, in the words of a leading monetarist, 'suppliers receive information about the prices of their own goods faster than they receive information about the aggregate price level'. But the upshot is that unemployment can only be reduced – by the government or anybody else – when people make mistakes about the rate of inflation: when, in the jargon, they make expectational errors about the future course of inflation.

But . . . the rational expectations hypothesis tells us that people do not make expectational errors *systematically*. They correct their mistakes, and learn to make correct appreciations of the inflational effects of government policy actions. The conclusion is obvious and important. If the government can only affect the level of output and employment through errors about the inflation rate (which is what the 'natural rate' theory says); and if people do not make systematic errors about inflation (which is what REH tells us); then it follows that the government cannot systematically affect the level of output and the level of employment. Government policy, in particular employment policy, is thus proved ineffective. This is the central theoretical argument of the 'new classical macroeconomics' against government policy intervention, and hence for a policy of *laissez-faire*. (Of course, the same argument cuts both ways: if employment cannot be above the full employment level, it cannot be below it either. This makes the existence of long-term recession rather difficult to explain.)

As a basis for discussing economic policy, theories such as these seem almost entirely inadequate, for reasons which will be discussed in the next section. However, the objections should be neither to the idea that economic agents behave rationally, nor to the idea that the expectations which they hold are of great importance. On the contrary, it is correct and important to emphasize that expectations of what the future might hold can be of great economic significance currently. It is ironic, however, that the economist who first really stressed this was none other than J. M. Keynes. The theme of expectations and uncertainty about the future runs right through his major work, though it has been neglected by many of his followers. Of course, the thrust of the 'new classical' approach is to introduce the concept of expectations and to remove uncertainty, but they are nevertheless right to emphasize that expectations about the future include expectations about the effects of current policy. This is particularly important when one turns from the theoretical world of general equilibrium to the real economic environment in which we live. This environment is characterized by concentrated economic power: large firms control the vast majority of output, large banks control the financial system, large unions dominate the labour market. A relatively small number of decision makers effectively control a very large number of important economic decisions, in the course of which they can and do weigh up the likely effects of government policy, and adapt their actions accordingly. The Ford car company, for example, is said to employ economists whose sole task is to predict exchange-rate changes (they are supposed to be very good at it). The decisions taken by such firms, on the basis of their expectations, have effects. In a sense, however, economic policy has always concerned itself with such matters, for a perennial theme in policy making is the need to sustain 'confidence'. When people use this word they are invariably referring to the need to induce a certain set of expectations (usually profits) in large corporate managements. To speak of expectations in this sense is meaningful and important; to use the existence of expectations to prove the necessary ineffectiveness of policy is quite another matter.

THE 'NEW CLASSICAL MACROECONOMICS' AND ECONOMIC POLICY: SOME PROBLEMS

The 'new classical macroeconomics' has been increasingly influential in recent years, both within the economics profession (though there remain many sceptics) and among those who make or comment on policy. This writer is firmly among the sceptics, though certainly the 'new classical' system has performed one signal service. It has set out, in a thorough way, the theoretical basis of 'free-market' policy making. This section will be doing something that the apologists of the free market rarely do, namely taking a look at the underside of the theory, at its weaknesses. In the light of these weaknesses it seems difficult to see rational justification for any form of *laissez-faire* economic policy.

The first major problem for the 'new classical' system lies in the restricted nature of the theoretical model on which it is based. That model only works on the basis of some extreme simplifications, such as that all prices are not only flexible but adjust more or less instantaneously to shifts in supply and demand. However in outlining these stringent 'assumptions' (in Chapter 6, pp. 128–9) the dimensions of this problem have, if anything, been understated. For example, the full general equilibrium model requires a very large number of 'futures' markets (markets in which trades are undertaken today for completion in the future) if it is really to work. But the assumptions (perfect competition, perfect knowledge, price flexibility, etc.) are sufficient to clarify a major difficulty for the 'free-market' model. The difficulty is this: if any of these assumptions do not hold *in general*, then a general equilibrium may exist, but it will not be one in which full employment is achieved, or in which efficiency is possible, or in which the social outcomes can be claimed to be the 'best possible'. In fact, there is an interesting result in 'welfare economics' known as the 'second-best theorem'. It shows that if any *one* of these conditions is violated (i.e. if there is 'imperfect competition' in only one market) then in order to achieve the 'next best' result to the 'best of all possible worlds' optimum, intervention is required throughout the economy, quite possibly in *all* markets. In other words, it is no use having a bit of competition, a bit of the free-market economy, or a bit of *laissez-faire*. It is a case of everything or nothing: if the initial assumptions do not hold *in their entirety*, then *none* of the beneficial outcomes which are beloved of Conservative economists and their journalistic hangers-on necessarily follow.

Now clearly no serious person could claim that these assumptions or conditions hold in the UK economy, or any other for that matter. The monetarist response to this tends to be to acknowledge that the economy does not work like the 'model', but then to suggest that this is only because we tolerate 'imperfections' (such as monopolies or trade unions). Therefore we should rid ourselves of rigidities and imperfections in markets – which are the only true cause of unemployment, recession and so on – and the economy would work as the model suggests. However, this ignores the fact that many of the assumptions not only do not hold, but *could not possibly hold*. Some of the assumptions are straightforwardly impossible: no conceivable economic organization could deliver perfect knowledge, absence of uncertainty or instantaneous price adjustment. Others are unrealistic in a different sense. Such things as imperfect competition (i.e. oligopolistic or monopolistic industries), or economies of scale, or 'externalities', are not 'imperfections'; they are precisely the product of the natural development of the economy. They are not just the basis of the way our economy functions, they are the outcome of it, and it is pointless to fulminate against them. Other 'imperfections', such as taxes, or the way in which public goods – like television or defence – are provided, are simply part and parcel of the institutional structure of our society; this is a matter which is systematically avoided by general equilibrium theory, which explicitly ignores the institutional organization of economies. (This may be theoretically justifiable in my opinion, so long as the results are not used in pronouncements about policy.)

However, it is not simply in its assumptions or axioms that the free-market model is impoverished in policy terms. It is also restricted in the very nature of the theoretical system which emerges. The crucial economic policy debates in recent years have concerned firstly, monetary policy, and secondly, government economic activity. How far does the general equilibrium approach and its 'new classical' variant, illuminate matters here? Recall that, in the Walrasian system, equilibrium is achieved simultaneously and instantaneously via the 'auctioneer'; he sets up all the trades in the economy, which occur all at once. Money is not necessary to these trades. Certainly it is easy enough to introduce money into the analysis: you simply call one commodity – any commodity – 'money', and reckon the prices of all goods in terms of it. But the Walrasian economy is essentially a 'barter' economy – it would work adequately without money and a financial system. Much the same can be said of government. The Walrasian model of the market economy generates full employment, maximum efficiency, optimum welfare and presumably peace on earth. There is virtually nothing for a government to do, apart from ensuring that contracts are enforceable, and providing some public goods. The supporters of free-market economics are therefore in the peculiar position of advocating detailed monetary and government policies on the basis of a theory which requires neither money nor government.

Perhaps related to these weaknesses is a further difficulty. This is that the problems which we face in the real world are simply not problems in the model. Consider inflation: in real life it poses problems. It affects the distribution of income, for example, because it hits so unevenly. In recent years the prices of basic commodities have increased faster than those of luxury goods, and this has made the poor poorer in real terms (since even where their incomes have kept pace with the general rate of inflation, they have risen slower than the prices of the basic goods on which most of their incomes are spent). Yet in the monetarist, 'new classical' model, inflation has *no* real effects – all prices change in proportion, including wages, and everyone is affected identically. No one either benefits or loses, there is no effect on output or employment. So why on earth is it a problem? In particular why is it necessary to advocate recession-inducing economic policies in order to reduce it? (Actually there is a 'cost' of inflation in the monetarist approach, which it is almost embarrassing to record. It is a 'shoe leather' cost: as inflation proceeds we wish to hold less cash, because the value of money is diminishing. So we keep it in the bank since the interest earned will maintain the value of our cash even though prices are increasing. But because we are economizing on cash we must make more frequent journeys to the bank for cash, thus wearing out shoe leather. This, for monetarism, is a significant cost of inflation. It is for this that, at the time of writing, three million British unemployed are doing their bit in the struggle against inflation.)

Similar things can be said of unemployment as an economic problem. Unemployment can only exist because of a too-high wage rate in the new classical system, and this cannot be more than temporary. Consider the current unemployment in the UK. This can only be the result of 'expectational errors' – past or present – on the part of workers. The government is adopting a policy of monetary restriction; this leads to falling wages. Workers think, mistakenly, that their real wages are falling because money wages are in effect falling. Because of this expectation of falling real wages workers wish to work less. Soon, however, they will see that all prices are falling, and that real wages are not falling, and they will offer to work more. Any unemployed who are not in this position can, however, still get a job by accepting a lower real wage. Thus all unemployment is either temporary or voluntary in the monetarist model. These interpretations have been seriously offered in explanation of the current recession in Britain.

These kinds of weaknesses clearly raise doubts about the applicability of the model to questions of practical policy in the real world of the economy. The matter of 'applicability' is a problem in itself, to do with the grounds on which monetarists think that their results can be used in practice. What is involved is a complex issue of scientific method, which certainly cannot be treated adequately here. But a certain amount can be said. The difficulty is this: too many monetarists think, like many people, that a theory consists simply of a statement about the world, which can be easily shown to be true or false. Actually any really adequate theory is much more than this, it is much more complex. A fully developed theory must do many things. It must elaborate a range of general concepts which set out its problem area, or 'domain', and it must develop further concepts in order to solve the puzzles and perplexities of the theory. It must specify what is to count as evidence, and it must have methods of assessing the relevance and meaning of evidence. It must have criteria for deciding what will count as an explanation or a proof. And finally it must set out the conditions under which its results can be used.

General equilibrium theory, despite its many achievements, fails in a number of these areas, but most importantly in the last. Far too many 'equilibrium' economists simply assume that the theory does actually describe the real economy (or the real economy as it would be without distortions). They also assume, again without serious argument, that results obtained with the drastically simplified model are actually applicable to the messy and complex world of policy making. To accept such ideas at the present stage of development of the theory requires, however, not a scientific approach but its opposite: an act of faith.

Yet these easy and unjustified assumptions are an integral part of the arguments for *laissez-faire*, and for less extreme forms of free-market policy making. The 'rational expectations' approach seems to go even further, by assuming not only that the monetarist version of general equilibrium is true, but also that it is obvious. To be precise, it assumes that we can draw inferences about the real workings of the economy which, if we are intelligent and rational, would lead us to monetarist conclusions. Quite apart from the way this consigns opponents of monetarism to an outer darkness of irrationality and stupidity, this is a fanciful notion. Can one, for example, draw inferences from money supply figures which will correctly predict, in detail, the future course of inflation? The answer is simple: no. One wonders what remains of the basis of claims of policy ineffectiveness.

The final word on the policy pretensions of general equilibrium theory can best be left to Professor Frank Hahn of Cambridge, one of the very best of the modern general equilibrium theorists:

I have always regarded competitive General Equilibrium analysis as akin to the mock-up an aircraft engineer might build. My amazement in recent years has accordingly been very great to find that many economists are passing the mock-up off as an airworthy plane, and that politicians, bankers and commentators are scrambling to get seats. This at a time when theorists all over the world have become aware that anything based on this mock-up is unlikely to fly, since it neglects some crucial aspects of the world, the recognition of which will force some drastic redesigning. Moreover at no stage was the mock-up complete; in particular it provided no account of the actual working of the Invisible Hand . . .[2]

ALTERNATIVES
IN GENERAL EQUILIBRIUM

The central weakness of general equilibrium theory lies, it has been emphasized, not so much in the theory itself as in the rather blithe use which is made of its results. True, the theory is sketchy and restricted in many ways, despite its mathematical complexity; and it is also true that criticism could be directed against the equilibrium approach as a whole. But there are developments of general equilibrium theory which move beyond the naiveties of its monetarist and new classical variations. This section will briefly outline some of these alternative positions within general equilibrium theory; it will discuss first the *interpretation* of general equilibrium, and secondly its *development*.

General equilibrium theory is frequently interpreted as a descriptive theory of the capitalist economy. Another account has been offered, however, by Professor Hahn, in which general equilibrium is seen not as an investigation of the capitalist economy as such, but rather of its effects on economic 'welfare'. Since Adam Smith, a persistent refrain in economics has been that market systems work ultimately to the benefit of all. They produce what was described in Chapter 6 as an 'optimum', a 'best possible' solution to the economic problem of what should be produced, and how, and of who should get what. It turns out to be relatively simple to show that a Walrasian general equilibrium is such an optimum. It is a 'best possible' arrangement in the sense that nothing could be changed without making someone worse off.

Now suppose that the focus of the analysis is shifted. Instead of treating general equilibrium theory as an analysis of market economies with certain interesting 'spin-off' conclusions about economic welfare, let it be treated directly as a theory of welfare. Turn the analysis on its head, as it were: start with full employment, maximum efficiency and general economic bliss, and then ask, what characteristics do markets have to have for these desirable ends to be achieved? What would a market economy have to look like if these results were to be produced? General equilibrium tells us the answers to these questions. It tells us, for example, that the economy must consist of a large number of markets and futures markets (many more than exist in any real economy); that these markets must be fully competitive – no one can set prices in them; that prices must be flexible; that there must be perfect knowledge and an absence of uncertainty; and so on, and so on. These 'answers' are of course simply the 'initial assumptions' described in Chapter 6, looked at in another way. What conclusions can be drawn from this interpretation?

The broadest conclusion is that general equilibrium theory, far from being a foundation of free-market economic policy, is actually a disproof of the practicality of such a policy. General equilibrium theory formulates the conditions necessary for a valid *laissez-faire* policy; since those conditions are not met, then policies which have the 'market mechanism' as their basis should be labelled 'handle with care'. In particular we should be careful about the argument that government interventionist policies cannot improve on *laissez-faire*, as Professor Willem Buiter has recently pointed out: 'While economists – in their less guarded moments – frequently advance variants on this argument, it has no sound foundation as a generally valid proposition, either in economic theory or in careful empirical observation.'

This kind of interpretation, it should be said, is hardly common among general equilibrium theorists. In the main they remain committed to the idea that the objective of the theory should be to describe the principles on which the real economy works. Where this has been taken seriously it has led to attempts to make the theory in some sense more 'realistic'. Here there are two broad strategies. The first involves a straightforward modification of the 'initial assumptions' in favour of a measure of realism. If it is assumed, for example, that prices and wages are not flexible – that they are 'sticky' and unresponsive to changes in demand – then it is simple to show that 'disequilibrium' positions exist for the economy. These positions are characterized by unemployment and restricted output; since firms cannot sell the quantity of output they would like to sell, and workers cannot sell the quantity of labour they would like, these positions are known as 'quantity-constrained' or 'quantity-rationed' equilibria.

One obvious Conservative objection to this is to say that the 'quantity constraints' are due only to the inflexibility of prices, to rigidities which the government should attempt to remove. The second major strategy, therefore, accepts the possibility of flexible prices, and shows how quantity constraints can still emerge. One way of doing this is to introduce real time into the analysis: if the economy adjusts to equilibrium in a series of steps, through time, then at each of the steps there will be a certain level of unemployment or unsold output and/or unsatisfied demand. This is, again, relatively straightforward once we move away from the instantaneous adjustments of the Walrasian model. Another approach is to acknowledge that agents actually have to set prices and that they do so in conditions of uncertainty, and in particular without knowing how a price change might affect any quantity constraint that they face. As with the introduction of time into the analysis, this is reasonable and plausible, and leads to 'quantity constraints' even with flexible prices. Unused resources and unemployment can be a more or less permanent feature of such an economy. These types of equilibria turn out to have strange features: for example, it may be possible to increase output and employment by increasing the money supply . . .

These kinds of results are now fairly well known, and acknowledged, in general equilibrium theory. They push that theory directly into Keynesian territory, for it was Keynes who initiated the analysis of states of equilibrium with unemployment (a result which, prior to his work, was considered impossible). In doing so they undercut the monetarist claim that its economic basis, general equilibrium theory, licenses an economic policy of non-intervention and *laissez-faire*.

CONCLUSION

In assessing economic policy pronouncements it is important to understand the basis on which they are made. Economic policies which emphasize the operation of free markets are invariably based – either explicitly or implicitly – on general equilibrium theory, for it is the most complete available model of the free-market economy. The status of that theory is therefore of considerable importance.

But the theory has many problems. In recent years there has been considerable debate within the economics profession over results – especially concerning economic policy – which have been 'proved' on the basis of general equilibrium theory. However, even though many dispute these results, it remains true that the overwhelming majority of economists still accept and teach a broad view of the market system which is consistent with general equilibrium theory or derived from it. The consensus is that markets work, more or less well, and that some form of 'market economics' is the appropriate framework for both theory and policy; it is an article of faith that free markets produce desirable outcomes.

But the theory simply does not support such conclusions, especially in the field of policy. This is why I believe that Professor Hahn was quite right when he suggested, a few years ago, that 'the vulgarizations of General Equilibrium which are the substance of most text-books of economics are both scientifically and politically harmful'.[3] The problem is that the vulgarizations have, with a vengeance, stepped out of the pages of the textbooks, and out of the lecture theatres where they can do only intellectual damage, into the world of policy making.

Policy making in Britain has been marked by a disastrous over-confidence in the capabilities of the market economy, and a careless belief in the essential correctness of market economics. Objecting to all this does not mean that markets are useless or inefficient, nor need it mean that governments either can be or should be all powerful in the economic domain. On the contrary, the arguments advanced here against 'free-market' economic policies involve no presumption that 'planning' of some sort could work any better. It does mean, however, that greater care should be taken in assessing the role of private enterprise and market forces in economic recovery. Furthermore it means that the economic role of the government should be put on the agenda once again: if general equilibrium analyses of the economy show anything, it is that it is very unrealistic to place any great faith in market forces alone. The crucial questions for Britain concern the forms, objectives, limits and control of intervention. It is not simply general equilibrium theory, but economics as a whole, which is unfitted to answer such questions.

8

Keynes and Intervention

In view of the fact that monetarist and 'new classical' ideas are often presented – especially in the policy field – as a counter-revolution against a prevailing Keynesian orthodoxy, it may seem strange to discuss them in apparently reverse order, with Keynes coming after the monetarism which is ostensibly a reaction to his thought. Yet there is a good reason for this sequence. Keynes, like modern monetarists, saw his work as a theoretical revolt against an established economic orthodoxy, which he called 'classical economics', a heading which lumped together such writers as Marshall, Jevons and Walras. Now modern monetarism is in large part a reassertion, or more accurately a reformulation, of the central ideas of this older orthodoxy against which Keynes set his face. Hence the term 'new classical macroeconomics'. Because monetarism is very much a revival of an older doctrine, it continues to make sense to discuss Keynes and Keynesianism as a rejection of the 'free-market' economics which monetarism has resuscitated.

There is a problem in outlining and discussing Keynesian economics, however. Just as monetarism is not a unified doctrine, but rather a range of often discrepant ideas sharing a broad vision of the efficacy of markets, so Keynesian economics is not one theory but many. Within the varieties of Keynesianism, however, there is very little in the way of a core of shared concepts. The result is a diverse set of ideas and theories which are not easily summarized; some parts of Keynesian economics converge towards the neoclassical system, with its emphasis on the market mechanism, while others veer off towards Marxian economics, with its picture of a dynamic yet unstable economy in which markets fail to harmonize different needs and interests, and instead reflect a world of power, politics and struggle.

Between these extremes lies an enormous variety of intermediate positions which defy description, let alone systematic analysis, in one chapter or even one book. However, the differences between them boil down to quite fundamental – and in some ways quite simple – disagreements about the properties of market systems. As we saw in Chapter 6, the neoclassical view holds that markets coordinate economic activities by conveying information. This information concerns supply and demand conditions – conditions of production on one side, and consumer needs on the other – and the signal which conveyed the relevant information was the changing price of the product in the market. But do things really work like this? And if they do not, what are the consequences for the economy as a whole? Is it possible for market economies to generate not full employment but recession, not wealth but unsatisfied needs? In one way the answer to such questions seems very straightforward: one only needs to take a look around. But in analytical terms things are not so plain, since we are concerned with the theoretical implications of a particular model of the economy, rather than the often confused and confusing evidence of the real world.

Before going on to the theory, it is worth saying something about why controversies about it exist at all within Keynesian theory. After all, Keynesian economics, unlike monetarism, is based on a specific text by a specific author: John Maynard Keynes, of course, and his book *The General Theory of Employment, Interest and Money*. It seems strange, therefore, that there should be disputes among Keynesian economists as to the meaning of Keynesian economics, as to its core concepts, as to what ideas are necessary to Keynesian theory and what are not. Presumably Keynesian ideas are defined by the text of the *General Theory*, and controversies about the meaning of Keynesian economics can be resolved by an appeal to that text. Unfortunately things are not so simple. In some ways the *General Theory* is in the great tradition of pathbreaking scientific texts, meaning that it combines analytical innovations of great power, scope and complexity with passages which are confused, internally contradictory, generally tricky to decipher or just plain wrong. This mixture of advances and problems is characteristic not just of Keynes, but also of most of the major texts of scientific breakthrough.

An important implication of all this is that the labour of understanding, of working out and constructing the meaning of texts is an integral and normal part of scientific practice, in economics as in other disciplines, and it cannot really be dodged. Within Keynes's work the central problems revolve around the fact that the work is presented as an explicit rejection of what he called 'the postulates of the classical economics' yet appears to involve an equally explicit acceptance that sometimes those very postulates are valid. The issues here are frequently fudged both in textbooks of economics and popular and journalistic representations of Keynes, yet they are crucial to any real understanding of the status of modern Keynes-based economics. They hold the key both to the continuing relevance of Keynes, and to the areas where his work may be an unreliable guide to policy.

KEYNES'S CHALLENGE TO MARKET ECONOMICS

On the basis of its account of market systems and the 'market mechanism', neoclassical economics reaches three main conclusions: firstly, that capitalist economies are basically stable (they are not subject to major fluctuations in output and employment). Secondly, they tend towards a full-employment level of output. Thirdly, in consequence, there is no real case for government intervention to ensure stability and growth and to promote full employment. Within the neoclassical approach, deviations from full employment and stability are ultimately the result of market imperfections, meaning that somewhere along the line supplies and demands (of goods, or of labour) are out of alignment because prices are not moving smoothly enough to equate supply and demand. Unemployment is a consequence of wage rates being too high. The level of output is closely related to profitability, to the amount enterprises find it profitable to produce: the way to get them to produce more is to cut their costs (especially of labour) and to raise their margins of profit. This leads in practice to a concentration on what are often called 'supply side' policy measures: wage restraint and tax cuts, to raise the post-tax return from production and hence increase the incentive to produce; ideas like these have been a familiar theme of Thatcherite policy in the UK and 'Reaganomics' in the United States.

Within this approach, then, the level of output is determined by decisions by producers, in which costs of production are the crucial element. The emphasis is, therefore, on factors governing the supply of goods rather than the demand for output. Behind this lies a theoretical argument, to the effect that demand is not a constraining factor in the output of goods and services. This position is set up by open or covert reference to a hoary economic principle known as 'Say's Law', normally expressed as 'supply creates its own demand'. The underlying idea can be put in a number of ways. For example, the basic motivation behind offering a good for sale in a market is to earn the wherewithal to buy some other good: thus the supply of some good is in effect a simultaneous demand for some other good. This point applies to labour as much as to commodities, and the conclusion follows that the overall demand for goods is equal to the quantity which people wish to supply. Another way of getting to the same result is to note that the price of any commodity can be decomposed into the incomes earned in producing it. The total value of cars, for example, produced annually in Britain is equal to total costs of production plus profits. But these costs (wages, and other inputs) and profits in fact constitute an income for someone or other – for workers, or suppliers of materials, or shareholders in the firm. So the sum of these incomes is equal to the total value of output, and this is true not just for car production but for the production of each and every product or service in the economy. It seems to follow that demand is not a problem for the sale of output as a whole: the process of production creates exactly enough incomes to buy the total output. Of course there may be problems for individual products, for which demand may be inadequate, but there is no possibility of a shortage of overall demand.

It is here that Keynes's objections begin: his argument is that demand *is* a problem, and that we cannot simply invoke Say's Law to get round it. To begin with, if we are concerned with the level of employment, then this will depend on the number of workers firms wish to employ. But this is a matter not just of the wage rate (the price of labour in the labour market), but also of the amount of goods that firms can expect to sell to consumers. But the amount of goods that consumers will be able to buy will itself be dependent upon their incomes, which depend in turn on their wage rate and the number of them in employment. There is therefore, a complex interdependence between wage rates, incomes, the demand for goods, the demand for workers and the resulting levels of employment and unemployment. None of this is adequately reflected in the simple demand-and-supply approach to unemployment of neoclassical market economics. One criticism, for example, of the neoclassical approach is to point out that when it suggests wage cuts as a solution to unemployment, it is implicitly assuming (a) that this will not affect the overall demand for goods, and (b) that the demand for goods is already at a full output, full employment level. But suppose this is not the case? Then unemployment will result not just from factors in the labour market, but because the overall level of demand is not sufficient to encourage enterprises to produce the maximum output of which they are capable: there is, in short, 'demand failure'. Say's Law does not hold, and rather than supply creating its own demand, demand is a complex phenomenon, determined by many factors; moreover it can determine the level of supply and output. It is this demand problem, and the recognition of demand failure, which forms the connecting thread between the varieties of Keynesian doctrine: in one way or another, all see the problems of unemployment and recession as caused by it. The differences lie in the way in which they describe the emergence of demand failure, and the reasons which they give for the persistence of unemployment once demand failure has occurred.

Before going on to describe the Keynesian approach to recession and unemployment, a preliminary but important point should be made about the time horizon of the analysis. Economists often distinguish between two sorts of time-period, namely the short run and the long run. The difference is that in the short run the economy operates with the available, given stock of capital and equipment, so its level of output is in large part determined by the extent to which that array of equipment is actually used. In the long run it is possible to change the stock of equipment itself, both in composition and quantity. In the long-period analysis, therefore, changes in the potential output of the economy are considered. Now the Keynesian approach is quite firmly *short term* in character: it assumes that potential output is given and fixed, and concentrates on the actual output which is achieved; this is because, in one of Keynes's better known remarks, 'in the long run we are all dead'. One might want to quibble with this as a principle for policy analysis (after all, we are not all going to be dead at once, with any luck); nevertheless we do live in the here and now, and output *now* is of great importance. The point here is that Keynesian economics is abstracting from questions about the long-term development and structure of the economy; it explicitly brackets out, therefore, the issues concerning growth and change which were raised in the first section of this book. Some of the implications of this will be discussed below.

The question of demand failure has two aspects. The first concerns the impulses which generate output fluctuations, recession and un-employment. The second concerns the mechanisms which keep an economy in an unemployment state. But before describing these processes, and the debates to which they give rise, we need to outline the make-up of 'demand' in the economy as a whole.

AGGREGATE DEMAND

Keynes and Keynesians are concerned not so much with the demand for individual commodities, as with total or 'aggregate' demand in the economy. Typically, four components of aggregate demand are dis-tinguished.

1. *Consumption* demand: for goods to be consumed more or less immediately, by individuals or households. This can include durable goods such as cars or washing machines, which are rather arbitrarily classified as consumption goods if individuals buy them and invest-ment goods if firms buy them.

2. *Investment* demand: essentially for goods which will yield an income in the future – machines, equipment, buildings, inventory, etc.

3. *Export* demand: that is, demand for all types of British goods outside Britain.

4. *Government* demand. This is in turn divided into demand for *current* goods and services (typewriter ribbons, civil servants' pay) and *capital* transactions (buildings, equipment, etc.).

In addition to these components of aggregate demand there is a further market which must be mentioned since it has important interactions with these 'goods' markets, and affects aggregate demand. This is the so-called 'money market'. Within this market money is exchanged for financial assets. A simple form of such a market is an ordinary deposit account: we hand over money to a bank, and receive in return an account on which interest is paid; this asset can be reclaimed as money simply by a withdrawal. In an economy like Britain's, the money market is exceptionally complex, with a very wide range of financial assets on offer, ranging from building society accounts, to shares, to insurance policies, to government bonds. Each of these types of asset comes in a wide variety of forms. In the simple Keynesian system it is assumed that there is a market for only one asset, government bonds, which are in effect I O Us issued by the government: in return for money, investors get a regular interest payment and a promise to repay the total after some specified time.

Now let us try to see some of the ways in which these types of demand and market can interact to generate demand failure. In doing so we will concentrate on two forms of demand only: consumption and investment.

CONSUMPTION AND INVESTMENT

Suppose we consider a simple economy which produces two types of goods, namely consumption goods (for immediate or more or less immediate consumption) and investment goods (for future use). As these goods are produced they will generate incomes, in the form of wages and profits, to the workers and capitalists who produce them. These incomes will be equal to the value of output. Now with their incomes, people can basically do two things: they can spend them, or they can save them. In the case of saving they are postponing expenditure until some time in the future.

It is easy to see that if this economy is to be in equilibrium, that is if it is to be stable, and without forces operating to change the level and types of output and employment, then there must be a definite relation between what people decide to do with their incomes, and what the economy is actually producing in terms of consumption and investment goods. For the consumer goods producers to be producing exactly the right amount of output, so that they do not have unsold stocks, and so that people do not have unsatisfied demand, the consumption goods output must be equal to the amount which people decide to consume out of their incomes. In this way there is exactly enough – no more, no less – consumption goods demand to buy the consumption goods output. If consumption goods demand is greater than the output of consumption goods, we can assume that output will rise to meet the demand (providing that the economy is not already at maximum output). Conversely, if demand is inadequate to buy consumption goods output, then output will contract. So it follows that consumption goods demand and output will tend to equality.

This implies that investment must be based on that part of incomes not consumed – on savings, in fact. If total output is equal to total incomes in value, and if consumption output equals consumption expenditure, then the amount of savings must equal the amount of investment. The amount of income which people decide not to consume must somehow provide the demand for investment goods, either by being spent directly on them, or by being recycled through the financial system to be spent on investment goods. But how does this happen? What is it which makes the savings of the economy just adequate to finance the investment which is being undertaken (in new factories, machines, and so on)? Clearly savings and investment will not be equal all by themselves – except by some very unlikely accident – since decisions to save and to invest are made by two quite different sets of people. It is individuals who save, but firms who invest. Only by some bizarre chance will they decide to save and invest exactly the same amount. So what kinds of mechanism operate to keep savings equal to investment, and thus keep the economy in balance?

In the system of neoclassical economics, it is argued that this problem is solved – as are most problems within it – by the operation of the price system and the market mechanism. Savings and investment are seen as the supply of, and demand for, investible resources. The price of these resources is the *interest rate*, the basic function of which is to equate savings and investment. If people decide to consume less and save more, then the supply of investible resources has increased, and we might expect the price – the interest rate – to fall. Like all price changes, this is a signal. On the one hand it signals that investment resources are cheaper, and can therefore be expected to earn a greater return. More abstractly, perhaps, it signals that people are postponing consumption now for consumption some time in the future, and so enterprises should invest to be able to produce in the future. So enterprises invest more, and a new equilibrium emerges, with lower consumption but higher savings and investment and a new interest rate. Overall demand remains exactly what it was – the fall in consumption is offset by increased investment. People's savings decisions, therefore, do not affect aggregate demand. This is what Alfred Marshall – in many respects the founder of the English neo-classical tradition – presumably had in mind in a remark quoted by Keynes: '. . . a man purchases labour and commodities with that portion of his income which he saves just as much as he does with that he is said to spend'. In this approach, therefore, output and income stay at full employment levels, and the interest rate is the mechanism which makes savings equal to investment, thus keeping output and incomes in balance, and the economy stable.

Keynes's work is an attempt to disrupt this story of full-employment stability, to rethink it in ways which make it possible to understand the occurrence and persistence of recession. Two central strands of his argument concern the nature of the interest rate – what it is and what it does – and the consequences of any fluctuation in consumption spending. Let us begin with the interest rate, and then trace the way in which changes in consumption demand can generate a recession and unemployment in which no forces are in play to get the economy out of its unemployment predicament.

In the first place, Keynes contests the idea that the interest rate is the price of investible resources in the broad sense; it is not determined by the supply and demand for investment. Rather it is a monetary phenomenon. It is the price of *money*, and is determined in the money markets. As such it is governed by the supply of money (determined by the government and the nature of the banking system) and the conditions governing the demand for money (such as people's need to finance transactions, and the advantages of holding money rather than interest-bearing financial assets). Out of these interacting supply and demand conditions an interest rate will emerge. 'Savings' do not enter the equation here: Keynes's crucial point is that changes in the volume of savings do not in themselves change these monetary conditions which determine the interest rate. So increases or decreases in savings do not produce interest rate shifts which adjust the level of investment so that it is equal to the new level of savings. But this equality must be brought about if the economy is to be in equilibrium. This brings us to Keynes's fundamental idea, which is that the equality of savings and investment is brought about not through variations in the interest rate, but through increases or decreases in the amount of total national income. Perhaps the best way to see the process is to consider the effects of a fluctuation in consumption, and then to examine what happens to the savings–investment relation.

THE DEVELOPMENT OF A RECESSION

Suppose that people decide, for whatever reason, to consume less and to save a higher proportion of their income. The immediate result of this will be twofold: in the first place savings will now be higher than the going level of investment; and in the second place there will be a fall in the sale of consumption goods, as people consume less in order to save more. Consequently firms in consumption goods industries will have stocks of unsold goods. They will therefore reduce their outputs of such goods in response to the falling demand. As these firms reduce output there will as a consequence be falls in the incomes of those producing; firms will lay off workers until they have just enough to produce the new, lower, level of output. So there will be a lower level of overall income in the economy. But as incomes fall we might expect further falls in the level of consumption; and as consumption falls firms will cut back output and employment further. This next round of output restrictions means further falls in incomes and then consumption. The economy thus enters on a downward spiral, in which the first-round effect of a fall in consumption spending is 'multiplied' by second- and third-round effects. In effect, the system has 'positive feedback', for the original disturbance is amplified by the way in which falls in consumption and income reinforce each other to generate a major disturbance. Clearly this contrasts sharply with the 'negative feedback' of the neoclassical theory, in which a consumption cut – meaning an increase in saving – leads to interest rate falls which increase investment and thus dampen down the effects of the initial disruption to stability.

In the Keynesian approach, therefore, a fall in demand produces economic 'echoes' which enlarge the demand problem yet further. This effect is known within the Keynesian system as the 'multiplier' relation: the multiplier describes the ultimate change in income resulting from some initial change in aggregate demand. Of course multiplier effects are not argued to continue *ad infinitum*: a cut in consumption will not lead to an ultimate income of zero. Rather the system will settle down to stability at some new – and lower – level of income. The main determinant of this point will be the savings–investment relation. Remember that the downward spiral began because people decided to consume less and save more; thus investment and savings were no longer equal and a general demand imbalance emerged in the economy. This generated falls in output and income. However, as income declines, not only does consumption decline, but also savings begin to decline: people who are earning less tend to save less. Eventually, income will fall to a point which reduces savings back to the original level of investment. At this point consumption demand will once again be equal to consumption output, and the system will be stable, in equilibrium. The actual level of output at which this occurs will be determined by two main forces: people's decisions as to the amount they wish to consume out of income, and the level of investment which enterprises wish to undertake. But it is investment which is the crucial, 'active', element: once the level of investment is fixed, then income will either grow or fall to make savings equal to it. It will fix a level of aggregate demand to which output and income will adjust. But in the Keynesian system there is no necessity for this to be at a full employment, full output level; the economy may well settle down at a level where savings and investment are equal, but output is well below the maximum attainable.

Note the crucial difference between this account and the neoclassical approach. Each involves a mechanism which equates savings to investment, but these 'adjustment' mechanisms are very different and entail very different economic outcomes. In the neoclassical world it is the interest rate which adjusts, forcing investment and saving into line; income remains unchanged. In the Keynesian theory, the burden of adjustment is on income, which falls until a new equilibrium point is reached. In the neoclassical story there is but one equilibrium point: at full employment. For Keynes there are many possible equilibria, depending on the aggregate demand situation: full employment is but one possibility among many, and by no means the most likely. Left to itself, there is no guarantee that the economy will generate the right volume of demand: indeed the chances are overwhelming that it will not. Thus the neoclassical system of economics is what Keynes referred to as a 'special case' – the case of a full employment level of demand. His own account therefore outlines the 'general' case – thus the title '*General* Theory' – in which unemployment is the rule rather than the exception. In his own words,

I ... argue that the postulates of the classical theory are applicable to a special case only and not to a general case ... Moreover the characteristics of the special case assumed by the classical theory happen not to be those of the economic society in which we actually live, with the result that its teaching is misleading and disastrous if we attempt to apply it to the facts of experience.[1]

Before moving on to the various interpretations and constructions which have been put upon Keynes's work, a further point should be made about the picture of 'demand failure' which has been sketched. This is that, in principle, this kind of demand failure can arise from any of the components of aggregate demand. The case of a change in consumption spending has been described. But similar results would have occurred with a fall in investment, with sudden cuts in government expenditure (though here the picture is complicated by questions of finance), or with falls in exports. Given that all of these categories of expenditure are capable of fluctuation, then a case begins to emerge for intervention – in practice, by government – to maintain levels of aggregate demand at a volume corresponding to satisfactory levels of employment.

From this follows the basic Keynesian policy principle: that the government does have an economic task to perform. But it is a limited one, of 'demand management' in response to any prospective demand deficiency.

9

Rewriting Keynes:
Variations on the General Theory

The publication of the *General Theory* in 1936 had a major impact on the economics profession and its thinking about persistent unemployment, but that impact was complicated by the difficulty of understanding all of the elements of Keynes's argument. Years of discussion and debate followed, not because of the well-known penchant of economists for debate, but because of real problems and confusions in Keynes's text. Almost immediately fellow economists began to publish papers and books either interpreting Keynes's work as a whole, or subjecting parts of it to critical analysis. Because of the complexity of Keynes's work, some of these interpretations were necessarily simplified, concentrating on quite specific aspects of the argument. Joan Robinson's *Introduction to the Theory of Employment*, published as a guide to students in 1937, focused on the determination of the interest rate and levels of investment, though in some respects it was even wider in scope than Keynes's book. By far the most important of these post-Keynes interpretations was a paper by J. R. Hicks, published in the journal *Economica* in 1937, in which he developed some relatively simple diagrams to display what he took to be the main thrust of the argument in the *General Theory*.[1] Within the rather narrow world of professional economics, the paper became a smash hit, and was rapidly reproduced in textbooks. This is still the case. To the present day, when students learn the analysis of the economy as a whole, and the 'Keynesian' system, they almost invariably learn not Keynes, but Hicks's version of Keynes. Even after the monetarist counterrevolution, there is hardly a textbook which does not employ Hicks's diagrams, and generations of economics students have been trained – and have gone on to practise professionally – without ever reading Keynes. So one way of understanding the modern debates about Keynes would be to see them not as concerning Keynes directly, but rather as being about the validity of the Hicksian interpretation of Keynes, and its pervasive effect within the world of economics teaching. So the following pages begin with the Hicks model of Keynes, and go on to the theories and debates which it has engendered.

THE HICKS MODEL

In the Hicks version, Keynes's account of the economy involves the operation of two overall markets: a *goods* market, in which consumption and investment goods are bought and sold, and a *money* market, in which financial assets are traded. In the money market people are essentially making a decision as to whether to hold their wealth in the form of interest-yielding government bonds or non-interest-bearing money. Hicks's model is essentially a simple and elegant way of showing the interaction between these two markets, so that the equilibrium level of income can be depicted.

Let us take first the goods market. Once again, government expenditure and exports will be left out of the picture: aggregate demand is therefore made up of consumption spending and investment demand. So national income will be equal to the total of consumption plus investment. But remember that investment is the 'active element' here: for any given level of investment, national income will adjust, so that it generates exactly the right amount of savings. In other words, people will make some decision about the proportion of their income they will consume and the proportion they will save; given that decision, income will adjust to make savings equivalent to investment. It follows that whatever determines the amount of investment will determine the size of national income. Now Keynes's analysis of the investment problem is a complex one, but one theme in it stresses the role of the interest rate. Keynes, like the neoclassicals, suggests that a fall in the interest rate will produce higher investment, and a rise in interest rates will lower investment. Hicks makes the interest rate effectively the *only* determinant of investment in his model (some of the objections to this will be discussed below), and this leads to a simple relation between the rate of interest and the level of

income. As the rate of interest falls, investment rises, aggregate
demand rises and income rises. The rise in income will be just sufficient to generate a new level of savings equal to the higher level of
investment. This means that every equilibrium point in the goods
market, that is every point at which investment equals savings, will
also correspond to a particular level of income, and to a particular
value for the rate of interest.

The first of Hicks's diagrams (fig. 2) illustrates this idea. On the
vertical axis, the symbol 'r' means the rate of interest, and on the
horizontal axis, the symbol 'y' means national income: lower interest
rates are associated with higher income and vice versa.

Figure 2. Hicks's 'IS' curve

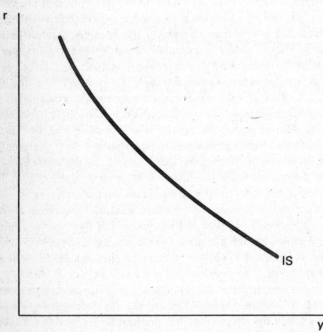

Hicks calls this curve the 'IS' curve. It traces out the combination of
rate of interest and national income at which investment is equal to
savings and the goods market is therefore in equilibrium. To repeat,

it simply says that, given people's consumption decisions, a lower interest rate means more investment, which means a higher level of income. At every point along the curve investment will be equal to saving, and so we have the quintessentially Keynesian idea that equilibrium can occur at almost any level of income.

Because the curve traces out a range of possible incomes, however, we have no way of knowing which will emerge as the *actual* level of income. That will depend on whatever the interest rate in fact turns out to be. So the question is, what determines the interest rate? As indicated, for Keynes the interest rate is a monetary phenomenon, emerging from the money markets. Hicks's model also depicts this process, once again showing a relationship between the interest rate and national income.

Hicks's version of Keynes's money market theory runs as follows. If there is a given amount of money in the system, then people can do two things with it. They can use it to finance transactions, or they can hold it as an asset (since money is a store of value). For any given level of national income, people will require a certain amount of money to finance current transactions. As income rises, they will need more 'transactions cash' and as income falls they will need less. If the money supply is fixed, then the amount of money available for holding as an asset will simply be whatever is left after the 'transactions demand for money' has been satisfied. So as income rises, the quantity of money available for holding as an asset falls; and vice versa when income falls. Now the alternative to holding money as an asset is to switch it into some other financial asset, namely interest-bearing government bonds. Without going into the details of the way the bond market operates, it is argued that there is an inverse relationship between the return on bonds (which is the interest rate) and the amount of 'asset money' there is in the system, after the 'transactions demand' has been taken care of. The larger the amount of asset money, the lower the interest rate; if the amount of asset money falls, then the interest rate rises. Once again this implies a definite relationship between the interest rate and the level of national income. If the money supply is fixed, then the higher the level of income, the higher will be the requirement for 'transactions' money, the lower will be the amount of 'asset money' and the higher will be the rate of interest. In the money market there will be a direct relationship between the rate of interest and the level of income. The second of Hicks's diagrams (fig. 3) illustrates this.

Figure 3. Hicks's 'LM' curve.

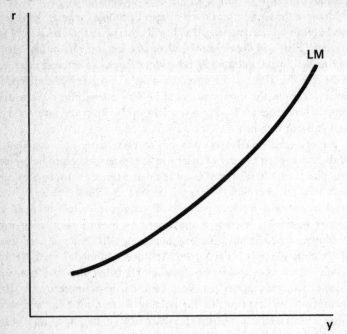

This time we are tracing out all the combinations of interest rate and income which keep the money market in equilibrium, meaning that the supply of money is just equal to what people want to hold, both as transactions and asset money. Hicks called this curve the 'LM' curve.

Because Hicks's two diagrams involve the same variables (the rate of interest and the level of income) they can be put together (fig. 4) to find the combination of interest rate and income which will deliver simultaneous equilibrium in both markets.

The equilibrium point is given by the intersection of the IS and LM curves: at this intersection, the rate of interest (marked as r*) and

Figure 4. Equilibrium.

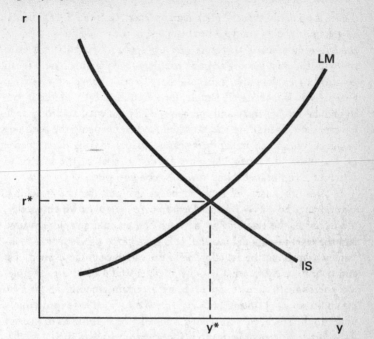

income (y*) are at the only values which give equilibrium in both markets. Thus we have determined the actual level of income which will emerge from the interaction of goods and money markets. And, to repeat, the central point of Keynes's work is that this equilibrium point is variable. It depends, for example, on the particular nature of people's savings and consumption decisions, on the decisions of entrepreneurs as to how much they will invest, on the supply of money in the system, on the decisions of people in financial markets as to whether to hold money or bonds. There is no guarantee whatsoever that the equilibrium level of income which emerges will be sufficient to employ all of the available workforce. It may well be an equilibrium at a low level of income and a high level of unemployment.

THE CAREER OF THE HICKS MODEL

There is no doubt that the Hicksian approach – or the IS–LM model as it is most widely known – has been one of the real success stories of modern economics. The reasons are very straightforward: it is easy to teach to students, there is no great problem in expanding it, and it can be used to explore the implications of a wide range of economic alternatives. It is relatively simple, for example, to open up the model to include foreign trade and the balance of payments, and to include government expenditure and taxation. And by changing the positions of the curves and changing their shapes (that is, making them steeper or shallower) it is possible for students to analyse the effects of different assumptions about how the economy works.

In fact, the uses of such a model go well beyond teaching. Underlying the curves on the diagrams are equations which specify, for instance, the relationship between the amount people consume and the level of national income. It is possible to use statistical techniques to spell out the actual value of the variables in these equations, and then to calculate what national income would be if, for example, the government were to cut taxes by a certain amount, or raise its expenditure by printing money, or whatever. These procedures underlie the so-called 'forecasting' models which are used to predict our short-term economic futures; the government uses such a model, the 'Treasury model', which consists of about 800 main equations. So, although the diagrammatic approach I have outlined above is extremely basic, it is capable of being extended in very sophisticated ways.

The question is, however, to what extent are these diagrams an adequate representation of the ideas Keynes was concerned with? Recall that Keynes saw his work as a distinct break with the neoclassical system; in many ways his views on neoclassicism were scathing. The problems with the Hicks model begin with the fact that it is quite unclear just how far the Hicks version reproduces this rejection. Is the Hicks version of Keynes really inconsistent with the neoclassical approach which Keynes claimed was so mistaken? Or is it in fact simply a *variant* of neoclassical market theory, in which the demonstration that the economy can generate permanent unemployment and recession is achieved by sleight of hand? These questions arise because it is possible to make the Hicks model generate results which are in effect those of the neoclassical system.

In the neoclassical view, for example, employment depends on the real wage rate, and unemployment is a consequence of wages being too high. This leads to the idea that unemployment can be cured by wage cuts, an idea which seems incompatible with Keynes's account which is based on demand failure, on an inadequate level of demand for output. Yet it is possible to use the Hicks approach to suggest that from a position of unemployment, wage cuts will indeed do the trick and restore full employment. This has been such a central part of recent debate, that the issue is worth examining.

WAGE CUTTING AND UNEMPLOYMENT

Firstly, the discussion of wage rates and unemployment always makes the distinction between money wages and real wages. Real wages are the actual amount of goods that can be bought with the money wage; broadly speaking it is the money wage divided by the price level. If money wages are unchanged and prices rise, then real wages are falling, and vice versa. Now the simple 'supply and demand' theory of labour always makes employment depend on the real wage; but with constant prices, clearly a cut in money wages will be a cut in the real wage. So all it takes is for workers to accept a cut in money wages and employment will increase.

Keynes directs a number of criticisms towards this idea. In the first place, there is the question of whether the demand for products is independent of the wage rate. In the simple neoclassical story it is necessary to assume that prices of products, and the quantity of them which is demanded, are not going to be reduced by any reduction in wages. Now, this may be reasonable for a single product, but it is certainly unreasonable to think of the whole economy like this. If wages fall, then costs will fall, and the process of competition will force firms to lower prices in line with costs. If prices fall in the same proportion as money wages, then real wages (i.e. the money-wage/ price ratio) will be constant, so what incentive is there for firms to hire more workers? On the whole, of course, prices would not fall as

much as wages – because wages are not the only cost of production –
but even so, Keynes argued in the *General Theory*, neoclassical economics had really given no serious thought to what would happen to
prices in the event of a general wage cut.

However, neoclassical theorists have produced a range of answers
to these objections. These tend to rely not on the direct effects of
wage cuts – though it is still maintained that wage cuts directly
increase employment – but on various indirect effects. The most
important indirect effects are as follows.

1. If wages and prices fall, this means that the purchasing power of
money, and wealth generally, has increased. The money balances held
by money holders will have increased in real terms, in terms of what
they can buy. So money holders become more wealthy, and will
consume more, thus increasing demand. Wage cuts will therefore not
lead to a demand problem. (This process is known in economics as
the 'real balance effect'.)

2. Output will rise because wage and price cuts will have an effect
on exports, which will become relatively cheaper abroad. So employment will increase as a result of the effect of wage cuts increasing
exports.

3. As wages and prices fall, the amount of money needed in the
system for business transactions will fall; so the 'real' quantity of
money in the economy will rise, if the money supply is unchanged.
This will cause the interest rate to fall, which will increase investment
spending and thus demand will be maintained.

These answers to Keynes gave rise to a very particular interpretation of his work. This is that Keynes's work, far from being a new
'general' theory is in fact just a variant, a special case of the old
neoclassical system. Keynes gets his results only by imposing restrictions on the old neoclassical theory: in particular that wages are not
flexible, that they do not shift in response to changes in supply or
demand. If they did, if workers would accept wage cuts when there
was unemployment, then there would be no unemployment. In addition, Keynes imposes other sorts of restrictions, such as the idea that
investment is not particularly responsive to changes in interest rates.
In essence, Keynes makes the mistake of not recognizing mechanisms
(1) and (3) above. His work therefore makes no break, at a theoretical

level, from the neoclassical economics he affects to supersede; it is the same system, but with a few arbitrary and unwarranted assumptions – notably that wages are 'rigid' – tacked on.

These kinds of assessment of Keynes's contribution were intensively explored in the dominantly neoclassical economics profession of the United States after the Second World War, being summed up at length in such works as Patinkin's *Money, Interest, and Prices*. Two sorts of conclusion emerged. One was that Keynes was irrelevant, the only serious economic theory being the neoclassical general equilibrium system described in Chapter 6. The second suggested that Keynes had a point, of limited theoretical significance it is true, but of considerable practical importance. But these conclusions have also given rise to fierce criticisms, so that at present there is simply no overall consensus on what Keynesian economics actually is. There are only factions, the most important of which are discussed below: they can be called, respectively, the 'neoclassical synthesis', the 'Cambridge school', and 'new Keynesianism'.

THE NEOCLASSICAL SYNTHESIS

One particular economist dominates the neoclassical synthesis: Paul Samuelson, whose textbook *Economics* has been sold by the million to generations of students. The central device of the neoclassical synthesis, as the name suggests, is an attempt to reconcile Keynes with the neoclassicism he ostensibly rejected. This is done by admitting the core of the neoclassical objections – by admitting that wage cuts would restore full employment, for example – but arguing that in the real world wages are not, in practice, flexible. Keynes is wrong in a theoretical sense, but he is right in the sense that the world actually works the way he says it does: wages are rigid, prices are not generally flexible, etc. As a practical doctrine, and as a guide to policy, Keynes is useful: he shows how we can expand aggregate demand up to the full employment level. But on a theoretical level, the neoclassical analysis of markets is valid.

The acceptance of such ideas within the economics profession has led to a teaching approach which is anomalous, to say the least. Students are normally taught an economics which is divided in two:

into *micro*economics, which deals with the market and production decisions of people and firms, and *macro*economics which deals with the economy as a whole. The microeconomics component of teaching is almost purely neoclassical: it emphasizes the role of markets, of flexible prices, and suggests that market systems are efficient and welfare-maximizing. The macroeconomics part, however, suggests quite the reverse: it deals with the occurrence of unemployment, trade cycles, recession and instability. Not surprisingly the two do not mesh very well.

It would be wrong to suggest that this neoclassical version of Keynes, in which his work is integrated with the market economics he hoped to supersede, is a straightforward distortion. Keynes certainly did not work out the microeconomic implications of his ideas. Moreover, he himself suggested that his thought was compatible with the neoclassical model. At the very end of the *General Theory* he explicitly made the suggestion that his work applied only to periods of unemployment. His ideas, he suggested, should be used as a guide to getting the economy back to full employment, and then the neoclassical analysis would apply once more.

This passing remark by Keynes has been taken up by many British Keynesians, who therefore seem to have Keynes's warrant for a belief in free markets which is hardly less extreme than some monetarists. But this is hooked up with a belief in a particular form of state intervention, namely that the government should simply try to expand demand, and let the market do the rest. However, is this all that Keynes has to say? We turn now to the theorists who argue that although Keynes flirted with neoclassical ideas, the central thrust of his work was very different.

THE CAMBRIDGE SCHOOL

In England such writers as Joan Robinson, Richard Kahn, Nicholas Kaldor and G. L. S. Shackle, mainly but not exclusively based in Cambridge, have consistently argued that the Hicks version is a misleading one. Specifically the neoclassical synthesis finds no place for a number of important problems which Keynes discussed at great length in the *General Theory* and which are central to his analysis.

Here just one of the crucial Cambridge objections to the Hicks model will be emphasized. This is that it is a *static* model, like the general equilibrium system, in fact. It concentrates on the factors determining income, output and employment at one moment in time. It is, as it were, a snapshot of the economy at the instant of equilibrium.

This approach does indeed make some of Keynes's work almost incomprehensible. To take an example, in 1937 Keynes published an article in an American scholarly review, the *Quarterly Journal of Economics*, to explain the 'simple fundamental ideas' of his just-published book. The article makes odd reading for anyone brought up on the Hicks model. In the first place it begins with a longish, rather philosophical, discussion of the nature of 'uncertainty'. We live, says Keynes, inside a historical process, a progression from past to future. We cannot predict this future. It is not that we know what might happen, and can make some estimate of the probability of things occurring (as in throwing a dice, where we know that some number will come up, and can assess the probability of any particular number turning up). Rather, the problem is either that we cannot reliably assess the probability of some possible event (such as the third world war occurring next year), or simply that we do not know what events might occur. What kinds of ecological problems will the next generation face? Will a cheap substitute for oil be discovered by 1995? On such matters we just don't know what is on the historical agenda.

Such considerations, Keynes goes on, are of great economic importance. This is because a large number of economic decisions are made with respect to the future. The most important of these are investment choices: when firms invest in new plant and equipment, they are constructing the capacity to produce output in the future. They do so, of course, because they aim at making profits in the future. But such a decision must involve a range of assumptions about what the future will hold: for example, that the interest costs of the capital being used will not rise significantly, that the machinery being installed will not become rapidly obsolete, that demand for the product to be produced will not suddenly evaporate, and so on. But none of these things can be known: they are *uncertain*. Uncertainty, argues Keynes, also pervades the money markets: when wealth holders decide to keep their wealth in money rather than bonds, they do so because they are worried that bond prices might fall, and they will lose out. This decision, however, has effects on the interest rate, so that interest rates are also affected by uncertainty and the vague and shifting expectation of what the future holds in store. But, of the various factors which affect income, Keynes writes, 'it is those which determine the rate of investment which are the most unreliable'. Investment is based on

expectations that have no foundations in circumstances, but take their cues from the beliefs of others, and that will be sustained by hopes, undermined by fears and continually buffeted by the 'news'.[2]

There is, it follows, no reason for investment determined in this way to correspond to the 'full-employment' level. On the contrary, it will do so only by very unlikely accident. Thus 'full, or even approximately full, employment is of rare and short-lived occurrence ... an intermediate situation which is neither desperate nor satisfactory is our lot'.

This distinction between a world which is static and certain, and one which is historical and uncertain is at the core of the Cambridge objection to the Hicksian approach. From it flow complex issues and problems which cannot be treated here. Underlying everything, however, is the belief that the static equilibrium approach of Hicks – a method based on describing the equilibrium position of the economy at a moment in time – should be abandoned. Rather we should be thinking in dynamic terms, of an economy moving through time, in which changes – in the stock of capital, for instance – are happening constantly. Finally we should be thinking in terms of an economy in which uncertain expectations exist, and should bear in mind their complex political and economic effects. These ideas, the Cambridge school argue, are Keynes's central theme and lasting contribution. The problems arise from the fact that although Keynes was thinking of *dynamic* problems – of a changing, shifting, unstable economy – he did so with an analysis which was really *static* in method. It was borrowed, in fact, from Marshall, whose ideas he was attempting to displace. It is the resulting confusions which have given rise to the debates and differences, and to the bizarre result of a textbook Keynes being assimilated with his neoclassical enemies.

'NEW KEYNESIANISM'

Cambridge criticisms of the neoclassical version of Keynes had been made since 'Keynesian' economics first came to dominate economics during and after the Second World War. But in the late 1960s a new line of criticism began to emerge, based not just on the problems of uncertainty and so on, but on more fundamental questions about the nature of market economies. Associated with the names of Professors R. W. Clower and Axel Leijonhufvud (both of the University of California at Los Angeles), the new critique of neoclassicism based its account of effective demand failure on the failure of markets to act as advertised in the neoclassical system. It has given rise to an increasingly substantial academic literature aimed at exploring the ways in which markets do and do not really coordinate economic activities.

Like the Cambridge critique, the new Keynesianism begins with a straight rejection of the Hicks I S–L M model, which as Leijonhufvud remarked, 'seems to me a singularly inadequate vehicle for the interpretation of Keynes's ideas'. This inadequacy stems from the way the Hicks model can be grafted on to a neoclassical theory so that, for example, wage cuts can cure unemployment. Against this, the new Keynesian approaches argue that Keynes's work is founded on basic objections to the neoclassical story of the market mechanism.

To understand the Clower–Leijonhufvud arguments it is necessary to take a step back to the Walrasian general equilibrium system described in Chapter 6. There we saw that, if all markets in the economy are in equilibrium, and if complete and 'perfect' competition reigns, then full output, full employment and general bliss will be the result. The problems lie in finding the equilibrium prices which will deliver this result. Walras used the device of an 'auctioneer' who by a process of trial and error – comparing offers and bids – worked it all out. This trial and error process was called *tâtonnement*, and through it the full set of equilibrium prices emerged.

The problem, however, is that the real world doesn't work like that. What are the implications, then, of the absence of an 'auctioneer' and the absence of *tâtonnement*?

In the first place, what happens if we are out of equilibrium? This means, by definition, that supplies and demands of some goods are not going to be equal. At disequilibrium prices, though, some traders will be unable to sell all of the goods, or all of the labour, that they would like to. But this must mean that their incomes – which are earned by selling goods – must also be constrained; these traders are earning less than they would like to be earning. And it follows that their demand for other goods will also be curtailed. So right away the economy has run into a demand problem – the quantities of goods which people actually can purchase are less than those they would really like to buy. Professor Clower therefore distinguishes between *notional* demand – the demand for goods which would exist if the economy was in a full-employment equilibrium – and *effective* demand, which is the amount people can actually demand, given their incomes. And it is easy to show that where anyone fails to make their desired sales, then the lowering of their effective demand in other markets will lead to 'multiplier' effects through which the initial disturbance is amplified. Unemployment, and less than full output, will be the result.

This kind of unemployment follows simply from the failure of the economy to find the set of equilibrium prices at which the full-employment level of trading will take place: as Leijonhufvud remarks, 'to make the transition from Walras's world to Keynes's world, it is sufficient to dispense with the assumed tâtonnement mechanism'.[3]

So we have an unemployment position characterized by the existence of people who would like to work but cannot, *as well as* a form of unsatisfied demand for the goods these people might make. The unemployed would like to buy goods, but cannot because of the lack of purchasing power deriving from their own unemployment. There is a 'communication' failure: the unemployed have no mechanism for sending a message to firms, to say that if they were hired, they would buy goods. But in the absence of a sign that demand is increasing, firms will not increase output, and therefore will not hire more workers. The price system – which in the neoclassical theory conveys information and coordinates activity – is simply failing here. It doesn't convey the information needed to connect potential demand with the ability of the economy to produce: '*The market signals* presupposed in general equilibrium analysis *are not transmitted*,' as Leijonhufvud puts it.

Note that such a recession does not result from wages being 'too high', and it cannot be cured by wage cuts. This is because a car firm, for example, will increase output and employment only if it thinks demand is rising. An offer by workers to work for less is not, in itself, a signal that demand is increasing, and therefore will not increase overall employment. The general problem here has been described recently by Professor M. L. Weitzmann:

> The market system suffers from a 'failure to coordinate' the desired consumption and production plans of all agents because the unemployed lack the means to communicate or make effective their potential demands.
>
> In a modern economy, many different goods are produced and consumed. Each firm is a specialist in production, while its workers are generalists in consumption. Workers receive a wage from the firm they work for, but they spend it almost entirely on the products of other firms. To obtain a wage the worker must first succeed in being hired. However when demand is depressed because of unemployment, each firm sees no indication that it can profitably market the increased output of an extra worker. The inability of the unemployed to communicate effective demand results in a vicious circle of self-sustaining involuntary unemployment. There is an atmosphere of frustration because the problem is beyond the power of any single firm to correct, yet would go away if only all firms would simultaneously expand output.[4]

These kinds of 'coordination problems', as a source of effective demand failure, are only one part of the 'new Keynesianism'. Their significance lies in the fact that they take the Keynesian attack right to the heart of the general equilibrium system, to its theory of the market mechanism and its beneficent results. It is at this point that some modern Keynesians join up with general equilibrium theorists such as Hahn (see Chapter 7) in contesting the often rather facile use by monetarists of the ideas of general equilibrium.

CONCLUSION

It was suggested in the introduction to Part Two that the confrontation between 'monetarists' and 'Keynesians' over the past few years has been a rather spurious one. This is because the real theoretical dividing lines lie not between these doctrines but within them. When we look at the theoretical underpinnings of these doctrines it is relatively easy to trace the beginnings of such internal divergences: they concern the way markets, and the 'market mechanism' are understood. Do market systems operate smoothly and efficiently, to coordinate and harmonize the economic activities of people? Or are they clumsy and inflexible, a poor basis for economic decision-making?

The issues discussed in the previous chapters may seem abstract and hardly relevant to Britain's current problems. But they are of great policy relevance, since politicians, policy makers and commentators are often circumscribed in their thinking about economic problems by ideas about the way they think the economy really works. In Britain the most important of these ideas has been a belief in the market mechanism. A bizarre feature of economic and political debate over the past few years has been the way in which the thirty post-war years have been labelled as years of ever increasing state intervention, with an ever increasing distortion of free markets. The 'Keynesian' policy makers of those years have been condemned as full-scale interventionists, trying to guide the economy from above, with devastating results. In fact their belief in markets was scarcely less extreme than that of the monetarists.

So question one on the agenda is whether economic theory gives us any grounds for a belief in free markets, and free market economic policies, as a basis for solving our problems? The answer seems to be 'no'. Keynesian theory, and the work of some general equilibrium theorists, suggests that market economies are *not* the self-stabilizing, welfare-maximizing machines which neoclassical economics would have us place our faith in. This point seems to have been demonstrated fairly conclusively, and most economic theorists would probably accept it. But where does this leave us in terms of policy, in terms of the choices which face Britain if it is to escape its current predicament?

The inadequacies of free-market theories and of the policies based on them open up the question of state intervention. Both Keynesian and some general equilibrium theories indicate that an unguided economy is unlikely to perform well. But this general point does not mean that we can jump to the conclusion that any particular form of state intervention is justified. Keynesian theory has very little to say on *how* the economy should be managed. In the past, Keynesians have tended to support fiscal policies – essentially policies based on state expenditure and tax decisions – to maintain aggregate demand; the key idea was to maintain an 'adequate' level of demand, and then allow the economy to take care of itself.

But policy interventions of that type seem to offer little in the face of the problems outlined in the first section of this book. These problems are specific ones concerning manufacturing performance, and the R & D, investment, engineering and educational inputs to that performance. Keynesian policies of demand management are aimed elsewhere; they are pitched at an abstract level which brackets out the specific problems of industrial organization which face Britain. For this reason it is necessary to explore such problems directly, without relying on policy panaceas derived from the highly abstract preoccupations of theoretical economics. It is not that theoretical economics is not important, not a worthwhile and necessary activity. It is simply that it is time for politicians and others to stop thinking that it can offer simple answers.

PART THREE

WAYS OUT?

What Went Wrong?

The account of Britain's economic crisis presented in the first part of this book was essentially descriptive: it outlined the key processes in Britain's economic decline without seeking to explain their final causes. The concern was with what happened rather than why it happened. The account had this emphasis because of the striking way in which economic discussion in Britain often fails to sort out what the crucial issues actually *are*. Frequently, debate takes the form of assertions about who caused some particular ill-defined problem, with no clarification of the nature of the problem itself, let alone of how the causal mechanisms work. So in concentrating on the problems an attempt has been made to avoid the game of naming the guilty men. Partly this is because there are frequently no guilty men to name: many problems occur because of the structure of the economy, rather than because of particular actors within it. But also it is usually unclear how pinning the blame helps to elucidate solutions, which is what we really should be interested in.

Unfortunately, many of the attempts to explain Britain's predicament also imply a programme of action to solve the problems. Where the explanations are dubious, as they often are, this can lead at best to no apparent solution and at worst to misguided solutions which are likely, if anything, to make matters worse. So before going on to look at some policy measures aimed at promoting industrial recovery in Britain a critical look will be taken at some of the main explanations which have been on offer over recent years. All of them have limitations in one way or another, and can easily constitute obstacles rather than aids to clear thinking about Britain's difficulties.

In what follows, three types of explanation of the UK's problems are assessed. The first argues that British managers and industrialists have failed. They have lacked enterprise, they have lacked the tech-nological skills of foreign managers, they have not invested enough: they are bad 'entrepreneurs'. This approach is known in the economics literature, therefore, as the 'entrepreneurial failure' thesis: it pins the blame on British capitalists.

The second thesis argues that Britain's trades unions and working practices are at fault in various ways. British industry is 'overmanned'; it is strike prone, and unions are too rigid in their opposition to the changes in work practices which technological change involves.

The third thesis looks not at particular people, but at an economic process. It argues that Britain's problems stem from insufficient investment. This thesis is not necessarily separate from the previous two, in that poor management and bad industrial relations are fre-quently cited as the cause of low investment. But in either version inadequate investment is the immediate cause of Britain's problems, and raising investment would serve to overcome them.

ENTREPRENEURIAL FAILURE

The hypothesis of 'entrepreneurial failure' has had a long and happy run. It has been a mainstay of academic explanations of British decline since the late nineteenth century, and has also had a significant popular impact. As recently as 1982 it surfaced in a series of television programmes called – rather predictably – 'The Betrayal of Britain' on ITV; and reappeared almost immediately on the BBC, as part of the series of reflections on Britain, by the then head of the London School of Economics, Professor Ralf Dahrendorf. The theme has a number of variations, but a typical version runs as follows. The massive and spectacular growth of the UK economy in the early nineteenth century – the industrial revolution – was the result pri-marily of vigorous entrepreneurship. Go-getting owner-managers, alert to every opportunity, occasionally going to excess (eighteen-hour days for seven-year-old children, etc.) but otherwise entirely admir-able, pushed Britain to world leadership. They built up fortunes, and deservedly so. But what of their descendants? They alas, lacked the go-getting spirit; frequently they just wanted to use their fortunes to become country gentlemen. They did so, and this meant that the enterprises which had produced their fortunes became stagnant. Firms became moribund at the top, as the vigorous entrepreneurship of previous years disappeared. This story often ends with moralizing conclusions of the 'clogs to clogs in three generations' variety.

When we get down to specifics, the charges against late-nineteenth-century entrepreneurs are as follows. Firstly, they neglected to take up technological improvements which would have raised productivity and maintained a higher rate of growth. Critics usually point to certain developments in chemicals technology, steel production and textile manufacture where innovations which were adopted elsewhere were not taken up in Britain. Secondly they lacked engineering expertise, and failed also to employ enough engineers and managers with a technical training. Thirdly, they were unadventurous in marketing.

The problem with this argument is that, although it is not difficult to find examples which seem to accord with the general thesis, its implications are rarely fully spelled out. In recent years, however, a number of economists and historians have tried to set up the argument in a rather more rigorous way. Their objections to the entrepreneurial failure line begin by asking two questions:

1. What does it actually *mean* for the British economy to have 'failed' in the late nineteenth century? and

2. What would entrepreneurs have to do, or not do, to be responsible for this?

The answer to the first question is that Britain could be said to have failed if it had unused economic resources (of labour, for instance; if, in a word, there had been unemployment) which could have been used to produce extra output; or if it could have got more output with the resources of land, capital and labour it was using. In other words, if Britain had used the same inputs, were there products, activities, processes, technologies it could have used which were more productive than the ones it *did* use? The answer to the second question is that entrepreneurs would bear the responsibility for failure if they had failed to adopt these productivity-improving opportunities.

Now the evidence indicates that in the last quarter of the nineteenth century, when the slowdown in growth occurred, Britain did not suffer from large-scale unemployment, of the kind that has plagued it in the twentieth century, and in general resources do not seem to have been underutilized.

This leaves the question of whether productivity-increasing opportunities existed. From the point of view of enterprises, anything that increases productivity increases profits (at least in the short run). So the question becomes, did entrepreneurs have opportunities to make profits (by engaging in new activities, using new technologies) which they did not take up? Now the 'entrepreneurial failure' hypothesis normally lays emphasis on some quite specific technical missed opportunities: the open-hearth process in steel, the use of American production techniques (involving, for example, interchangeable parts) in mechanical engineering, a new technique (ring-spinning) in cotton manufacture, and the 'Solvay process' in alkali production (one of the most important of chemical processes). Added to this is a charge that British industry underemployed scientists and underinvested in research.

Those who reject the 'entrepreneurial failure' hypothesis advance two kinds of answer to these charges. The first is one of concrete, practical investigation. Was it actually more profitable to introduce these new techniques? Entrepreneurs are in business to make profits, so they can hardly be blamed for not taking up new techniques unless they are foregoing opportunities for profit. Various studies have argued that, in fact, these new techniques did *not* offer extra profits, and so businessmen can't be blamed for not adopting them. The second argument here is that if, say, some new process (in steel, or chemicals) was more productive and hence more profitable, entrepreneurs who adopted it would have made super-profits. Others would have noticed the ringing cash registers of the successful adopter (it is difficult to keep secrets in business) and would have followed suit. So, in these industries – which had in the main a large number of firms – only *one* adopter would suffice to change the whole basis of the industry. The fact that no one went for these supposedly profitable processes leads one to suspect that they weren't profitable at all.

On these kinds of grounds, then, British entrepreneurs of the late nineteenth century can be acquitted of blame for Britain's industrial problems. Certainly the structure of the world economy was changing, and the British people were to suffer heavily for British economic concentration on what were becoming outmoded industries; but it seems unreasonable to blame businessmen for not foreseeing all this, for not foreseeing, as one historian has put it, 'the trick which history was about to play on them'.

This is not to say, of course, that problems of entrepreneurship and the quality of management might not be important at other times and in other industries. Occasionally there is suggestive evidence. The British motorcycle industry declined at least partly in consequence of a failure to innovate. Yet this was not because the possibilities for innovation did not exist. Designers at BSA produced, in the early 1950s, new designs for bikes which anticipated the successful Japanese designs of a decade later. They were never put into production, and so there may be some evidence of 'entrepreneurial failure' in that industry. But this would require careful analysis. In general we should be suspicious of easy assumptions of managerial fallibility and entrepreneurial failure; suspicious also, presumably, of Mrs Thatcher's attempts to restore the values of Victorian entrepreneurship: if they never went away they do not need restoring.

THE UNIONS

The sins of trades unions are such a perennial theme of British economic and political discourse that it is difficult to know where to start. Three primary assertions are made:
- that Britain is 'strike prone', with an industrial relations climate which lowers output and inhibits technological change;
- that British industry is 'overmanned', and this is the cause of low productivity growth;
- that union 'monopolies' cause, like all monopolies, a rise in the price of the commodity being sold (in this case, labour) – British wage rates are thus too high.

The first thing that should be said about these assertions is that it can be difficult to resolve them simply by referring to the available evidence. In each case they involve international comparisons: Britain can only be strike prone, for example, if it has more strikes than comparable countries (obviously, if all have the same strike record, then Britain's poor relative performance is not explained by strikes). But the statistics we use to make such comparisons may not be consistent, and this poses comparability problems. Leaving such problems aside, the evidence is often ambiguous. For example, Britain is in general no more 'strike prone' than a number of other countries. It has considerably less days lost per thousand workers than, say, the USA, Italy or Canada. On the other hand, American strikes – in the car industry, for example – are often ritualized, semi-formal affairs, whereas British strikes are more random, more often unofficial and more damaging in terms of lost output. Finding a balance in the often conflicting statistical evidence can be no simple matter.

Such problems of evidence also appear in discussions of 'overmanning'. Although there are a number of studies which indicate that UK industries employ more workers for a given output than foreign industries, many appear to incorporate rather elementary weaknesses. A typical problem is that of 'ancillary workers', that is workers who perform some function within a plant, but take no direct part in production, such as cleaners. It is often unclear from comparative studies whether ancillary workers are included or not: thus reports claiming that British Steel uses more workers per ton of steel output than German plants tended to neglect the fact that ancillary labour was subcontracted out in the German plants – and not included in the labour figures – whereas all British ancillary workers were employed by BSC, and counted in. Furthermore, claims concerning 'overmanning' are only relevant if workers are using similar amounts and types of equipment; sometimes this is the case but more often it is not.

Quite apart from these statistical and interpretive difficulties there are some analytical problems. What, for instance, are strike proneness and overmanning meant to explain? We have seen in previous chapters that Britain's problems involve persistently low rates of growth: it is low growth rates of output and productivity that we should be trying to account for. But there is a crucial distinction to be drawn between factors which affect the *level* of productivity (i.e. of output per worker) and factors which affect the *rate of growth* of productivity. 'Overmanning' will affect the *level* of productivity: if Britain uses the same type of machines as country X, but twice as many workers, then the level of output per worker in Britain will be half that of country X. But the rate of growth of productivity is determined by such things as increases in capital per worker, improvements in the technical efficiency of machines and so on; overmanning will not necessarily have any impact here, and so rates of growth in Britain and country X will be the same. Similar considerations apply to strikes. Strikes and overmanning will not affect rates of growth unless they are getting consistently worse, relative to competitors. One rarely sees systematic evidence presented to this effect. It might be added, moreover, that so-called 'overmanning' does not necessarily make production in Britain more costly or less profitable. If overmanning is accompanied by relatively low wages (as it is in Britain compared with most of Europe), then overmanning may even be accompanied by cost advantages rather than disadvantages. Certainly neither strike proneness nor overmanning will suffice – at least not in the glib way they are usually deployed – as explanations of Britain's economic malaise.

INVESTMENT

'Investment' is that part of current income and output which is devoted to adding to the capital stock: that is, to increasing the quantity of machines, buildings, equipment and so on at the economy's disposal. In a general way, the size of the capital stock in different countries is central to understanding international differences in productivity. The reason why output per worker in Britain or Germany or France is so much higher than in India or Ghana is not that European workers are miracle men; it is simply that European workers have a substantially greater capital stock to work with. This rather trite observation can readily be transformed into an explanation of Britain's slow growth record. Britain's output grows slowly because its capacity to produce output grows slowly; its capacity to produce output, that is its capital stock, grows slowly because it invests less than other economies. Low investment is therefore the source of the problem.

Two kinds of evidence can be used to support this argument. Either we can look at rates of investment (that is, the proportion of national income used for investment) or we can look at the size of the capital stock per worker. In the long run these amount to much the same thing, since the amount of capital per worker is normally increased only by investing more over a period. But there are complications: a large part of the capital stock is inherited from the past, so it is not just *present* investment rates which matter, but also past rates: thus two countries may have similar investment rates now, but different capital stocks because of past investment decisions. Secondly, because the investment rate is a ratio, two countries may have the same rate of investment, but different absolute amounts of investment, and hence different sized capital stocks. If country A and country B both have investment rates of 20 per cent, but B's income is twice A's, then in absolute terms B will be investing twice as much as A. These considerations produce some analytical problems which will be outlined below.

But first some of the evidence. On *rates* of investment, the statistical sources make a number of important distinctions within the overall investment figure. Firstly, they distinguish between gross and net investment: that is, between total investment (which includes replacement of existing capital goods which have worn out) and new investment (the construction of completely new plant, equipment and so on). Secondly, they distinguish between overall investment (which includes, for example, domestic houses), industrial investment (including mining, oil, construction plant) and purely manufacturing investment. Thus in comparing Britain and West Germany, we might for some purposes – such as comparing technological levels in manufacturing – be interested mainly in net manufacturing investment. If we were interested in the Keynesian problem of the total level of demand we might consider gross investment for all sectors. A typical historical comparison of investment rates is as follows: it shows that gross investment in Britain was slightly less than in West Germany or Italy. But net investment – that is, investment actually devoted to increasing the capital stock – was very substantially less, particularly in manufacturing (see table 19).

In a more recent year, 1978, Britain invested about 18 per cent of GDP, as opposed to 21.5 per cent in France and Germany, and 30.2 per cent in Japan. A number of writers have taken such figures as the

Table 19. Investment rates in three European countries 1953–60

	W. Germany	Italy	UK
All industry			
Gross investment, % of GNP	16.6	16.3	14.5
Net investment, % of GNP	14.6	14.7	8.9
Manufacturing only			
Gross investment, % of GNP	13.3	13.8	10.7
Net investment, % of GNP	11.0	11.6	5.9

Source: A. Lamfalussy, *The United Kingdom and the Six*, London, 1963, pp. 92 and 94.

main explanatory factor in Britain's slow growth: we have invested less in total, and also less in net terms (which means that our capacity to produce has expanded more slowly than competitors').

This approach seems confirmed when looking at investment per worker, and the amount of capital stock which each worker has to work with. In both these areas Britain appears to lag, as tables 20 and

Table 20. Gross investment per head, 1974–7 ($)

	1974	1976	1977
Norway	1,900	2,800	3,200
Sweden	1,500	1,900	1,900
Japan	1,400	1,500	1,800
W. Germany	1,400	1,500	1,700
France	1,300	1,500	1,600
USA	1,200	1,300	1,500
UK	680	750	790

Source: A. Maddison, 'Long Run Dynamics of Productivity Growth', *Banca Nazionale di Lavoro Quarterly Review*, no. 128, 1979, p. 19.

Table 21. Manufacturing investment per employee ($)

	UK	Neth.	US	
1970	604	1,633	2,145	
1974	920	2,743	2,785	
1975	1,006	3,108	2,947	
	Sweden	France	Japan	Italy
1970	1,207	1,439	1,317	751
1974	2,443	2,288	2,141	1,469
1975	2,943	2,682	1,768	n.a.

Source: C. J. F. Brown and T. D. Sheriff, 'De-industrialization: a background paper', in F. Blackaby, ed. *De-industrialization*, London, 1979, p. 247

21 show. Table 20 deals with gross investment per person. A similar picture emerges when looking simply at manufacturing investment (see table 21).

Finally, these low investment rates appear to have resulted in low levels of assets per worker, that is low levels of capital per worker, as table 22 indicates in looking at different firms within the same industry in different countries.

Table 22. International comparison of assets per employee, 1976

	Assets per employee (£)
Motor industry	
British Leyland	8,505
11 Japanese firms [average]	42,020
Electrical engineering	
GEC (UK)	9,725
Siemens (Germany)	16,479
Hitachi (Japan)	34,680

Source: F. E. Jones, 'Our Manufacturing Industry – the Missing £100,000 Million' *Nat. West. Bank Quarterly Review*, May 1978, pp. 8–17.

This story of low investment can be multiplied using a wide range of statistical sources, and has led many people to argue, therefore, that low investment is at the core of Britain's economic difficulties.

Against it, two types of objection have been raised. The first argues that Britain's investment rates have not been notably lower than competitors, especially if we confine ourselves to the crucial category of investment in machinery and equipment. True, Britain invests less overall, but about the same in this area. A recent argument to this effect used data from OECD sources (table 23). On

Table 23. Investment as % of GDP, 1978

	Plant, machinery, transport	Total investment
Japan	10.9	30.2
UK	9.2	18.1
France	9.1	21.5
Germany	8.9	21.5
Italy	7.8	18.8
US	7.3	18.1

Source: *Lloyd's Bank Economic Bulletin*, No. 33, September 1981, p. 1.

directly productive investment, the argument runs, Britain is second in the league rather than at the bottom. Certainly it is less in absolute terms than other economies, because our GDP is lower, but the rates of investment compare well. The problem is that the returns from our investment seem much lower than competitors': our growth rate was much lower than, for example, the French growth rate, from a similar rate of investment. This leads the author to conclude that 'in relation to her growth performance, the UK may have been investing too much rather than too little'.[1]

A number of objections could be offered to this type of argument – we could tell a different story by looking at different years, say, or we could argue that it is absolute amounts of investment that matter for productivity, rather than rates (and here Britain is distinctly lower than comparable economies), or that past rates have been very low. However, the matter rests not just on statistics: there are analytical principles involved. These lead to another argument, which accepts that Britain has had low investment, but suggests that this explains nothing. Rather, low investment is the problem to be explained.

This latter argument has a number of facets. In the first place, it points out that the relation between investment and economic growth is a two-sided one. On the one hand, investment promotes growth by increasing the economy's capacity to produce output, and by increasing the productivity of workers. But on the other hand, investment *depends* on growth: it is only if demand and output are growing, and expected to keep on growing, that it is worthwhile investing in order to increase the capacity to produce. As the American economist Edward Denison has pointed out, 'a rapid increase in capacity is induced by rapid growth'.[2] Expanding markets are a primary motive for investment, so when the economy is growing only slowly, enterprises lack this crucial motive; thus low investment and low growth become mutually reinforcing. Such considerations recently led David Stout, economic director of the National Economic Development Office, to remark that 'I have come increasingly to take the view that British industrial investment behaviour has been much more of a symptom than a cause of our low growth rate.'[3]

Thus growth in incomes and demand produces opportunities for investment, and slow growth stifles such opportunities. But there is another sense in which low investment is an effect rather than a cause. 'Opportunities for investment' depend on more than fast growth: they depend also on firms and industries vigorously seeking out new activities. This search for new products and processes – a search which takes the form either of invention and innovation, or of using the available innovations of others – is what makes up the R & D activity whose importance was so heavily emphasized in earlier chapters. Research and development can be seen as the process by which areas for profitable investment are found; and from this derives the economic significance of the inadequate levels and types of R & D in Britain, which were charted in Chapter 4. This has led to an inability to find areas of investment able to generate both reasonable returns and a reasonable growth rate. To stress low investment as the source of our problems is, therefore, to put the cart before the horse. As David Stout points out, it is like telling someone who wants to be a long-distance runner to eat more (since it is noticeable that athletes eat more than other people). In fact, you need to start with training: it is only later that more food becomes necessary. From all of these perspectives, then, it is a mistake to think that low investment is the source of our problems, and a mistake also to think that simply jacking up the investment rate will solve anything.

CONCLUSION

In developing this critique of some standard explanations of Britain's past decline and present malaise, it should not be suggested that these explanations are completely without merits. The thesis of 'entrepreneurial failure', for example, is the subject of continuing debate among economic historians. Though it would be rash to predict the outcome of the debate, since there is much research still to be done, it could be argued that the idea that the British economy 'failed' is in some sense correct. And while it is probably also true that the blame for this cannot be pinned on entrepreneurs, there may nevertheless be managerial problems in British industry in the modern era. As for trades unions, while one may feel sceptical about the 'overmanning' idea, it would be foolish to claim that they bear no responsibility for the messy problems of the British industrial relations scene. But even if they are seen as incompetently led, obsessed with short-run questions, and blind to the effects of their actions on fellow workers this hardly means – as criticisms of the 'overmanning' thesis indicated – that they have caused long-run decline, industrial collapse, and deepening unemployment. It seems sensible to see industrial relations problems in much the same way it was suggested we view low investment: as an effect rather than as a cause of Britain's economic difficulties.

So none of these factors – entrepreneurship, industrial relations, investment – can be dismissed as problem areas within the British economy. On the contrary, they involve complex and seemingly intractable problems which must be overcome. The point, rather, is that the stories which are based on them do not stand up as single all-encompassing explanations of Britain's decline into crisis. We should have a care, therefore, not only with the explanations, but also with the panaceas which people are prone to base on them. The most important victims of simplistic explanations of Britain's problems are Britain's political parties. The Conservative project of 'restoring the balance of power in industrial relations', and the pride it takes in what is so brutally called the 'shake-out' of labour (i.e. increased unemployment), which is alleged to have reduced overmanning, is heavily based on the naiveties of the overmanning thesis which have been criticized above. The emphasis within recent Labour programmes on raising levels of investment is similarly short-sighted, quite neglecting the fact that investment rates by themselves explain very little. The tragic consequence of all this has been a concentration by British politicians on economic issues which are to greater or lesser extents peripheral to our real and urgent problems; in effect, they have not seen the wood for the trees. If the crisis is to be resolved, therefore, future policies must abandon what might politely be called the 'indirectness' of past and present policy measures. Policies should be based on a much more realistic assessment of our future prospects, and of the mechanisms which have made them so bleak. Furthermore, they should be aimed at the most direct possible solution of those problems.

Industrial Recovery: The Policy Problems

As British oil output declines in the late 1980s and through the 1990s, only a major expansion of some other export sector or sectors will prevent a stark decline in the level of real income in Britain. Failure to expand non-oil exports will lead to a more or less drastic depreciation of the exchange rate. Certainly this will make some British exports more competitive, but it will do so only to the extent that British costs – meaning primarily wages – do not rise in response to the increased prices of imports such as food. In addition, Britain's import bill will presumably fall as the falling exchange rate makes imports more expensive. But these mechanisms for maintaining balance of payments equilibrium have a real adjustment process underlying them, namely decreased consumption and decreased standards of living for the British population as a whole. The burden of the British crisis will then no longer be borne only by the unemployed; it will be felt by everyone.

Avoiding further falls in income, and alleviating Britain's chronic unemployment, requires growth in industries capable of both exporting and competing with imports inside Britain. We cannot hope for such an expansion in service industries such as financial services, tourism and transport which have provided the bulk of Britain's 'invisible' earnings in the past, for reasons which were elaborated in Chapter 5: these are not major growth sectors in the world economy, and in each of them Britain faces intensive competition. Britain's recovery therefore depends on a revival of manufacturing, for in this sector, although competition is intense, world demand and world trade are growing.

But such a revival seems very unlikely to occur as things stand: there is no sign of the large-scale increases in innovative and investment activity which would be required *now* for any recovery in the late 1980s or early 1990s (since there are significant lead times involved in most industrial manufacturing projects). Nor is it likely that such increases will occur on the necessary scale in the slowly growing British economy of the middle and late 1980s, since investment rarely expands in an environment of recession and depressed demand. Manufacturing recovery must therefore be engineered; that is to say, it must become a primary objective of economic policy.

But to say that the overriding priority for economic policy in coming years should be a reconstruction of Britain's manufacturing capability begs a number of difficult questions. To what extent, for example, can such a project actually be an objective of economic policy? What kinds of economic and institutional obstacles stand in the way of carrying it out? Are the available policy instruments adequate for the task; and if not, what kinds of measures are needed?

Policies for industrial reconstruction face two kinds of difficulties in economies like Britain. In the first place there are *economic* problems, to do with the economic mechanisms by which decentralized, private-enterprise market economies actually generate increased industrial investment and growth. Secondly, there are problems of *policy instruments*: the measures, powers and institutions through which the government can affect the economy, and which constrain the kinds of effects it can produce. When these economic and instrumental problems are examined against the background of Britain's problems, the need for new types of policy and new types of institution to carry them out begins to emerge.

THE ECONOMICS
OF INDUSTRIAL INVESTMENT

If output, employment and incomes are to grow in Britain, then the problems of low and poorly directed R & D activity, and low industrial investment, which are at the core of Britain's economic decline must be overcome. However, as we saw in Chapter 10, investment tends to follow growth in incomes and expenditure, not precede them. Enterprises invest in order to satisfy the demand generated by increases in income, they do not aim at generating income increases via investment.

In practical terms this means that as economies move out of recession, expanding consumption usually precedes expanding investment; these expansions of consumption demand are in effect the signal which tells enterprises that it is worthwhile to invest once again. In a market economy, in which all enterprises make investment decisions in isolation from each other, there are no general incentives other than demand expansion which will provoke investment increases.

This is why there is a fundamental difference between the growth patterns of capitalist and socialist economies. Socialist economies do possess a central planning institution which tells enterprises when and how much to invest: thus economic growth in those societies is 'investment-led'. This is why, historically, they have had both a good growth and employment record, but also a poor record on the provision of consumption goods: beginning with the process of investment means that incomes are being generated (i.e. for workers in the investment projects) before consumption goods are produced as the end-product of that investment. Maintaining high investment levels has thus meant that incomes have consistently outrun available consumption goods in those societies – hence the coexistence of high growth, high employment, steady income growth, and shortages.

It is another story in capitalist economies. Here, 'investment-led' growth tends to be the exception: not unknown, but rare. Rather, growth is initiated by an expansion of demand elsewhere. This need not be in consumption expenditure: 'export-led' growth has historically been very important, both in Britain (where our early nineteenth-century industrialization was fed by massive export demand) and in other economies. But in practice, particularly in the post-war era, attempts to stimulate growth in Britain and elsewhere have taken the form of policies to stimulate consumption demand, in the hope that investment would respond. The idea was to create a 'virtuous circle' of growth; increases in consumption leading to increases in investment, leading to increases in productivity and incomes, leading to further consumption increases and so on. For many years and in many countries, this more or less worked. But now we are trapped in a 'vicious circle' of decline. The question is, how to break out of it?

The main difficulty is that consumption-led growth appears not to be on the cards. This is because Britain's manufacturing performance is so poor that consumption increases have not fed through into increased demand for British products, and hence to investment in British industry. Consumption increases have been spent quite disproportionately on imports, especially of manufactures: as the British economy returned to slow growth in 1983, it was noticeable that increases in consumers' expenditure had no effect on British manufacturing output. It is therefore not open to British policy makers to engineer industrial reconstruction and investment via a consumption boom.

Unfortunately, the problem is not simply that we cannot stimulate renewed economic growth by a direct expansion of consumption in the economy. It would not necessarily help to act on investment, either. It has been emphasized above that in the normal operation of capitalist market economies investment tends to follow the expansion of consumption demand. But this has not prevented governments from attempting to act on investment. On the contrary, they have adopted a wide range of measures to increase investment, ranging from tax concessions to subsidies and so on. And such measures have had some effect. The problem, however, as previous chapters have emphasized, is not simply the amount of investment, but also the productivity of that investment. The fact is that investment in Britain has not produced the same increases in output that it has in other economies: it has not been as effective. This is because the projects in which investment has been embodied have not had the degree of research and development input which generates the design and production quality on which real market success is based. The fundamental British problem lies not at the point of investment, but much further back: at the R & D stage, when products are planned and the marketing and investment strategies for them are developed. As David Stout has put it:

In an economy in which relatively slow growth and declining manufacturing competitiveness are a century-old problem, spread across almost every sector, it is tedious but necessary to find out what has gone wrong market by market, and to direct policy to the recapturing of demand. Investment has its place in the vicious circle of slow growth, but it is not the right place to *break into* the circle when the productivity of existing capital is low.[1]

The central tasks are in the fields of product design, technological standards, and production quality. They are, in other words, not in the area of investment but rather in the development of projects which are worthy of investment. For this, however, the available policy instruments are inadequate.

INSTRUMENTS OF POLICY

These considerations suggest that the focus of economic policies for reconstruction should be quite limited – on the formation of viable projects within the manufacturing sector – yet those policies must also have economy-wide effect. Now although it is not unheard of for countries to adopt policies restricted to small groups of industries, yet which have large-scale effects – Chapter 12 describes such a policy – it is in fact unusual. Certainly Britain has no experience of such policies, at least in peace time. Rather, policies which have significant effects on the overall level of income tend to be general in scope and diffuse in impact. In the economic jargon, such policies are aggregative, meaning that they operate on the whole economy as an aggregate. In Britain, economic policy making is concentrated either on fiscal policies – which concern government tax and expenditure decisions, and are presented in the Budget each March – or monetary policy, which primarily affects interest rates. These policies affect everyone: they expand or contract incomes over the whole economy or a large part of it. Such policies form the centrepiece of both Keynesian and monetarist economic strategies, and are the main policy legacy of the doctrines discussed in Part Two of this book. Their limitations begin from the fact that they can break into the vicious circle of decline at one point only: that of demand. In practice they boil down to policies of deflation (monetarism) or reflation (Keynesianism). Now while it is true that the choice between these two strategies is an important one – it is difficult to see any recovery being sustained in a deflationary policy environment – it is also the case that the instruments with which they work are not suitable for solving Britain's industrial problems. Growth and reconstruction in specific, limited parts of the UK economy cannot be promoted with general policy instruments. What is needed is a specific policy instrument to enhance the supply potential of the manufacturing sector: an industrial policy.

AN INDUSTRIAL POLICY

'Industrial policy' refers to the whole complex of measures, instruments and institutions which has as its focus the *structure of industry* (that is, the kinds of sectors and activities, and their relative sizes), the *composition of output* (the types of products being produced), and the *technological basis* of industry. Like many countries, Britain has had some sort of industrial policy for many years. What it has not had, and what it requires, is an industrial policy to which all other government policy preoccupations are subordinated; which has clearly articulated objectives for reconstruction; which is adequately funded and staffed; and which has powers sufficient to attain the objectives which are set for it. This is not, it should be emphasized, an argument for a central planning agency on the Eastern European model. It is an argument for a coordinating agency of the type possessed, in some form or another, by all of the fast-growing economies of the post-war era.

The objectives of such a policy are implicit in the analysis presented in Part One of this book. If that analysis is even half-way correct, then Britain faces something akin to external collapse over the next decade or so. It may take five years to occur, it may take fifteen or even more: precise prediction would be rash. But as oil disappears, Britain's already low levels of income will decline catastrophically; the many effects of this will include an enforced contraction of such publicly funded institutions as the National Health Service. So the first objective of policy can be put very bluntly, and by itself it will be enormously difficult. It is to stave off this disaster.

From this follows the primary task for economic and industrial policy: averting disaster means developing a nucleus of industries whose technological levels and product ranges will enable them to survive and prosper in the competitive trading markets of the world. As oil declines in the 1990s, they must generate an increase in manufactured exports at a rate determined by the rate at which oil revenues are falling.

Maintenance of Britain's income levels while oil declines is, however, but a preliminary task. Long-term prosperity for Britain requires that existing income levels are not merely sustained, but are significantly raised. So the industries which are developed in the disaster-averting phase of reconstruction must support Britain's external accounts during a second round of reconstruction, in which the technological level and productivity of a range of subordinate, domestic, industries is substantially enhanced.

However, although the construction of a group of dynamic, externally oriented manufacturing industries is perhaps no more than a preliminary on the way to the solution of other, more serious problems, it is nevertheless the condition on which all else is based. The central problems for such a construction project lie in the field of product design, technological level, and standards of production. They are not in the field of investment, but rather in the area of generating projects which are worthy of investment. Of course, raising the funds and resources for large-scale investment will be difficult in itself. But first it is necessary to solve the problem of what to invest in. How can this be done?

A RECONSTRUCTION AGENCY

What is needed is an interventionary apparatus which will coordinate and fund, in collaboration with enterprises, a substantial programme of research and development in an integrated range of products. It must then translate these programmes into investment projects, which it will carry out. This work has six major aspects, which one government agency should oversee. They are:

- the scientific and technological aspects of industrial construction;
- the commercial appraisal of prospective projects (in which the expertise of businesses in assessing the commercial viability of projects will be crucial);
- the investment programme, in particular its timing, and the integration of one project with another;
  the financial aspects of investment, that is the provision of funds on an adequate scale and over adequate time periods;

– labour provision and training;

– finally the macroeconomic implications – it will be necessary for all these activities to be carried out within a well-worked-out conception of their macroeconomic consequences.

The task of a reconstruction agency need not be – in fact, cannot be – to carry out all of these tasks itself. In each of these areas there are adequate existing institutions, some of which will need to be expanded substantially. The central function of a reconstruction agency carrying out an industrial policy should be coordination and, where necessary, direction. Where other institutions are involved, their activities should be clearly subordinated to the overall needs of the industrial policy.

An industrial policy of this type, and a powerful government agency to carry it out, are perfectly feasible for Britain, as they have been for a number of successful economies over the past thirty years. Yet many in Britain have ignored examples from abroad, and have maintained serious objections to industrial policies. How valid are those objections?

OBJECTIONS TO INDUSTRIAL POLICY

In Britain there is a strong tradition that policies of industrial intervention are at best useless and at worst positively harmful; a great deal has been heard of such arguments in recent years, since they reflect the views held by the government. Three sorts of argument are advanced. The first – a very abstract one – is based on the kinds of free-market economic thinking outlined in Chapter 6. It alleges, on theoretical grounds which are rarely adequately spelled out, that since free-market economies tend towards optimal mixes and levels of output, it is folly to intervene in them. This 'optimality' property of capitalist economies is produced by individuals and firms reacting to the prices which are established in competitive markets. Since any intervention is going to alter those prices – by definition, since it aims at doing something the price mechanism is not already doing – then it will also make the optimal mix and level of output impossible to achieve.

The second argument varies this original argument by concentrating on those who would make the crucial decisions in an industrial policy. These people, it is held, will be civil servants. But why should bureaucrats be better at making economic decisions than businessmen? How are bureaucrats likely to have the information, the incentives, the experience, to make better decisions than industrial professionals? In fact, it is argued, there are no grounds for thinking that they will be more efficient, more forward looking, more entrepreneurial, than existing managers. Since industrial policy involves control by bureaucrats it should be rejected on efficiency grounds.

The final type of argument is more practical. It looks at industries where there has been considerable state intervention in Britain, and argues that they are characterized by inefficiency, inflexibility and waste. Industries such as steel and coal have been badly led, inflexible in response to changing circumstances, and have in consequence required massive subsidies. The story can be extended into other state-run industries such as shipbuilding and airlines; even where state-owned industries are profitable – such as British Telecom – they are argued to be considerably less efficient (in terms of providing services) than their free-market equivalents elsewhere (such as the Bell telephone network in the USA).

None of these arguments seem convincing, though all require an answer. Some of the problems of the free-market approach have been spelled out in Chapter 6. In the first place, such arguments almost invariably obscure the conditions which are necessary to make free-market systems deliver the goods: those conditions are so restrictive as never to be met in practice. At the theoretically abstract level at which this argument is made, there is in fact no great distinction to be made between free-market systems and planned systems. It is possible within economic theory to show that planned, interventionist economies can deliver exactly the same results, or better, than decentralized market systems. On a purely theoretical basis economic theory produces no presumption whatsoever in favour of free markets as opposed to intervention. Moreover, there are a wide variety of theories which claim that the isolated activities of individuals can always be improved upon by non-market forms of cooperation and collaboration – these approaches tend to draw on the insights of 'game theory' in the analysis of economic problems. Surely the reasonable conclusion here is that this argument cannot be resolved purely at the level of abstract theory.

On the question of bureaucrats running industries, there is certainly a problem. It can be agreed that bureaucrats are unlikely to run industries well, though they could hardly run them worse than some of Britain's free-enterprise businessmen. But the real point is, why should it be presumed that an interventionist industrial policy requires civil servants to run industry? The function of an industrial policy must be to provide coordination, collaboration and support, not to replace one set of managers with another. This point is very well put by Christopher Freeman:

> This is of course the strength of the 'free enterprise' argument – that only the managers of the firms in each sector have enough detailed knowledge and experience to make good decisions. The argument for the flexibility, speed and initiative of decentralised entrepreneurship remains extremely strong whether in private, public or mixed enterprises. No one should underestimate the dangers of bureaucratic delay and bungling often associated with over-centralisation. But in our view this does not absolve government from some responsibility for long-run strategy for investment and technology in each sector of the economy. Central overall responsibility needs to be combined with decentralised initiative in all mature industrial societies, whether capitalist or socialist, and we have to find a practical solution, not one based on doctrinaire positions.[2]

The final assertion, that state direction has in practice been a disaster in such British industries as steel, coal, airlines, shipbuilding and so on, is also problematical. Again it can be agreed that much of the British experience since the Second World War is a lesson in how not to carry out policies of industrial intervention. There have been two central mistakes. The first was to concentrate substantial economic support on essentially declining industries. Far too much in resources and effort has been devoted to a fruitless effort to prop up industries whose future was limited in any case, rather than attempting to promote other industries whose output and employment would substitute for those in decline. As indicated in Chapter 2, economic growth consists of transformations in the economy, and declining industries are as much a part of that process as emerging ones. The second mistake – though the word 'mistake' rather understates things – has been in the quality of the interventionist decisions which were made. The disastrous histories of Concorde and the nuclear power programme do not need repetition here: the main point is that the crucial decisions were made on the basis of fantasies about Britain's economic and political place in the world, rather than according to commercial and economic criteria. In the discussion of Britain's R & D record in Chapter 4 it was suggested that these types of errors were particularly significant in Britain because of the degree of government involvement in the provision and control of R & D resources.

The existence of these problems does not, however, indicate that there is no case for government industrial policy. It indicates the need for much more carefully considered programmes of such intervention. That is, the problems outlined above constitute an argument against a particular type of industrial policy; they are not an argument against industrial policy as such. Similarly, the argument for increased government involvement in, and support for research and development is not vitiated by the fact that it is the government which is largely responsible for Britain's R & D disaster in the 1950s and 1960s. The problem there lay in the principles on which the government intervened, not that intervention itself, as Freeman has pointed out:

... the major misallocation of government R & D expenditures in military, nuclear and aircraft applications over the past thirty years does not invalidate the general case for government sponsorship and encouragement of new technology, based on economic as opposed to prestige and military criteria.[3]

Force is added to these points if we bear in mind that virtually all of Britain's more successful competitors operate active industrial policies which, to greater or lesser degrees, and in a variety of forms, are of the type which has been advocated above. If industrial policies are doomed to failure, one is therefore tempted to ask, why are they such a conspicuous feature of the policy apparatus in West Germany, Sweden, France and above all Japan, the most successful country of the post-war period? Perhaps the simplest way of suggesting that policies of industrial reconstruction and intervention can work is indeed to point to the case of Japan, an economy which is in many respects similar to Britain. Chapter 12 consists, therefore, of a description and discussion of the activities of the Ministry of International Trade and Industry (MITI) in Japan, an institution whose economic role and long-term effects have been of central importance in promoting Japan's post-war growth.

Behind the Japanese Miracle

This chapter describes the contribution of economic and industrial policy, and of one industrial ministry in particular, to the extraordinary growth of modern Japan. Most of us in the West are familiar with the outlines of that growth, and with some of the paradoxes it has produced. Where 'Made in Japan' was once such a symbol of cheap, imitative and shoddy products that it became almost a catch-phrase – connoting both inferiority and presumption – it now stands for the highest standards of quality and reliability. Where once the Americans paternally fostered Japan's post-war reconstruction, they now stand aghast at the competitor which has emerged. Rates of growth of output and productivity in Japan are the highest ever recorded by a capitalist economy (they have been matched in the post-war world only by the Soviet Union) and moreover have been maintained over very long periods. Between 1960 and 1978 Japan's national income grew at over 8 per cent per year; at the end of that period annual income was over 400 per cent of its 1960 level. In 1980, while Britain's manufacturing output fell 10 per cent, Japan's rose by 6 per cent.

This growth success manifests itself in Japanese domination of a wide range of markets. As we all know, in certain consumer products, Japanese firms virtually have the field to themselves: in cameras, video recorders, motorcycles, audio equipment and so on. But Japan is equally innovative and successful in industrial technologies such as machine tools (particularly 'numerically', i.e. electronically, controlled tools), special steels, chemicals, plastics, special-function ships and newer technologies like industrial robots and fibre optics. In cars and trucks, many national industries – including the British – exist only

214 · THE BRITISH ECONOMIC CRISIS

on Japanese sufferance. Japanese manufacturers voluntarily restrict their exports of vehicles, since both they and the Western governments who pressure them into it know that with unrestricted free trade they would decimate the car firms of the West.

This economic growth has been based on unrelenting transformation of the economy, on the structural and technical changes which were identified in Chapter 2 as the basis of industrial growth. In the 1950s Japan produced and exported the labour-intensive products of the few consumer industries which had existed in the pre-war world and survived the chaos of the war: textiles, clothing, simple metal manufactures, shoes, toys and so on. In the late 1950s the focus of the industrial drive shifted on to more technically advanced and capital-intensive industries and products: synthetic fibres, motorbikes, ships, petrochemicals, cameras. In the 1970s these technologies were extended into new product groups such as cars and domestic appliances, as well as electrical and electronic products such as television and stereo equipment. In the late 1970s came another change of direction, into the widespread application of electronic and microelectronic technologies: video equipment, computers large and small, robots, numerically controlled machine tools. In each of these areas – with the possible exception of computers, though here the situation is still unclear – Japan is world leader.

This success may hold lessons for Britain, since it has occurred in an economy which has faced and overcome problems not too dissimilar from those which confront Britain today. Like Britain, Japan is a small, heavily populated island group, with a resource base inadequate for industrial production, and a consequent need to import food and raw materials. Like Britain, its national income is heavily dependent on its export success; like Britain it must generate a trade surplus in manufactures. Unlike Britain it has been successful in doing so. But just as Japan's success is unique, so are the policy methods and institutions which it has brought to bear on its problems. The post-war economic success of Japan has been that of an economy guided and managed by the state to a degree unparalleled in modern capitalism. If we are to learn anything from Japan, it must be from its techniques of industrial policy.

THE BACKGROUND
TO JAPANESE GROWTH

A major difficulty in thinking about Japanese economic performance lies in disentangling the effects of particular policies and institutions (which might be transplanted elsewhere) from the specific and distinctive cultural traits of Japan (which are unlikely to be exportable). If it is the latter which are responsible for Japan's economic success, then there may be no useful lessons to be learned.

Sorting out these issues of policy as against culture is very difficult for a Western observer. European images of Japan, as Endymion Wilkinson pointed out in detail in his *Japan versus Europe*, involve a very complex set of conceptions and images. There are ideas of Oriental exoticism which evoke aesthetic admiration from some and racial contempt from others; there are images of a feudal warrior society becoming a modern militarist power still embodying the samurai values of its feudal past; there are ideas of a people at once culturally refined and capable of great cruelty. Some of these conceptions are foolish, no doubt, but some more or less accurately depict features of a society with very different cultural forms and traditions.

As Japan has emerged as a major world economic power there have been many who have ascribed its success to the way in which some of these supposed cultural features have been filtered into the economy. One of these factors – alleged to have a number of economic manifestations – has attracted considerable attention in the West. We might call it 'mutual commitment'. It is suggested that although Japanese society is hierarchical, having economic and social divisions like most societies, these divisions are submerged beneath a sense of cultural sameness, an identification of interests above and beyond personal interests. Great mutual loyalty springs out of this, and it has considerable economic consequences. In the first place, it makes possible consensus policies organized around a national interest. But its most striking manifestations are found within the Japanese enterprise, which has two quite distinctive features.

The first of these features is the so-called 'lifetime contract', an undertaking by firms to guarantee jobs until retirement for their workers; as a formal commitment, this is almost completely absent from the Western industrial scene. At the same time there is an exceptional degree of loyalty by workers to the firm. Workers feel a primary loyalty to the employing company: they sing company songs, wear company uniforms, and so on. The climate of industrial and social harmony which results from all this is, we are sometimes told, the crucial determinant of Japan's extraordinary performance.

To these advantages of cultural and economic nationalism and a docile workforce can be added other features, largely historical. The importance of very large corporations (*zaibatsu*), for example, which have long dominated the production system; and the close cooperation between such firms and the Japanese state which was a feature of Japanese industrialization following the Meiji restoration in 1868.

It would be difficult, I think, to overestimate the importance which Westerners attach to such specifically Japanese cultural and social phenomena when they seek to understand Japanese growth. And it is not only Westerners: Professor Morishima of the London School of Economics, in his book *Why Has Japan Succeeded?*, ascribes exceptional importance to the 'Japanese ethos', and traces it back to the way in which Confucian religious ideas were modified in the course of their import into Japan from China. 'While Chinese Confucianism is one in which benevolence is of central importance,' he writes, 'Japanese Confucianism is loyalty-centred Confucianism.'

Now while it would be foolish to deny that cultural differences can and do have important economic effects, it does seem that there are many problems in looking to such factors as the primary cause of Japan's growth performance. Although the whole matter is a very complex one, two issues are particularly important. The first is whether this mutual loyalty, and consequently social harmony, really are a general feature of the Japanese economy and society, or whether they are in fact relatively recent developments which stand in need of explanation. The second question is whether the apparently unique Japanese enterprise relationships (lifetime contracts/worker loyalty) explain Japan's performance, or whether they could equally well be seen as effects – rather than causes – of that perfomance. More generally, do we need these 'culturalist' explanations, or can everything be well explained by economic factors of a rather more ordinary kind?

Consider first the question of whether Japan really is a society of mutual commitment, of consensus, of social harmony. One might question whether it is a harmonious society today – given, for example, the organized violence associated with the protests over the second Tokyo airport – but it certainly was not in the fairly recent past. The inter-war years, as Robert Reich has pointed out,

were marked by bitter struggles between factions in the army and navy, between the military and the large industrial groups called zaibatsu, between tenant farmers and landlords. Trade unions were suppressed by the authorities. Lifetime employment had little meaning in an industrial system in which most factory employees were young female textile operators whose working lives were two to three years, and in which half the population were poor peasants. National industrial policies were barely able to maintain stability after the financial panic of 1927, the invasion of Manchuria in 1931, the fascist attack on capitalism in the 1930s, the war with China from 1937 to 1941, the Pacific war, the economic collapse of 1946, the post-Korean war recession of 1954.[1]

The general picture which emerges of Japanese society prior to the beginnings of the 'economic miracle' is one of a factionally and socially divided system. It prompts the thought that it is economic growth which makes possible the emergence of a consensus, not vice versa.

Similar points might be made about the distinctive features of Japanese enterprises. Such phenomena as lifetime contracts are made possible by Japanese industrial success, they are not the basis of it. They are not an option open to Western managers, given the insecurity of their economic environment, and the risks which their enterprises face. Lifetime contracts are best viewed as an expression, by Japanese managers, of confidence in continued growth, an expression of a belief that they do not face significant risks which threaten their corporate future. The real question is, why do Japanese corporate managers feel this way? What is it about their economic environment which promotes their confidence? And while worker loyalty may well be part of the 'Japanese ethos', we should remember that economic security, and particularly employment security, is very highly valued by people everywhere; once workers are guaranteed a degree of security, their loyalty to the firm that provides it may not be all that surprising.

In other words we may not need notions of cultural and national solidarity, or the idea of a 'Japan Incorporated' to which they give rise, to understand Japan's growth record. Rather we need to look at the economic environment within which Japanese firms operate, an environment which is set by the government. There are two aspects to this policy environment. The first is the general macroeconomic policy framework, which will be described only briefly. The second, much more important, is industrial policy and the activities of the ministry which carries it out.

THE JAPANESE POLICY FRAMEWORK

The general approach by Japanese policy makers has three distinctive features. The first is a firm rejection of some orthodox ideas on international trade, concerning both the types of goods which Japan should be producing and exporting, and the desirability of free trade as opposed to protection and import controls. The second is an equally firm commitment to the expansionary demand-management ideas associated with the economics of Keynes. This has taken the form not so much of the public expenditure programmes with which we are familiar in the West, as tax and expenditure policies designed to encourage investment (including government investment); but monetary policies also have been managed with an eye to maintaining low interest rates and easily available credit for investment. The final aspect is a kind of two-faced attitude to competition within the economy: in general the Japanese economy has combined a high degree of government intervention with the promotion of competition. Competition has been encouraged where it was felt that this would enhance efficiency; but it has been firmly discouraged where it would threaten the prospects for growth. More will be said about this – in the shape of concrete examples – below.

All of these areas are of great interest, but one which deserves further comment, especially in the light of Britain's trade problems, is international trade policy. It is necessary to begin here by saying something about the basic economic theory of trade.

The theory of international trade has generated perhaps the most consistently successful economic 'law' of all time (successful, that is, in terms of its acceptance by economists and politicians): the law of comparative advantage. Without going into details, the theory of comparative advantage is held to demonstrate three related points. The first is that countries should not produce all the types of goods which they are capable of producing, but rather should specialize. Specifically, they should specialize in lines of production where they have a relative cost advantage. This does not mean goods in which a country has an absolute cost advantage, but rather in goods whose costs compared to more expensive lines are lowest, compared with competitors. Secondly, these costs will be determined by the relative availability of labour and capital; specifically, countries with a substantial amount of capital should specialize in capital-intensive goods, while countries with a large volume of labour should specialize in labour-intensive goods. Finally, countries should engage in free international trade – completely unrestricted by tariffs or other barriers – in the products of the resulting specialization. If these precepts are followed, world output, consumption and welfare will be maximized. Such propositions are, therefore, an essential underpinning for the doctrine of free trade which is such a major component of free-market economics.

But though it has been widely accepted and admired (Paul Samuelson, challenged to produce an example of a proposition in any social science which was both true and non-trivial, answered, 'the theory of comparative advantage'), the doctrine has always had its critics. There have been two principal lines of objection. The first is that if it was followed to the letter it would be likely to cement countries inside an existing division of international activities which they might not find to their long-term benefit. The second is that free trade makes it very difficult to establish and build new industries where that industry already exists, at a more advanced level, in other countries. The already existing industry is likely to have a competitive advantage – since firms' costs tend to decrease both with time and with size – and there have always been, therefore, arguments in support of the protection of 'infant industries'.

The free-trade doctrine was rejected by the Japanese economic administration throughout the post-war period, but particularly during the years of construction. Discussing the decisions of that period, Mr Y. Ojima, vice-minister for International Trade and Industry, said that it was

> decided to establish in Japan industries which required intensive employment of capital and technology, industries that in consideration of comparative costs of production should be the most inappropriate for Japan, industries such as steel, oil refining, petrochemicals, automobiles, aircraft, industrial machinery of all sorts, and electronics including electronic computers. From a short-run, static viewpoint, encouragement of such industries would seem to conflict with economic rationalism. But from a long-range viewpoint, these are precisely the industries where . . . demand is high, technological progress is rapid, and labour productivity rises fast.[2]

This attempt to construct a new industrial basis for Japan's trading position in the world was accompanied by a range of import controls to protect these industries in their formative period.

But while it is one thing to set out the kind of industrial objectives listed by Mr Ojima, and to provide the trade and domestic policies to back them up, it is quite another thing actually to set up the industries. That required another set of policies and a specific institution to carry them out. We turn to that now, for it is here that we can find the main determinant of Japan's growth success.

MITI: THE MINISTRY OF INTERNATIONAL TRADE AND INDUSTRY

It is difficult to exaggerate the importance of the Ministry of International Trade and Industry (MITI) in Japan's economic success, or the extent of its activities. MITI is responsible in Japan for the development and coordination of the main industrial sectors, and in particular those concerned with manufactured exports. Since its foundation in 1949 MITI has guided and in some cases controlled the import and use of foreign technology, the availability of foreign currency to firms, the process of research and development, the collection and exchange of technical information between firms, the number of firms in particular industries and the entry of new firms into industries, the expansion or contraction of whole industries, the availability of investment funds for firms from the Japan Development Bank and private banks, the application of monopoly and competition policy, the development of tax measures to promote growth, and long-range programmes of research in advanced technologies. It has also produced regular growth projections which form the basis of economic policy decisions by government in coordination with other ministries, and has played an important role in setting pay and income norms around which firms and unions negotiate.

It should not be assumed from this list of activities and powers that MITI is all powerful, either with respect to firms in the economy, or other ministries. It attempted to consolidate the car industry around Nissan and Toyota, for example, and failed. It has been in repeated conflict with the government's Fair Trading Commission, which has limited some of its activities. Moreover, its statutory powers are quite limited, and there are a number of major industries in which it has had little involvement. Nevertheless, its impact has been very great. The following sections describe the objectives and functions of MITI, its structure and its methods; finally, a concrete example of its role in one particular industry is given.

Objectives and tasks

'Industrial policy,' remarks the Japanese economist Ryutaro Komiya, 'is government policy that changes the allocation of resources among industries, or the levels of certain types of productive activity among firms within individual industries. It is designed to encourage production, investment, research and development, modernization and reorganization in some industries and not in others.'[3] The primary objective of MITI is to use such a policy to promote economic growth of a type which will also generate a substantial balance of trade surplus in manufactures.

Structure

MITI consists of a central secretariat made up of nine bureaux, each of which has a number of sub-agencies. All are well staffed by highly qualified civil servants. (Ronald Dore remarks on MITI's 'ability to recruit from the very brightest of the nation's talented graduates. Many of those recruits will have classmates in leading industrial firms, and career lines from the MITI bureaucracy can also run into leading positions in politics and public or private corporations.'[4])

Five of the bureaux deal with broad industry groups: heavy industry, chemicals, textiles, coal and mining, and public utilities; they are, as Komiya remarks, 'the real makers of industrial policy'. There is a sub-agency for each particular industry within these broad industry bureaux. Thus the Heavy Industry Bureau has agencies for steel, machine tools, cars, electronics, aircraft, railway equipment, and so on: the list is a very full one. As well as the five industry bureaux, there are four which deal with policy areas; they are the Bureaux of International Trade, Trade Development, Enterprises and Pollution and Safety. In collaboration with the minister's personal secretariat these bureaux work on general policy guidelines for the ministry as a whole.

Corresponding to each MITI bureau and sub-agency are powerful industry associations, with representatives from all of the important firms in each industry. Each industry association has close links with the appropriate MITI sub-agency. Policy is not, therefore, made within MITI alone: it is made in a process of continuous interaction between MITI and the appropriate industry association. To this interaction businessmen bring the expertise and detailed knowledge which few bureaucracies are able to gather or assess. But MITI brings something which few businessmen are able to develop: an understanding of the technical and economic links between a developing firm or industry and other industries, and of the links between particular industries and the wider development of the economy.

Finally, MITI has a number of specialist advisory councils, which bring in wider expertise on specific problems. They are, says Naoto Sasaki, 'composed of experts in matters deliberated by the respective councils, leaders of the industrial communities concerned, general consumers, leaders of the financial community, and talents from a wide variety of social strata such as workers, educators, mass media specialists and experts from the government agencies and offices concerned'.[5] The number of these councils varies: in 1970, for example, there were twenty-seven. It is generally agreed that their reports are extremely influential in the formation of policy and legislation.

The final link in the structure of industrial policy formation is the banks. The most important of these is the government-owned Japan Development Bank, but private banks with loan commitments to particular industries also take part in the collaboration between the MITI sub-agency and the relevant industry association. As we shall see, the MITI relationship with the financial system is an important mechanism of its industrial control.

Methods of policy implementation

The particular measures available to MITI have changed over the years, as the economy has grown and changed its structure, and as the problems facing it have changed also. The following account concentrates, therefore, not so much on measures which are necessarily in use at this moment as on the broad spectrum of measures which have been used over the whole of Japan's reconstruction and growth period. Over these years MITI has had six types of policy instrument available to it. They were and are as follows.

1. The ability to control the import and use of foreign technologies. Over a long period, any firm wishing to use a foreign patent had to obtain MITI approval on a case by case basis. But also, during the years of foreign currency shortage, MITI had the power to allocate foreign currency for technology imports, and thus to control the types of technology which were imported.

2. The ability to modify competition and monopoly policy within any sector, and thus to control the number and size of firms in that sector. Competition often increases efficiency, but it can also increase risk, which inhibits the long-term investments needed for growth. MITI has always promoted growth at the expense of competition. But at the same time MITI has promoted the diffusion of new technologies from one firm to another – even where they are rivals – if this did not threaten the stability and growth of the industry.

3. The ability to enact regulations on tax incentives or subsidies in order to encourage particular industries.

4. The ability to draft and enact laws concerning import controls, tariff rates, export subsidies and foreign investment in Japan.

5. The ability to encourage and control particular investment projects by controlling the availability of funds for such projects, either

through the Japan Development Bank or through the private banks with which MITI has close links.

6. It can carry out particular research and development projects on its own account where these are not likely to be profitable for private firms within a reasonable time period. Such work has included, for example, major computer development projects; some recent priorities will be mentioned below.

These policy instruments are used vigorously and flexibly in many combinations in a wide variety of industrial circumstances. But MITI has four basic types of intervention, and it is an important point about Japanese industrial policy that all four are operated simultaneously. The first deals with the creation and sustenance of new industries, which, to the outside observer, has probably been the central aspect of Japan's post-war growth. Next are programmes of industry modernization, especially in sectors with a large number of small firms. Here MITI has encouraged the development of large-scale plants and enterprises, to reap the productivity benefits of economies of scale. Thirdly, there are policies to control capacity in particular industries, that is, to prevent excessive investment. Examples here include oil refining, petrochemicals and steel, all of which – at least in Japan, and for complex reasons – are prone to overcapacity. In many countries – including Britain – overcapacity has forced these industries into abrupt redundancies and the scrapping of capital equipment; MITI has consciously tried to prevent the emergence of such problems in Japan. Finally, by no means the least of MITI's intervention packages concerns declining industries. Policies here include subsidies over the period while industries are reduced in size or phased out, government purchase of obsolete equipment for scrapping, aid to workers in moving to other areas, and grants and subsidies for retraining. This is crucial to Japan's continued growth for, as suggested in Chapter 2, economies must manage the process of decline and de-industrialization at least as well as they manage the process of creating new industries. Both complement each other in economic growth.

Constructing a new industry: an example

This section draws on the work of Professor Terutomo Ozawa in describing MITI's role in the construction – or more accurately reconstruction – of the Japanese synthetic fibre industry. It points up a number of important aspects of MITI's role.

Japan developed a textile industry in the late nineteenth century on the basis of imported British technology. In the late 1930s the industry was shaken by the development of artificial fibres such as nylon and viscose in Britain, the USA and Germany. But patent information was quickly obtained from IG Farben in Germany, and during the Second World War a number of companies developed nylon production capacity. But the industry was shattered by the effects of the war: its personnel and production facilities were dispersed and more or less wiped out.

Both the American occupation administration and the Japanese government saw the rebuilding of the textile sector as an important aspect of post-war reconstruction. The task became one of the first undertaken by MITI (at that time called the Ministry of Commerce and Industry). The procedure it adopted became typical of its methods: it oversaw the import of foreign production technologies of the latest type from a range of foreign producers; it carefully selected the firms which would be allowed to enter the industry; it restricted entrants in the early phase of development (so as to maintain profits and reduce risk) but nevertheless maintained a definite programme of entry (so as to maintain competition and keep firms on their toes); it provided low interest loans to firms via the Japan Development Bank and other banks; it provided R & D backup to develop and improve the imported technologies; and it also promoted the development of domestic technologies.

All of these objectives are set out in MITI's policy document, published in May 1949, called 'A Policy for a Prompt Development of the Synthetic-Fibre Industry'. It is worth quoting at length, since it sets out a framework which has been followed many times since:

1. Objectives:
In the light of the export requirement of Japan's textile industry, it is imperative for the Government to foster the synthetic-fibre industry. Japan's technological capabilities in some synthetic fibres are already near the state of full-scale commercialization with a good prospect for developing trade competitiveness. In order to achieve the output goals of synthetic fibres set forth in Japan's Five-Year Economic Reconstruction Plan, capital

and technological resources shall be allocated in a concentrated manner so that plants of efficient size are constructed.

2. Measures:

a. As a first step, encouragement shall be given to the construction of plants for two types of new synthetic fibers, i.e. polyvinyl alcohol fibre (vinylon) and polyamide fibre (nylon).

b. One company shall be selected as a first-entrant firm for each of the fibres mentioned above, so that it can benefit from scale economies. As the market develops, other firms shall be assisted to enter the industry in tandem.

c. Preferential construction funds shall be provided on the condition that once a plant is complete and successfully operated, it shall be open to visits by other companies and research institutions (at some appropriate remuneration), so that newly acquired knowledge and experience are disseminated for the development of the synthetic-fibre industry.

d. In order to foster the second and subsequent entrant firms the Industrial Technology Agency of the Government shall guide and assist the development of alternative production technologies other than those used by the first entrant.

e. The development of those industries which supply raw materials and intermediate inputs for synthetic fibres shall be encouraged.[6]

Of the two fibres one (nylon) required imported technology, while the other (vinylon) was developed in Japan. Two firms were selected, one for each fibre. Toyo Rayon, the firm which would produce nylon, concluded a long-term licensing agreement with DuPont of the USA in 1951: for 300 million dollars it got the right to use the DuPont patent for fifteen years. But Toyo Rayon received relatively little in the way of detailed technical information – for its money it got 'only three sets of documents: patent documents, process specifications, and technical service manuals'. It ran into serious difficulties actually producing nylon of adequate quality. During this period, while the technical problems were being solved, MITI held off further entrants to the industry. But when Toyo Rayon moved into profit in 1954, it licensed another entrant, Nippon Rayon, this time using a Swiss technology.

Throughout these years MITI encouraged domestic research into the development of new artificial fibres – to lessen Japan's dependence on foreign technology – and also authorized a joint venture between Asahi Chemical and Dow of the USA to develop a new fibre called 'Saran'. At the same time it closely monitored developments abroad, the most significant of which was the development of polyester fibres by ICI. MITI quickly sponsored a Japanese producer of polyester, who made enormous profits; a number of other producers followed, using different types of polyester technology, in the 1960s. The pattern of development, and the wide variety of technology sources, can be seen in table 24. The general formula is for a pioneer entrant to be protected for several years, and then for a rapid entry of further firms:

Table 24. *Entry pattern of Japanese firms in synthetic fibres and their technology suppliers*

Company	Year of entry	Technology supplier
Toyo Rayon	1951	DuPont (USA)
Nippon Rayon	1954	Inventa AG (Switzerland)
Toyo Rayon/Teijin	1958	ICI (UK)
Kanegafuchi Spinning	1963	Snia Viscosa (Italy)
Teijin	1963	Allied Chemical (USA)
Kureha Spinning (merged into Toyobo in 1966)	1963	Hans J. Zimmer AG (West Germany)
Asahi Chemicals	1963	Firestone (USA)
Toyobo	1964	Chemtex (USA)
Kurashiki Rayon	1964	Chemistrand (USA)
Nippon Rayon	1964	Inventa AG (Switzerland)
Kanegafuchi Spinning	1967	Snia Viscosa (Italy)
Asahi Chemical	1969	Rohne-Poulenc SA (France)
Mitsubishi Rayon	1969	AKU (Netherlands) and Glanzstoff AG (West Germany)

Source: T. Ozawa, 'Government control of technology acquisition and firms' entry into new sectors: the experience of Japan's synthetic-fibre industry', *Cambridge Journal of Economics*, 1980, no. 4, pp. 139–41.

There have been, as Professor Ozawa notes,

many benefits from the strategy, with the staggered-entry formula particularly enhancing the Japanese firms' ability to absorb sophisticated foreign technologies. To be qualified as an early entrant, a firm had to demonstrate its technological and financial capabilities. Therefore the industrial groups competed in searching for new promising technologies, conducting preparatory research, finding an appropriate foreign licenser, and securing the necessary investment funds ... the staggered-entry formula also served to strengthen the bargaining position of Japanese firms in negotiating with technology suppliers, because only one (or, at most, a selected few) was permitted to enter a new industry at a time.[7]

Among the benefits of all this was the fact that Japanese firms were 'often able to come up with significant technological improvements' to the imported techniques. Certainly the results were impressive: Japan overtook Germany in the production of synthetic fibres in 1953, Britain in 1956, and became second only to the USA. Throughout the 1960s, output grew at nearly 27 per cent per year.

In the 1970s the world textile industry became more competitive and less profitable, particularly in advanced countries like Japan. MITI, unlike government agencies elsewhere, did not try to fight this, and encouraged a kind of planned decline of the industry. Some firms were encouraged to go out of fibres and into new products; others were encouraged to merge to decrease the number of firms in the industry. In the face of slowing demand, the Japanese economy has moved out of fibres and into other products with a flexibility notably absent from other economies – in particular Britain.

The 'MITI formula' of staggered entry, of substantial financial assistance, and of the use of a wide range of technology sources, can be traced in a number of successful Japanese industries. The above description of synthetic fibre development could easily be multiplied – well-known examples are petrochemicals, shipbuilding and alloy steels.

MITI AND
RESEARCH AND DEVELOPMENT

Earlier chapters emphasized the importance of industrial research and development (R & D) in generating the product and process innovations on which modern economic growth is based. How does the Japanese economy perform in this area, and what is the role of MITI in its research and innovative activity?

Throughout the 1950s and 1960s, in its period of reconstruction and then rapid growth, the Japanese economy relied heavily on technology imports; the above account of synthetic fibre development underlines this. It is important to recognize that the search for available foreign technologies is itself a research and development activity. Any search for new techniques is R & D, and the process of seeking out available and useful foreign techniques is part of this.

MITI played a crucial role in encouraging firms to search for the best foreign technologies. It had two specific powers which enabled it to affect the general technical direction taken by the economy: it could control import licences, and it could control the issue of foreign currency needed to pay for imports. It set specific guidelines for technology imports: in 1950, for example, MITI issued a list of thirty-three important technologies it wished to see imported and developed. All but three were technologies for heavy industry. Almost all were geared towards industries or processes which held out the prospect of export markets. It was not until the early 1960s that the emphasis shifted to consumer goods technologies. However, it should be noted that this control over imported technologies has not been a permanent feature of MITI's policy arsenal; it was used primarily in the 1950s and early 1960s, when Japan was very short of foreign exchange. As Japan began to generate large trade surpluses, and hence an ample supply of foreign currency, MITI's control over imports was no longer so necessary and was reduced.

Of course technologies can also be developed domestically; it is important to remember, as two recent writers have pointed out, that 'the usual emphasis on importing technology tends to obscure the fact that the Japanese economy is research intensive'. There are three significant features of this domestic R & D effort.

The first is that *none* of Japan's resources go into military R & D. It is claimed in Britain and the USA, both of which spend significant sums on military research, that such work produces important commercial 'spin-offs'. There appears, however, to be little in the way of convincing evidence for this frequently made assertion. Certainly the Japanese emphasis on 'civilian' R & D with a predominantly commercial orientation seems to have worked.

The second distinctive aspect of Japanese R & D is that it is overwhelmingly applied to process and product development in a rather direct way, rather than being applied to basic scientific research. It is difficult to assess the effects of this, as Peck and Tamura point out in a recent Brookings Institute study of Japan:

It is unclear . . . what role the most advanced science plays in the technological change necessary for economic growth – and thus how much Japanese industrial progress is hindered by the comparatively low level of support for basic research in Japanese universities. Basic science is likely to be published extensively and to be freely available worldwide, and a long gestation period is likely to be necessary before its industrial application. Still there are suggestions that the lag between scientific discovery and economic application is growing shorter, so in developing new products it may become increasingly important to have the latest research easily available.[8]

But many argue that the connection between basic scientific research and high technology industrial activity is by no means as close as is often thought; consequently, Japan has got the emphasis of its R & D about right, given its economic priorities. The point here is that it is MITI which has set those priorities and is therefore responsible for the essentially pragmatic character of Japan's R & D effort.

The final distinguishing feature of Japan's R & D is that a very large part of it is carried out by private firms and is funded by them; this proportion is much higher in Japan than in Western economies. Naturally this prompts questions about the impact of MITI in this apparently largely private research activity. It would be wrong to conclude, from the mere fact that firms carry out a large amount of Japan's R & D, that MITI's role is insignificant. MITI bureaux do formulate a clear picture of the strategically important sectors for the economy, and do have a role in guiding R & D within those sectors.

The principal mechanism of control is MITI's close links with the Japan Development Bank and with commercial banks. Since Japanese firms rely to a much greater extent than their Western counterparts on bank lending as a source of finance, control of project lending by MITI is a powerful instrument in any attempt to control the direction of R & D and investment expenditure.

Important research is also carried out in Japan under the direct auspices of MITI. MITI's Agency of Industrial Science and Technology carries out about 2 per cent of all industrial R & D, concentrating on projects which are likely to generate substantial technological advances for large parts of the economy, yet not be appropriate for private firms to carry out. This may be because they are too expensive, too risky or too long term. Recent projects include desalination plants, an electric car, large-scale information processing systems, a new generation of jet engines, a remotely-controlled undersea oil drilling rig, and a comprehensive integrated traffic control system for cities.

CONCLUSIONS

The Japanese economy has been unique in the post-war world both in its remarkable growth record and in the institutions through which that growth has been organized. The Japanese example seems to undercut, in a most decisive way, assertions to the effect that state intervention inevitably has damaging economic effects, and that *laissez-faire* and the free-market system offer the only hope for economic prosperity. However, it is by no means the case that an economy like Britain either could or should imitate Japan. There are complex problems in assessing precisely what impact MITI has had on the Japanese economy, let alone why it has had any impact, and whether its activities are either desirable or capable of reproduction elsewhere.

There are those who argue that we cannot ascribe Japan's growth record simply to MITI's industrial policy, because we do not know what would have happened in the absence of MITI. Perhaps, without MITI, Japan would have grown spectacularly in any case. This view does not seem particularly convincing. In the first place, MITI is simply the most extreme example of a phenomenon which is found in all of the more successful advanced economies, namely a coordinating mechanism which promotes innovation and investment across industries, and reduces the risks associated with such activity. The mechanisms differ in other successful economies – Scandinavia, West Germany, France – but they are there. This coordination process is conspicuous by its absence in the really slow-growing economies of the post-war period – Britain and the USA. It should also be noted that Japanese industries in which MITI has not intervened have tended to be much less successful. In addition to the synthetic fibre case described above, there was another synthetic fibre, acrylic, for which firms did not require foreign technology or MITI support. The result was, in Ozawa's words, 'a disastrous experience from the industry's viewpoint', and it was only after MITI intervention that the industry was stabilized. Finally, one might suggest that innovation and investment decisions have their greatest overall effect when they are coordinated both as to level and direction; when they are left up to the isolated projections of firms they are unlikely to have the coherence or sense of strategy which only a central institution like MITI can impart.

Then there are those who argue that Japan's economic growth has involved unacceptable social costs. MITI has systematically diverted the resources of Japan's economy into the pursuit of industrial growth. Some argue that while this has raised incomes dramatically, it has also meant that the social welfare systems which we take for granted in the West are either non-existent or utterly inadequate in Japan. Furthermore, Japan's growth has entailed major pollution and other environmental costs. A typical assertion is that of C. J. F. Brown: 'Japanese achievements have involved the sacrifice of other objectives which are so highly regarded in the West as to make emulation impossible.' This conclusion prompts various thoughts. Should we, for example, think in terms of 'emulation' at all? And does applying lessons from Japan necessarily mean the sacrifice of welfare systems and environmental protection? We should remember that Japanese growth occurred on the basis of a very poor society which completely lacked a welfare framework. There may well, therefore, have been a straightforward choice between growth and welfare; or rather, no choice at all, since welfare systems are impossible without a high level of income. But this may not be a problem, or not so much of a problem, in a society in which the basic welfare apparatus is already in existence (even if it is rather decrepit).

Finally, there is the question of whether Japan's industrial policies and methods are so specific to its unique culture and society that they cannot be transplanted. Ronald Dore, for example, suggests that 'the unusual features of Japanese industrial policy derive not so much from specific imitable policy measures as from the ability of the bureaucracy, closely attuned as it is to thinking in industrial circles, to generate a consensus around particular interpretations of the national interest.' Well, granted that consensus is important in economic policy, *how* is it generated? Do we need, for example, to refer to the notions of cultural homogeneity and nationalist sentiment mentioned earlier in this chapter? They certainly are inimitable. But we should remember that consensus cannot be achieved without a framework of discussion, debate and bargaining in which goals are worked out and methods of achieving them agreed. Japanese industry certainly has such a framework in the shape of MITI; but it also has powerful policy instruments to generate growth, and this in itself is likely to promote consensus. Japanese consensus, therefore, may not be so much a cause of its growth record, as an effect of an economic policy which is recognized to have widespread benefits.

Under the circumstances – namely an impending economic crisis – it seems foolhardy in the extreme to write off in advance any lessons we can learn from Japan. The evidence seems very strong: the heavily interventionist industrial policy which has been described has worked spectacularly well in the face of economic problems not unlike those which face Britain today; we should draw the appropriate conclusions.

From Recovery to Reconstruction

What are the key trends in the British economy, and what are its future prospects? How credible are the Thatcher government's views on these issues? Above all, does the manufacturing decline matter, and, if so, what are the measures or mechanisms that will restore the situation? In this chapter we shall try to draw together the general argument of this book, in relation to these kinds of questions.

First, let us restate the fundamental problem. British manufacturing industry has made major and even heroic efforts to cope with the hostile economic situation imposed on it by events in the 1970s and by Margaret Thatcher in the 1980s. But despite this, its competitive position has eroded. The most graphic indicator of this is the trade balance in manufactures: after three hundred years of being a net exporter, Britain now imports on a massive scale. Table 25 tells the recent story:

Table 25. UK trade balance in oil and manufactures (constant 1980 prices, £million)

	1978	1980	1982	1984	1986
Oil	−2,212	315	3,987	5,318	3,420
Manfactures	6,217	5,457	2,095	− 2,735	−4,111
Visible Balance	−641	1,361	1,821	−3,036	−5,849

Source: *UK Balance of Payments 1987*.

In 1987 the trade deficit in manufactures was £7.4 billion, and in 1988 approximately £15 billion: the situation had deteriorated rapidly. The basic problem was not that manufactured exports did not grow, but that imports grew much faster, as Table 26 suggests.

Table 26. UK trade in manufactures 1978–86 (1980 prices, £ million)

	1978	1980	1982	1984	1986
Exports	31,695	34,880	34,898	40,411	45,625
Imports	25,478	29,432	32,803	43,146	49,736

Source: *UK Balance of Payments 1987*, Table 2.2, Price Indices, Table 4.1.

It is obvious that oil has played a major part in offsetting this manufacturing decline (whether it may have caused it is another question, which will be looked at below). And, in general, the manufacturing decline would not be a problem if major oil exports were to continue into the indefinite future. But will they? Britain's oil exports are basically determined by the difference between North Sea production and our own domestic consumption of 65–70 million tonnes per year. How will North Sea production change in the future? Estimating what will happen to oil output in the future is very difficult, since recoverable reserves are not known with certainty, and output and further exploration depend on oil prices, whose future is unpredictable, to say the least. However, we do have a set of Department of Energy projections, whose accuracy we can check by comparing them with actual outcomes in recent years. This comparison is made in Table 27 below.

Table 27. Projected and actual North Sea oil output (million tonnes oil equivalent)

	Projected range	Oil outcome
1985	120–135	122.4
1986	120–135	121.2
1987	115–130	117.6
1988	105–125	117.0
1989	95–120	
1990	85–115	
1991	70–105	

Sources: Ranges: 1985, from Department of Energy, *Development of North Sea Oil and Gas, 1985*; 1986, from Department of Energy, *Development of North Sea Oil and Gas, 1986*, Appendix 14, p. 96; 1987–91, from Department of Energy, *Development of North Sea Oil and Gas, 1987*, Appendix 14, p. 100. Output: 1985–7 *Monthly Digest of Statistics*, 506, Feb. 1988, Table 8.10; 1988, my estimate from output to July 1988.

The projections include a small amount for condensates and gases, but it can be seen that the oil outcomes have tended to fall in the lower end of the projected range. If this continues, then Britain's exports of oil will fall to approximately zero by 1991. Even if, as is very possible, the decline is less dramatic, it is none the less inexorable and the effects will be great: the windfall of oil is steadily being removed from Britain's balance of payments. It is clear that, in the years ahead, Britain faces balance of payments problems of major proportions. How will it cope?

The government's view on these matters is optimistic. In early 1986 the Prime Minister was asked in the House if she would 'list the achievements of Her Majesty's Government from 1979 to date'. She opened her reply as follows:

> The rate of inflation is almost half the level the government inherited, with further falls in prospect. The United Kingdom is in its fifth successive year of growth with GDP at an all-time high; and output is expected to have grown faster in 1985 than all other EC countries and the United States. Investment reached a record level in 1984 and is expected to have risen by a further 4 per cent in 1985. The balance of payments current account has been in surplus for six successive years. Manufacturing productivity has risen at an average annual rate of 6 per cent in the last five years – higher than France or Germany – and company profitability is at its highest for two decades. Employment is rising, with about 700,000 more people in work since March 1983.

The Prime Minister also placed considerable emphasis on the restoration of 'sound public finances' (meaning a fall in the PSBR); on tax reduction and reform; on the privatization programme; on education and training initiatives; on 'a large number of measures designed to improve the operations of markets'; as well as touching on a wide range of defence and diplomatic issues. Linked with this optimistic view is the idea that this new Britain will easily adjust to the decline of oil; the exchange rate will depreciate, making British exports cheaper; and manufacturing will grow.

Clearly a prime-ministerial statement of this kind can be something of a holiday pronouncement, delivered with an eye to its party-political effect; it need not reflect the full complexity of the government's view of the situation. The latter may well involve large doubts and perplexities, and considerably less optimism than the Prime Minister characteristically displays in public. Yet the themes running through Mrs Thatcher's remarks are to be found consistently in official statements and can reasonably be treated as a point of departure for an 'optimistic' view of the British situation. How valid is this view?

The simplest critique of the Prime Minister's position would merely draw attention to limitations in the evidence used, or to problems in its interpretation. Thus, by that time, five years of growth had not sufficed to return the UK to the growth trend of the 1970s; gross investment in aggregate was high, but manufacturing investment was not, and net investment was negative, as it had been through most of the 1980s; the 700,000 new jobs were mostly temporary or part-time service jobs, and had been insufficient either to stop unemployment rising or to return to the employment levels of the 1970s. Rising productivity is also susceptible to various interpretations. As Buiter and Miller have pointed out, this might simply be a rational response to the perceived permanence of the 1979–82 contraction:

Assuming that, on balance, productive capacity gets scrapped and labour laid off in inverse order to its efficiency, the average level of productivity of the surviving capacity will be raised. None of the resources that continue to be employed, however, need to be used more productively for this statistical improvement to occur.[1]

But this kind of critique is limited for various reasons. The main problem is that criticisms of individual elements of the Prime Minister's approach, however well supported they may be, tend to conceal the broad assumptions about economic performance which underlie conflicting interpretations of the situation. For example, consider the choice of base year which is implicit in the Prime Minister's statement. She is, in the main, describing developments not since 1979, but since 1981. By starting from 1981 of course obscures the effects of the massive 1979–81 recession, and therefore allows the presentation of a reasonable growth record. How should this be understood? On the one hand it may be treated as a kind of partisan 'lying with statistics', but it may also have a perfectly

238 · THE BRITISH ECONOMIC CRISIS

respectable rationale. Suppose one treats the first two years of the Thatcher administration as years of transition, in which the UK economy made a step adjustment to a new kind of growth path, based on higher productivity, less overmanning, a leaner, fitter industry, etc. In that case, the manufacturing decline of 1979–81 is in large part a response to the development of oil, which led to the collapse of an always non-viable section of industry. So current unemployment could be seen as reflecting the well-known fact that labour markets adjust more slowly than other markets. In which case it is reasonable to start with 1981, because that was, as it were, the year of rebirth.

Such ideas are very much part of the 'official view'. The idea that oil underpins the manufacturing trade decline, for example, is perhaps most systematically stated in official evidence to the Lords Select Committee on Overseas Trade (the 'Aldington Committee'). A joint memorandum to the committee from the Department of Trade and Industry (DTI), the Treasury and the Foreign Office argued, quite correctly, that 'a surplus on one element of trade must either be balanced by a deficit on another element or by the export of capital overseas through the accumulation of overseas assets'. In practice, the argument goes, the movement into surplus on the oil account has been paralleled by overseas investment and a deficit in manufacturing, because manufacturing was price-competitively weaker than other industries:

The extent to which the adjustment has fallen on the trade balance in manufactures reflects the relative competitiveness of manufacturing industry compared with that of other elements of non-oil trade (agricultural products, some services, etc.) and also the relative importance of manufactures in imports and exports. An important role has been played in these adjustments by the relative price-competitiveness of United Kingdom and foreign goods. The price-competitiveness of UK manufactured goods was adversely affected when the relatively high growth rate of unit labour costs in the UK in the 1970s and early 1980s was combined with the exchange-rate appreciation which occurred in 1977–80. This combination meant that the exchange rate was appreciating strongly in real terms ... The appreciation of the real exchange rate seems likely to have owed a great deal to the existence of North Sea oil resources.[2]

Now, there is much which might be disputed in this – particularly the account of exchange-rate appreciation, which completely ignores the effects of the monetary policies that were the real basis of appreciation from 1979 – but the key point is that the analysis is couched in terms of straightforward adjustments through the price mechanism: oil exports caused an exchange-rate appreciation that reduced manufactured exports to the point where a deficit emerged. The fact that manufactured exports were in decline long before oil was discovered, let alone in production, is overlooked in this view. Overall, in its reply to the Report of the Aldington Committee, the government was of the opinion that the absolute decline in manufacturing output was a step adjustment in which a basically non-viable part of UK industry, which had been artificially kept in existence, disappeared:

Manufacturing output fell at the beginning of the decade as the economy belatedly adjusted to correct long-standing weaknesses at a time of world recession.[3]

From this perspective, therefore, declines in manufacturing output, investment, R & D, and so on, in the 1980s do not indicate fundamental weakness. Manufacturing is basically strong, and the emphasis is thus on the manufacturing deficit as an adjustment to the effects of oil production on the exchange rate. This leads fairly directly to the view that the structural change in the balance of payments is readily reversible through the same mechanism:

When oil production declines, some reversal of recent trends is expected. The real exchange rate will respond to the declining contribution of oil, opening the way for an improvement in the balance of trade in other sectors.[4]

This point was reiterated in oral evidence given by representatives of the DTI and the Treasury, and most notably by the Chancellor himself, responding to 'concern in some quarters about what is going to happen as North Sea oil output declines':

... the balance on non-fuel trade, including in particular trade in manufactures, will tend to improve, in part responding to a fall in the real – and I emphasize the word *real* – exchange rate, some of which has already occurred. The most important development which would sustain and strengthen this process would be a further deceleration in domestic unit labour costs.[5]

In general the position adopted by ministers and officials in evidence to the Aldington Committee was, therefore, that oil was unlikely to decline as fast as forecast, and that its gradual decline would lead, through exchange-rate depreciation, to offsetting adjustments in the shape of a manufacturing recovery, both in output and the trade balance. How valid is this view?

Given the likely decline in oil export volumes, it follows that a great deal will depend, in coming years, on the extent and speed of adjustments to a depreciated exchange rate in the non-oil economy. Let us assume – and this may be a rather heroic assumption – that the depreciation will indeed be a steady one, and that there will not be substantial capital movements as current account deficits emerge. Then there are two main problems: 1. what do we know about the degree of responsiveness of manufactured exports to depreciation, 2. to what extent does UK manufacturing have the capacity to respond to depreciation? These questions should be addressed against the background of the scale of the adjustment problem. Suppose that by 1991 oil exports decline by approximately 20 million tonnes per year, but that exchange-rate depreciation halves the long-term real rate of growth of manufactured imports from 4.8 per cent to 2.4 per cent. If all other exports and imports remained constant (for example, if there were no increases in raw material imports), and the balance of real services did not continue to decline, then to achieve equilibrium in current accounts would require a 2.9 per cent per annum real-growth in manufactured exports. The actual real-growth rate in 1974–85 was 1.6 per cent, so an 80 per cent increase in the real-growth rate of exports is called for. How might this occur?

The 'official view', described above, follows what might be called the textbook account of balance of payments adjustment with flexible exchange rates: assuming constant prices, there is a depreciation which leads people to switch their expenditure between imports and exports and between traded and non-traded goods. Imports fall, exports rise, and output expands in both traded and non-traded goods. Eventually a new equilibrium is reached, with a changed economic structure and a return of the exchange rate to its pre-depreciation level.

But the textbook theory is not necessarily as straightforward as it appears. On the credit side of the balance of payments, depreciation increases exports and output in traded goods if the following four conditions are met:

1. Producers respond to depreciation with lower foreign prices rather than increases in domestic margins.

2. Demand for UK goods is 'price elastic', meaning that the percentage increase in the volume of goods traded is greater than the percentage decrease in price (otherwise, for example, total export earnings would fall rather than rise following a depreciation).

3. There exists unused domestic capacity in traded goods.

4. The depreciation is a real depreciation, i.e. its domestic inflationary effects are controlled.

Implicit in all this is the assumption that the complex of factors which make up a lack of price-competitiveness is at least being maintained. In the short run it is reasonable to assume that exporters respond to exchange-rate fluctuations with changes in margins. A sustained depreciation, however, opens up the possibility of increasing the volume of exports. But do export volumes respond significantly to exchange-rate changes? The fact is that the economic evidence suggests that, for Britain at least, they do not. The economic evidence to suggest that the British manufacturing trade balance responds to depreciation is simply not there. Here, perhaps, we ought to remember that while the UK manufacturing trade balance has been collapsing in the 1980s, the exchange rate has not been appreciating; on the contrary, the collapse has occurred despite more or less continuous depreciation.

In general, the modern evidence is consistent with the conclusion that Kaldor drew from his study of trade patterns in the 1960s and 1970s, namely that

the comparative export performance of the main industrialized countries remained remarkably impervious to very large changes in effective exchange rates ... Britain and America, who seemed to be losing out to the new industrial giants, Germany and Japan, continued to do so after the real exchange rates between them underwent drastic alterations.[6]

Next, there is the question of the supply capabilities of manufacturing in the face of depreciation. The investment and R & D mentioned in previous chapters do not suggest confidence in the ability of British manufacturing to expand its market share in the fast-growing areas of world trade, which are in research-intensive products. The National Economic Development Office has argued that recent UK investment has been

disproportionately directed towards cost-cutting and labour-saving mechanization rather than exploitation of new products and markets embodying new design, technology and higher value added: the investment showed substantial gains in labour productivity but almost no productivity gain when capital was also taken into account. This has meant that the UK has held on relatively better than elsewhere in several traditional industries usually characterized by relatively standardized and price-sensitive products . . . [7]

This suggests that insofar as depreciation will expand export volumes, it will be most effective in product areas that are in general slow-growing and in which competition, especially from developing-country producers, is increasingly strong. Britain is very unlikely to be able to compete in the innovation-intensive product groups that form the fast-growing categories of world trade, especially among the advanced economies who carry out the bulk of such trade.

Taken together, these considerations imply that depreciation must be a very doubtful route for any significant expansion of export earnings from manufactures, and the official view that non-oil industries will steadily respond to depreciation with increases in output and exports is excessively optimistic.

The interesting question, however, is why? Why does the UK have such an insatiable demand for manufactured imports, and why has its share of world trade in manufactures slumped so badly over the years (despite competitive devaluations)? As previous chapters have argued, the most convincing work here directs attention to the technological performance of UK industry and relates poor innovative performance (in terms of R & D inputs and/or patent-based outputs) to trade shares. The most detailed recent study of UK technological performance argued that

first, technological leads and lags are major determinants of the relative efficiencies, competitiveness and incomes of firms and countries. Second, such technological leads and lags emerge largely as a result of differences in cumulative and firm-specific investments in technological activities including design, R & D, production engineering and learning by doing . . .

These authors went on to show that extremely low relative growth rates of R & D in Britain were in large part the result of deliberate choices by firms and that

variance between UK sectors in their technological competitiveness was reflected in their trading performance.[8]

If these arguments are correct, and the view taken here is that they are, then to help resolve trade problems new, innovatory policy measures, instruments and institutions need to be considered in the areas of industrial and training policy, with the objective of significantly strengthening the UK manufacturing supply side. The key implication of the arguments above is that the latter cannot be a *result* of fiscal expansion or depreciation, but that, on the contrary, supply-side improvement is a precondition for growth. Past policy efforts in these areas have been clumsy and unsuccessful, but they still represent the crucial, if as yet imperfectly examined, policy option in tackling the external and employment issues facing the UK.

What are the policy implications of this? At its most basic, the policy decision facing government in the late 1980s/early 1990s concerns whether to accept this continued decline, or whether to attempt to overcome it. Two polar extremes of policy can be considered. Firstly, economic matters could be allowed to take their course, and the social consequences could be contained and, if necessary, policed. Accepting and managing decline need not necessarily constitute a *laissez–faire* policy: it could involve a high level of intervention and economic management, based on, for instance, special employment measures to ameliorate the effects of unemployment, selective or general import controls, and so on. Nor is it necessarily a low-risk policy: despite J. K. Galbraith's view that Britain is a good place for economic experimentation because of the stability of its democractic institutions, the social pressures of real-income decline are likely to be very great. The second policy extreme is one in which everything is sacrificed to the necessity for industrial reconstruction: consumption is restricted, investment promoted, and living standards and welfare provision kept low until conditions are improved, possibly many years later. For a parallel we could perhaps look to the experience of a number of countries during the reconstruction following the Second World War. However, these are not the only alternatives, but rather lie at either end of a spectrum of policy choices. Let us presume that government over the next decade opts to attempt to overcome Britain's seemingly chronic economic difficulties, rather than to accept and manage decline. What kinds of constraints does the situation impose on the range of policy options, and what kinds of policy measures are available, given the main problems to be faced?

Perhaps the most important point is that there is one policy which is *not* available, namely a fiscal and/or monetary expansion of the 'traditional' post-war Keynesian type: that is, a policy of reflation based on increasing public expenditure, making tax cuts or establishing lower interest rates. This is an important issue, since there are many proposals for a recovery policy that are implicitly or explicitly based on such a reflation. Perhaps the most serious among these is the programme of the Employment Institute, set out in its *Charter for Jobs*, which advocates a 'less deflationary' fiscal policy to reverse the fiscal contraction, which it sees as the prime cause of unemployment in the 1980s, accompanied by a cautious monetary policy to contain the exchange rate and the inflationary effects of expansion. It can readily be agreed that the continuation of a cautious monetary policy is necessary, but fiscal expansion can be at best slight. The reason for this lies in the trading problems discussed above: growth of incomes in Britain has the effect of feeding disproportionately through into imports; thus, since a fundamental problem is the trade balance, and since expansionary policies further upset the balance, expansion is not available as a major option.

An important policy conclusion flows from this. Since the Second World War, where British economic policy has been 'active' in character, its targets and instruments have been essentially macroeconomic in concept. Demand management policies, though they cannot be described as a single instrument, have enabled a number of targets to be linked: employment policy, growth policy and output have been seen as simultaneously determined through the complex of government budgetary and monetary measures. Other policy instruments have been employed primarily in a subordinate role, typically to circumvent the external or inflationary implications of a set of fiscal–monetary policies. But this linkage between objectives is no longer viable, if it ever was. The problems of mass unemployment, of competitive trading collapse, of R & D and investment, and of social services provision are likely to require quite new policy instruments – in industrial policy, in education and training, in special employment measures. In some of these areas, important work has already been done. But much remains undeveloped, not only in the construction of policy instruments and measures in the UK, but in making such measures consistent between policy arenas, and in the institutional framework through which they could be implemented. An important reason for this is that there is little in the way of a basic conceptual framework which might guide such policy. However, if the main arguments of this book are correct, and the mid-1980s optimism of the government indeed turns out to be unfounded, then it is these conceptual, institutional and instrumental problems that will dominate the economic agenda in the years ahead.

Sustainable improvement in British economic performance can only happen through a thorough-going reconstruction of the 'supply side' of the British economy, of its technologies and the products that it produces. However, this will not occur using present policies, deeply though the Thatcher government is committed to allegedly 'supply-side' solutions to Britain's difficulties. The great merit of the Thatcher government is that it is the first for many years to recognize that some kind of transformation of the British economy is required; moreover, Mrs Thatcher and her economic ministers have correctly identified the source of the difficulties in productivity and international competetiveness. They are right to emphasize that a reflation of demand will not in itself solve anything, and that income increases depend on growth in productivity and output. The tragedy of the situation is that the correct perception of the overall problem is accompanied by wildly inaccurate diagnoses of why the problems have emerged, and, perhaps in consequence, by policies which are at best ineffectual and at worst ludicrously inappropriate and damaging.

A true *laissez-faire* policy is quite impossible, as Mrs Thatcher and her ministers well know (they have not been slow to intervene in the economy, or to expand state power where their objectives have required it). However, the problem is that even the tentative steps which they have taken towards a non-interventionist, free-market economy do nothing but exacerbate the long-term deficiency of the British economy, which lies in the field of strategic direction and coordination. It is the absence of effective coordination and purpose among the leading sectors of British industry, the failure of government to take the problems of industry seriously and to make overcoming those problems the core priority for economic policy, that has led Britain to its present impasse. The Thatcher government's belief in the 'market mechanism' is more extreme than that of previous governments, but it is not different in kind. All have placed excessive faith in the ability of the market to manage the job of economic and industrial development.

However, the market mechanism is not working, and there is a definite role in market economies for the government to integrate and coordinate the activities of the crucial sectors. This role springs from three aspects of complex industrial economies, namely the *interdependence* between industries, the *future-oriented* nature of investment, and the *riskiness* of large-scale R & D and investment projects. Interdependence springs from the fact that the outputs of one industry frequently form the inputs of another: the motorcar industry, for instance, cannot expand without a concomitant expansion of the steel, glass, rubber and electrical components industries. Making overall output plans compatible may therefore require a coordinating agency; this is particularly the case for *future* output plans that require investment. There is little point investing for output expansion in one industry if others are likely to remain stagnant. Finally, the uncertainty associated with large-scale projects requires that information and risks be shared. Many forms of coordinating agency are possible, but in practice the simplest and most effective are those of government.

These costs of reconstructing Britain's scientific, technological and industrial base will probably be heavy, and will impose real sacrifices on most of the British population. Reconstructing British manufacturing industry will be neither easy nor cheap. However, if nothing is done, the costs of the impending crisis will be considerably heavier, and will not be temporary but permanent. On the other hand, if the period of reconstruction is likely to be arduous and even austere, at least we know the task can be accomplished, since there is a precedent for it: in 1940, in the face of a desperate military crisis, Britain carried out not only a military reorganization but a profound and successful economic restructuring which ensured its survival. It is going to have to do the same again.

References

Part One

CHAPTER 2: GROWTH AND TRADE — COMPONENTS OF THE CRISIS

1. S. Kuznets, *Modern Economic Growth Rate, Structure and Spread*, London, 1972, p. 1.
2. S. Kuznets, *Six Lectures on Economic Growth*, Illinois, 1959, p. 33.

CHAPTER 3: THE LONG DECLINE

1. D. S. Landes, *The Unbound Prometheus. Technological Change and Industrial Development in Western Europe from 1750 to the Present*, Cambridge, 1978, p. 276.
2. *op. cit.*, pp. 289–90.
3. I. Drummond, 'Britain and the World Economy, 1900–1945', in R. Floud and D. McCloskey, *The Economic History of Britain Since 1700*, Vol. II, London, 1981, p. 290.
4. S. Pollard, *The Development of the British Economy 1914–1967*, London, 1979, p. 54.
5. N. Von Tunzelmann, 'Britain 1900–1945: a survey', in Floud and McCloskey, *op. cit.*, p. 240.
6. B. W. Alford, 'New industries for old? British industry between the wars', in Floud and McCloskey, *op. cit.*, p. 311.
7. R. S. Sayers, *A History of Economic Change in England 1880–1939*, Oxford, 1967, p. 51.
8. A. E. Kahn, *Great Britain in the World Economy*, New York, 1946, pp. 112–13, quoted in Alford, *op. cit.*, p. 320.
9. R. Church and M. Miller, 'The Big Three: competition, management and marketing in the British motor industry, 1922–1939', in B. Supple, ed., *Essays in British Business History*, Oxford, 1977, p. 173.
10. D. H. Aldcroft and H. W. Richardson, *The British Economy 1870–1939*, London, 1969, p. 123.

11. C. K. Hartley and D. N. McCloskey, 'Foreign trade: competition and the expanding international economy', in Floud and McCloskey, *op. cit.*, p. 69.

CHAPTER 4: THE POST-WAR BOOM
1. R. C. O. Matthews, C. H. Feinstein and J. C. Odling-Smee, *British Economic Growth 1856–1973*, Oxford, 1983, p. 7.
2. Lars Anell, *Recession, the Western Economies and the Changing World Order*, London, 1982, p. 29.
3. Angus Maddison, *Phases of Capitalist Development*, Oxford, 1982, p. 130.
4. Anell, *op. cit.*, p. 41.
5. C. Freeman, 'Technical Innovation and British Trade Performance', in F. Blackaby, ed., *De-industrialization*, London, 1979, p. 68.
6. K. Pavitt, ed., *Technical Innovation and British Economic Performance*, London, 1980, p. 6.
7. Sir Arthur Knight, 'UK Industry in the Eighties', *Fiscal Studies*, Vol. II no. 1, 1981, p. 3.
8. Freeman, *op. cit.*, pp. 68–9.
9. G. F. Ray, 'Comment', in Blackaby, *op. cit.*, p. 75.
10. T. de St. Phalle, *Trade, Inflation and the Dollar*, New York, 1981, p. 115.

Part Two

INTRODUCTION
1. J. M. Keynes, *The General Theory of Employment, Interest and Money*, London, 1974, p. 383.

CHAPTER 6: FREE MARKETS AND MONETARISM
1. Quoted in V. Walsh and H. Gram, *Classical and Neoclassical Theories of General Equilibrium*, Oxford, 1980, p. 142.
2. M. Friedman, 'The Role of Monetary Policy', *American Economic Review*, March 1968, p. 8.

CHAPTER 7: MARKET ECONOMICS AND ECONOMIC POLICY
1. F. T. Blackaby, 'Common sense about economic policy', Open University, Brooman Memorial Lecture 1981, p. 12.
2. F. Hahn, review of M. Beenstock, *A Neoclassical Theory of Macroeconomic Policy*, in *Economic Journal*, Vol. 91, 1981, p. 1036.
3. F. Hahn, 'The Winter of our Discontent', *Economica*, Vol. XL, 1969, p. 330.

CHAPTER 8: KEYNES AND INTERVENTION
 1. Keynes, *op. cit.*, p. 3.

CHAPTER 9: REWRITING KEYNES
 1. J. R. Hicks, 'Mr. Keynes and the Classics: a suggested interpretation', *Economica*, 1937.
 2. J. M. Keynes, 'The General Theory of Employment', *Quarterly Journal of Economics*, Vol. 51, 1937, pp. 209–23.
 3. A. Leijonhufvud, *Information and Coordination. Essays in Macroeconomic Theory*, Oxford, 1981, pp. 6–7.
 4. M. L. Weitzmann, 'Increasing Returns and the Foundations of Unemployment Theory', *Economic Journal*, Dec. 1982, pp. 787–8.

Part Three

CHAPTER 10: WHAT WENT WRONG?
 1. *Lloyd's Bank Economic Bulletin*, no. 33, Sept. 1981, p. 1.
 2. E. Denison, in R. Caves, ed., *Britain's Economic Prospects*, London, 1969, p. 273.
 3. D. K. Stout, 'Capacity Adjustment in a Slowly Growing Economy', in W. Beckerman, ed., *Slow Growth in Britain*, Oxford, 1979, p. 103.

CHAPTER 11: INDUSTRIAL RECOVERY
 1. Stout, *op. cit.*, p. 104.
 2. C. Freeman, 'Government Policy', in K. Pavitt, *op. cit.*, p. 320.
 3. C. Freeman, *op. cit.*, p. 322.

CHAPTER 12: BEHIND THE JAPANESE MIRACLE
 1. R. B. Reich, 'Playing Tag with Japan', *New York Review of Books*, 24 June, 1982, p. 37.
 2. Quoted in C. J. F. Brown, 'Industrial policy and economic planning in Japan and France', *National Institute Economic Review*, no. 93, 1980, p. 61.
 3. R. Komiya, 'Economic Planning in Japan', *Challenge*, May–June 1975, p. 13.
 4. R. Dore, 'Recent Trends in Japanese Industrial Policy', *Political Studies*, 1983, p. 109.
 5. N. Sasaki, *Management and Industrial Structure in Japan*, Oxford, 1981, p. 94.
 6. T. Ozawa, 'Government control of technology acquisition and firms'

entry into new sectors: the experience of Japan's synthetic-fibre industry', *Cambridge Journal of Economics*, 1980, no. 4, p. 146.

7. Ozawa, *op. cit.*, p. 148.
8. M. J. Peck and S. Tamura, 'Technology', in H. Patrick and H. Rosovsky, *Asia's New Giant. How the Japanese Economy Works*, Washington, 1976, p. 574.

CHAPTER 13: FROM RECOVERY TO RECONSTRUCTION

1. W. Buiter and M. Miller, 'Changing the Rules', *Brookings Papers on Economic Activity*, 1983, p. 357.
2. Department of Trade and Industry, 'Memorandum submitted by the Department of Trade and Industry, HM Treasury and the Foreign and Commonwealth Office', in House of Lords, *Report from the Select Committee on Overseas Trade*, Session 1984–5, 2, p. 3.
3. Department of Trade and Industry, *The Balance of Trade in Manufactures*, Command 9687, p. 4.
4. Department of Trade and Industry, 'Memorandum submitted by the Department of Trade and Industry, HM Treasury and the Foreign and Commonwealth Office', in House of Lords, *op. cit.*, p. 5.
5. HM Treasury, 'Minutes of Evidence', in House of Lords, *op. cit.*, p. 554.
6. N. Kaldor, 'The Effect of Devaluations on Trade in Manufactures', in *Further Essays on Applied Economics*, London, Duckworth, 1978, pp. 99–118.
7. National Economic Development Office, 'Evidence,' in House of Lords, *op. cit.*, p. 498.
8. Patel, P. and Pavitt, K., 'The elements of British technological competitiveness', *National Institute Economic Review*, 4/87, 72–83.

Index

FOR THE BEST IN PAPERBACKS, LOOK FOR THE 🐧

In every corner of the world, on every subject under the sun, Penguin represents quality and variety – the very best in publishing today.

For complete information about books available from Penguin – including Puffins, Penguin Classics and Arkana – and how to order them, write to us at the appropriate address below. Please note that for copyright reasons the selection of books varies from country to country.

In the United Kingdom: Please write to *Dept E.P., Penguin Books Ltd, Harmondsworth, Middlesex, UB7 0DA.*

If you have any difficulty in obtaining a title, please send your order with the correct money, plus ten per cent for postage and packaging, to *PO Box No 11, West Drayton, Middlesex*

In the United States: Please write to *Dept BA, Penguin, 299 Murray Hill Parkway, East Rutherford, New Jersey 07073*

In Canada: Please write to *Penguin Books Canada Ltd, 2801 John Street, Markham, Ontario L3R 1B4*

In Australia: Please write to the *Marketing Department, Penguin Books Australia Ltd, P.O. Box 257, Ringwood, Victoria 3134*

In New Zealand: Please write to the *Marketing Department, Penguin Books (NZ) Ltd, Private Bag, Takapuna, Auckland 9*

In India: Please write to *Penguin Overseas Ltd, 706 Eros Apartments, 56 Nehru Place, New Delhi, 110019*

In the Netherlands: Please write to *Penguin Books Netherlands B.V , Postbus 195, NL–1380AD Weesp*

In West Germany: Please write to *Penguin Books Ltd, Friedrichstrasse 10–12, D–6000 Frankfurt/Main 1*

In Spain: Please write to *Longman Penguin España, Calle San Nicolas 15, E–28013 Madrid*

In Italy: Please write to *Penguin Italia s.r.l., Via Como 4, I-20096 Pioltello (Milano)*

In France: Please write to *Penguin Books Ltd, 39 Rue de Montmorency, F-75003 Paris*

In Japan: Please write to *Longman Penguin Japan Co Ltd, Yamaguchi Building, 2–12–9 Kanda Jimbocho, Chiyoda-Ku, Tokyo 101*

Almost Everyone's Guide to Economics
J. K. Galbraith and Nicole Salinger

This instructive and entertaining dialogue provides a step-by-step explanation of 'the state of economics in general and the reasons for its present failure in particular in simple, accurate language that everyone could understand and that a perverse few might conceivably enjoy'.

The Rise and Fall of Monetarism   David Smith

Now that even Conservatives have consigned monetarism to the scrapheap of history, David Smith draws out the unhappy lessons of a fundamentally flawed economic experiment, driven by a doctrine that for years had been regarded as outmoded and irrelevant.

Atlas of Management Thinking   Edward de Bono

This fascinating book provides a vital repertoire of non-verbal images that will help activate the right side of any manager's brain.

The Economist Economics   Rupert Pennant-Rea and Clive Crook

Based on a series of 'briefs' published in *The Economist*, this is a clear and accessible guide to the key issues of today's economics for the general reader.

Understanding Organizations   Charles B. Handy

Of practical as well as theoretical interest, this book shows how general concepts can help solve specific organizational problems.

The Winning Streak   Walter Goldsmith and David Clutterbuck

A brilliant analysis of what Britain's best-run and most successful companies have in common – a must for all managers.

FOR THE BEST IN PAPERBACKS, LOOK FOR THE 🐧

PENGUIN BUSINESS AND ECONOMICS

Lateral Thinking for Management Edward de Bono

Creativity and lateral thinking can work together for managers in developing new products or ideas; Edward de Bono shows how.

Understanding the British Economy Peter Donaldson and John Farquhar

A comprehensive and well signposted tour of the British economy today; a sound introduction to elements of economic theory; and a balanced account of recent policies are provided by this bestselling text.

A Question of Economics Peter Donaldson

Twenty key issues – the City, trade unions, 'free market forces' and many others – are presented clearly and fully in this major book based on a television series.

The Economics of the Common Market Dennis Swann

From the CAP to the EMS, this internationally recognized book on the Common Market – now substantially revised – is essential reading in the run-up to 1992.

The Money Machine How the City Works Philip Coggan

How are the big deals made? Which are the institutions that really matter? What causes the pound to rise or interest rates to fall? This book provides clear and concise answers to these and many other money-related questions.

Parkinson's Law C. Northcote Parkinson

'Work expands so as to fill the time available for its completion': that law underlies this 'extraordinarily funny and witty book' (Stephen Potter in the *Sunday Times*) which also makes some painfully serious points about those in business or the Civil Service.

FOR THE BEST IN PAPERBACKS, LOOK FOR THE 🐧

PENGUIN POLITICS AND SOCIAL SCIENCES

Political Ideas David Thomson (ed.)

From Machiavelli to Marx – a stimulating and informative introduction to the last 500 years of European political thinkers and political thought.

On Revolution Hannah Arendt

Arendt's classic analysis of a relatively recent political phenomenon examines the underlying principles common to all revolutions, and the evolution of revolutionary theory and practice. 'Never dull, enormously erudite, always imaginative' – *Sunday Times*

The Apartheid Handbook Roger Omond

The facts behind the headlines: the essential hard information about how apartheid actually works from day to day.

The Social Construction of Reality Peter Berger and Thomas Luckmann

Concerned with the sociology of 'everything that passes for knowledge in society' and particularly with that which passes for common sense, this is 'a serious, open-minded book, upon a serious subject' – *Listener*

The Care of the Self Michel Foucault
The History of Sexuality Vol 3

Foucault examines the transformation of sexual discourse from the Hellenistic to the Roman world in an inquiry which 'bristles with provocative insights into the tangled liaison of sex and self' – *The Times Higher Educational Supplement*

A Fate Worse than Debt Susan George

How did Third World countries accumulate a staggering trillion dollars' worth of debt? Who really shoulders the burden of reimbursement? How should we deal with the debt crisis? Susan George answers these questions with the solid evidence and verve familiar to readers of *How the Other Half Dies*.